Jonathan Birchall was born in Britain in 1958 and raised as a somewhat uncommitted West Ham supporter in the suburbs of London. He graduated in Classics from Cambridge University and joined the BBC in 1988, subsequently becoming their Tokyo correspondent. He has extensive experience of working in East Asia, having also been based in South Korea, Vietnam and Singapore. Jonathan Birchall now works for the *Financial Times* in London.

ULTRA NIPPON

How Japan Reinvented Football

Jonathan Birchall

HEADLINE

First published in 2000
by HEADLINE BOOK PUBLISHING

First published in paperback in 2001
by HEADLINE BOOK PUBLISHING

10 9 8 7 6 5 4 3 2 1

ISBN 0 7472 6409 0

Typeset by
Letterpart Limited, Reigate, Surrey

Printed and bound in Great Britain by
Mackays of Chatham plc, Chatham, Kent

HEADLINE BOOK PUBLISHING
A division of Hodder Headline
338 Euston Road
London NW1 3BH

www.headline.co.uk
www.hodderheadline.com

清水

CONTENTS

For Mila, who made me do it

清水

PROLOGUE

We were glorious burning orange and gold in the floodlights. We were the dancing rhythms of samba tunes singing and swaying in the still cold December air. We were the just and the righteous, the guardians of the pure, the children of light. We were Shimizu S-Pulse, with our team there below marching out on to the green grass arena of the Nihondaira Stadium.

They were a cold mass of light and dark blue, waving their blue polythene bin liners up and down, and chanting over and over again to a hammered repeated beat. They were the slick and the clever, the cold and the calculating, the divers and the niggle-merchants. They were the evil Jubilo Iwata.

And tonight, in Shimizu's Nihondaira Stadium, the battle was on.

'J.League Championship, 1999,' boomed the loudspeakers as the teams marched out. 'Final game. Second leg.'

Up behind me in the stands was our leader, Mr Matsuda, with the rattling snare drum, waving us all on. There was Miss Hori, who likes Eric Cantona, on the *tamborim*, and Endo-san at the back with the big bass drum, and Yuki and Mizuho and Mr Mochizuki and all the friends. 'SHI-MI-ZU ESSS-PULSE!

SHI-MI-ZU ESS-PULSE!' we shouted and sang, as the only soccer samba band in Japan gave it everything they'd got.

Down on the touchline, in his blue and yellow tracksuit, we could see Perryman-san, once of White Hart Lane, Tottenham, England, and now of Shimizu City, Shizuoka prefecture, pacing up and down, ninety minutes away from the glory, bearing the burden of the hopes of a small city in Japan which wanted this win so hard you could almost see it in the cold night air.

Out on the pitch, they were warming up now, dancing across the pitch in a long line, led by Oki, the assistant coach: Sawanobori, the captain, the goalkeeper Sanada, Ichikawa at right-back, Nishizawa on the left, and Itoh in midfield. There were Yasunaga and Kuboyama, the fast striking forwards, and Toda and Kenta and Saito and Oenoki. There were our three Brazilian stars, Alex and Santos and Fabinho. And there was Paru-chan, our big yellow fluffy mascot, giving us his 'Get the Victory' sign.

Here we all were. Ninety minutes to win a victory over the mighty Jubilo Iwata. Time enough to put Shimizu on the map. 'SHI-MI-ZU ESS-PULSE!' we chanted, as the samba swung its rhythm across the waiting crowd.

清水

1 DREAM STADIUM

There are two good reasons to go to the Japanese port city of Shimizu in early March. The first is the unparalleled view of the sacred peak, Mount Fuji, Japan's national symbol, still covered with snow and looming faintly through the haze of the late afternoon. The second is the football. From where I was sitting in the main stand of Shimizu's Nihondaira municipal stadium, at about ten to four on a Saturday afternoon, I was in a position to see both.

The football hadn't yet started, although the preparations were well under way. Out on the pitch, in the thin sunlight, some two dozen neat-looking Japanese Sea Cadets in light blue shirts, white trousers and sailor hats, had deployed energetically around the centre circle, holding red and white semaphore flags.

The Sea Cadets were just part of it. Another forty ten- and eleven-year-old boys and girls in football kit had formed a huge V, pointing to the main stand. Each was clutching a bundle of orange balloons. The watching crowd was standing in respectful silence. No one was shouting obscenities, not even at the Sea Cadets. It really didn't seem like a football match at all.

3

The Sea Cadet commander blew his whistle and semaphore flags flashed as one. 'EESS,' boomed a big, deep voice through the stadium loudspeaker system. The whistle sounded. The flags flashed again. 'AITCH,' boomed the voice. Then came an 'I' and an 'EM', and another 'I', and a 'ZEE' and a 'UUU' as the flags rose and fell, spelling out the letters, and more and more letters after that. Then the flags stopped.

'SHIMIZU S-PULSE!' boomed the voice over the loud-speaker. The crowd cheered, a wild drumming broke out from the home end, a barrage of fireworks by the touch-line blasted silver ticker tape into the air, and the theme from *Rocky* swelled across the ground. As the orange balloons floated skywards, the two teams marched out, led by the match officials, into a snow of falling silver ticker tape. Welcome to the J.League.

'NINETEEN NINETY-NINE,' boomed the loudspeaker voice in heavily accented English. 'J.LEAGUE . . . FIRST . . . STAGE.' More cheering. NIHONDAIRA STADO . . . SHIMIZU S-PULSE . . . VERSUS . . . VERDY KAWASAKI.'

At the home end, behind the goal on my left, the crowd was arrayed in all its gold and yellow splendour like a medieval army. The rails were strung with banners in yellow, blue and orange, each with the names of favourite players, some written in big Japanese *kanji* characters and some in English. In the very centre of the stand, below the electronic scoreboard, there was a large red and white Japanese flag, bearing the names of the three S-Pulse heroes who'd played for Japan the previous summer in the French World Cup.

Below that stood the band. I wasn't expecting the band. No one had told me to expect a fully functioning, all-singing, all-dancing Brazilian-style samba band, more than thirty members strong, readying itself for action in the centre of the stand. Along the front of the upper level the fans were waving more oversized banners, with slogans mostly in English whose significance I didn't understand until much later – S-Pulse Pul Lovers, The S-Keepers, K's Club – swirling the flags to and fro in a wave of colour. Someone was waving a vast standard made from dozens of small green and yellow Brazilian flags. Over to the side, a huge Brazilian flag had been hung out, marked EU GOSTA S-PULSE, which turned out to be Brazilian Portuguese for I LOVE S-PULSE.

Down on the pitch, the S-Pulse team had lined up in their bright orange and yellow kit, led by their thirty-two-year-old captain, Sawanobori. Sawanobori, known to the fans as Nobori, was carrying his three-year-old son, who was wrapped in an oversized orange S-Pulse shirt, and leading his six year old along by the hand. The number 9, Kenta Hasegawa, aged thirty-three, had also brought his children along, as had Shimizu's thirty-four-year-old goalkeeper, Masanori Sanada. All three veterans are local boys. As the players posed for photographs, a seven-foot tall, bright yellow, fluffy rabbit with floppy ears pranced about on the side-lines, holding a bunch of balloons shaped like another giant V-sign.

The big voice began to announce the players' names, one by one, as their photos flashed up on the giant electronic scoreboard. The home crowd greeted each name with loud Latin-American-style 'Olés!' – which came out, owing to Japan's difficult relationship with letters 'l' and 'r', rather more like 'Oré!' – while throwing their yellow and orange banners into the air, and banging their samba drums.

'ANDO MASAHIRO,' boomed the loudspeaker.

'ORÉ . . . ORÉ,' responded the crowd. BOOM BOOM went the drums of the Samba squad.

It takes just over an hour to get to Shimizu from Tokyo, changing from the Shinkansen bullet train at the neighbouring town of Shizuoka on to the local green and orange trains of the Tokaido line for the fifteen-minute journey to Shimizu. During the journey, the trains run through an unremitting landscape of low-rise housing blocks and factories, pachinko parlours and twenty-four-hour convenience stores, broken only by glimpses of the sea on the left-hand side. Along the coast of Japan between Tokyo and Osaka, the countryside appears only in very small patches amidst the suburban sprawl.

As for Shimizu itself, well, when I first visited I have to admit I wasn't that impressed. The day I'd first arrived at Shimizu's small railway station, the most noticeable feature wasn't Mount Fuji but a series of squat white storage tanks, helpfully described on the tourist map in front of the station as an 'oil waste collection centre'.

The plaza outside Shimizu Station could be anywhere in Japan. There's a taxi rank, lines of parked bicycles and a Lawson's convenience store selling an assortment of instant noodles and styrofoam *bento* (lunch boxes). The usual gaggle of teenagers leaf guiltily through the magazines. There's a McDonald's and a small neighbourhood police kiosk, or *koban*. There's a Marui department store, a sort of Japanese Marks & Spencer. Welcome to Shimizu, home of middle Japan, home of Mr Average.

Except for the footballs.

Outside the railway station, the posts of the low, chain-link fence lining the pavement are topped with small metal footballs. The shop selling local souvenir sweet bean cakes has typical Japanese paper lanterns, also shaped like soccer balls.

I had boarded the bus with a line of people wearing orange and yellow Shimizu S-Pulse shirts and carrying orange and yellow Shimizu S-Pulse banners. It wasn't a rowdy crowd. There was no pushing or shouting. There were no policemen on horses with riot helmets. At least half of the people on the bus were young women, some of them with children.

The bus headed through the neat downtown streets, passing a bronze statue of three footballers in the centre of the road, and periodic statues of naked women which raised more questions than they answered. At the Angel porn shop, with its small pavement shrine to S-Pulse players, we turned down S-Pulse Dori, or S-Pulse Street. The pavement is inlaid with brass plaques carrying footprints of the team, and the manhole covers are football-shaped.

We drove down S-Pulse Street towards the waterfront, where you can see piles of red bauxite on the wharves by the alumina smelter, and the tall concrete silos of the Honen vegetable oil company. We stopped in front of the S-Pulse team headquarters and the S-Pulse shop to pick up more people wearing orange and yellow and cruised into the suburbs towards the splendid stadium on the green hills of the Nihondaira plateau. Dream Stadium 99 it said on the new edition of the team's yearbook, available outside. Also outside were booths selling orange and yellow scarves, team shirts, the orange and yellow plastic clappers beloved of Japanese sports crowds, and yellow fluffy toys by the score.

Back at the game the loudspeaker voice was working on down the list of players, from Toshihide Saito, another local boy, to the two central defenders, Kazuyuki Toda and Ryuzo Morioka. Toda had dyed his hair brown that month, although by the middle of the season it would have turned a steely bluish grey. Morioka had opted to start the season as a straw-coloured blond with a goatee. Roughly a third of the S-Pulse players had something going on with their hair – hair has always been a big thing in the J.League. The league serves as something of a hair-style testing ground for Japanese youth, waging an increasingly aggressive war against the uniformity of black, black, black. Leader of the pack was probably Hidetoshi Nakata, the great national midfielder, who turned out for Japan's first-ever World Cup appearance, against Argentina, the previous summer with his hair a delicate shade of orange.

'ORÉ . . . ORÉ . . . BOOM BOOM!' went the crowd and the drums.

Next came the first of Shimizu's Brazilians, the twenty-six-year-old number 8, famed for his Ruud Gullit-style dreadlocks and his smart suits. 'ALEXU,' boomed the loudspeaker, which is easier to say than Alessandro dos Santos. There are two other Brazilians on the team – thirty-eight-year-old midfielder Carlos Alberto Souza dos Santos, known as Santos, who that season had become the oldest player in the league, and Augusto Justino Fabio, known as Fabi or Fabinho.

'ORÉ . . . ORÉ . . . ORÉ . . . ORÉ . . . BOOM BOOM!'

That was almost it now, except for one more name. Up on the electronic scoreboard a big, creased, extremely Japanese face was beaming down on the yellow and orange crowd.

'KANTOKU!' went the big voice, indicating that this was the manager. 'STEPHEN JOHN PERRYMAN!'

'STEPHEN JOHN PERRYMAN,' boomed the big voice.

'ORÉ ... ORÉ ... BOOM BOOM!' went the fans.

The two teams had broken from the line-up; the small children, the bunches of flowers and the big, fluffy, yellow mascot had been removed, and the crowd, and the drums, were starting in earnest – 'ESS-PULSE ESS-PULSE, BOOM BOOM BOOM. ESS-PULSE ESS-PULSE, BOOM BOOM BOOM.' At the front of the crowd, standing at the head of the samba band, a single figure in orange held up both his hands and the whole stand hushed. The leader signalled and the drums began again, this time with the entire band sweeping into the full samba rhythm. 'BOOM, Ti-BOOM, Ti-BOOM BOOM BOOM' went the bass drums. 'Ching ching ti-ching ching. Ching ching ti-ching ching' went the metal section, as the crowd began to chant in rising arpeggios, 'Ooooo-ré Oooooo-ré Oo-ré Oo-ré! BOOM BOOM Oooo-ré Oooo-ré Ooo-ré Ooo-RÉ! ESS-PULSE!'

Now the whole stand was moving as one, jumping from side to side, the fans throwing their arms forward at the end of the chant, like a massive coordinated aerobics lesson. Verdy kicked off. Down by the dug-out, in his blue and yellow tracksuit, Steve Perryman had already sprung to his feet, characteristically cradling his chin in his left hand, his right arm clutched across his chest.

This was Perryman's fourth season managing in Japan. He'd spent the first three at S-Pulse as assistant to his old Tottenham team-mate and friend, Osvaldo Cesar Ardiles. Ardiles had left in November the previous year. Now Stevie was running the show, backed up by his trusty oppo, assistant manager Phil Holder.

All managers want to win all games. But, after spending the past two seasons as surprise performers, this season the pressure was on for S-Pulse. They had come second in the first stage of the league last season, and ended as runners-up in the Emperor's Cup, the Japanese equivalent of the FA Cup, beaten by the Yokohama Flugels in front of a 50,000 crowd at the National Stadium. This season the pundits were tipping S-Pulse as possible championship winners.

After beating S-Pulse, the Yokohama Flugels had become the

first J.League club to go bankrupt, and were forced into a controversial merger with their cross-town rivals, the Yokohama Marinos. Top foreign players and managers were being eased out to make ends meet.

In the circumstances, it didn't turn out to be a particularly relaxing match for Steve Perryman, or for the home crowd. S-Pulse looked the better team, but they seemed jumpy and nervous, unable to settle down. Verdy Kawasaki's Brazilian forward, Henrique, would periodically break through and throw the S-Pulse defence into chaos. S-Pulse almost gave away two goals. Then their dreadlocked Brazilian star forward, Alex, put one past the Verdy goalkeeper. Verdy were aggressively not convinced Alex was onside, and an examination of the post-game tape indicated that he probably wasn't, but that didn't stop a booking for Verdy's Brazilian defender, Julio.

'ALEXU . . . ALEXU . . .' chanted the crowd. This game was looking increasingly like a case of your Brazilians versus our Brazilians.

At the half-time whistle, I went in search of snacks as the aisles filled up with people obeying the rules against smoking while watching the game. This being Japan, the snack scene is particularly well developed. Throughout the first half, polite young women had wandered up and down the stands, dispensing Asahi beer in plastic cups. At half-time, people were queuing for corn-on-the-cob, barbecued on an open flame in a corner of the stadium, while more polite young women shouted 'irraishaimasse', 'at your service', with all the enthusiasm of waiters at the finest sushi restaurant. Such are the rewards of social order.

Unable to find a soggy hamburger or a sinister hot-dog, I bought a neat, plastic *bento* box with rice, fish and some other more uncertain pickled things, complete with disposable wooden chopsticks. In Europe, disposable wooden chopsticks would be considered potentially dangerous weapons.

At Nihondaira Stadium, fans can wash and brush up at a sink with an unbroken mirror. That wouldn't happen in Europe. The fifty-foot drop from the parapet of the walkway to the ground wouldn't happen in Europe either. And what of the garbage bins, neatly divided for burnable and non-burnable rubbish? Where else in the world can you watch football, and sort your trash?

As the second half got under way, I munched the remains of my rice and fish, sipped my beer and watched the drama. Perryman certainly wasn't any more relaxed. There he was, still standing by the dug-out, periodically shouting and waving, and periodically being joined by his translator. At fourteen minutes in, Verdy's Henrique blasted the ball wide with only Shimizu's goalkeeper, Sanada, to beat. At twenty-one minutes in, he broke through again and hit the post, apparently having developed some kind of deep aversion to actually scoring.

Then Hattori, one of Shimizu's new signings, went up for a header at the Verdy end, and missed what looked from the stands like an open goal. He'd missed a sitter, but the home crowd started to chant his name, 'HATTORI, HATTORI', perhaps to show how happy they were that he'd turned up at the ground at all.

Alex managed to score again, making it 2–0, but before Perryman could sit down, Shimizu's defences were torn apart by a volley from Verdy's Kobayashi – 2–1. S-Pulse continued to look like they could lose the match at a moment's notice; Perryman continued to jump up and down like a tic-tac man; and then, in the eighty-fifth minute, Shimizu's bald-headed Tasaka blasted in the home side's third goal, and it was all over bar more samba dancing on the terraces. Shimizu S-Pulse 3, Verdy Kawasaki 1.

The two teams gathered in the centre to wave to all sides of the stadium and to bow to the crowd. The S-Pulse team jogged to the home end for another round of polite bows, after which they ran to the edge of the field and started throwing small, yellow fluffy mascots into the stands. Alex, who had been stretchered off after a tackle in the closing minutes, was on his feet receiving the man of the match award and doing an instant interview for the local TV network, which was being broadcast around the ground. I noticed he had taken off his boots and was wearing a very naff pair of blue and white plastic sandals.

Across Japan that afternoon, the J.League was starting its

seventh season. The league had been designed during the years when Japan was on the up and up. Japanese companies seemed to be able to buy whatever they wanted and to pay whatever was asked – the Rockefeller Center in New York, Columbia Pictures, Van Gogh's 'Sunflowers'. Before the J.League, all Japan's soccer fans had was the semi-professional Japan Soccer League, the JSL. Forget samba, furry toys and weird club names. The JSL was populated by solid company teams with solid company names such as Mazda FC, Yanmar Diesel and Sumitomo Metals. Popular enthusiasm for football had soared briefly after Japanese soccer successes at the Tokyo and Mexico Olympics in the 1960s. In the early 1980s, an eleven-year-old soccer player called Captain Tsubasa, star of a *manga* comic-book series, became a national cult figure with young Japanese boys; but in the late 1980s, Japan was still mainly a baseball-playing nation.

'I sensed the need for a revolution in Japanese soccer, and that's how the J.League came about,' said Saburo Kawabuchi, the self-made shogun of Japanese soccer, a former player and now chairman and chief executive of the J.League, when I met him in the league's plush offices in downtown Tokyo.

'We used to have company-based clubs to create corporate identity and loyalty to the company. The J.League is based instead on creating European-style community-based clubs, rather than the old corporate style.'

But the new J.League didn't spring spontaneously to life, drawing strength from soccer-loving local communities across Japan. The league was created in perhaps one of the greatest mass-marketing events Japan, and probably the world, has ever seen. The operation was directed by Hakuhodo, Japan's second largest advertising company, an agency that wields enormous influence in the relatively conservative world of mainstream Japanese media. Hakuhodo concluded that Japanese people, and in particular young Japanese people, were ready for something different from baseball and sumo wrestling.

'First of all, soccer appealed to people because it is international, and not just inside Japan,' I was told by Kazumori Monma, who directed the J.League project at Hakuhodo. 'And secondly, we made an image of soccer as "casual" and "speedy" and "active". These are the things that young people in Japan like.'

Having signed up Hakuhodo, Mr Kawabuchi brought in another top-rank company. Sony Creative Products was given responsibility for overall product design, everything from choosing speedy and active team colours to cute-engineering the fluffy team mascots. The combined corporate force behind the launch of the new league achieved a runaway success.

Sony started selling team flags and the coloured plastic clappers-cum-megaphones beloved of Japanese baseball crowds at a hundred special J.League shops set up around Japan seven months before the first game kicked off. Orchestrated by Hakuhodo, the media went berserk as only the Japanese media can, obsessively reporting details of the newly arrived foreign stars brought in by the clubs to launch the league. The J.League's new theme song, 'Olé, Olé, We Are The Champs', was in the shops weeks before the first game, and became the only sound around in stores all over Tokyo.

On the back of rising popular hysteria, Mr Kawabuchi sold the television rights for J.League coverage for 10 million yen ($96,000) per game, against the previous paltry sum of 300,000 yen for Japan Soccer League games.

Some 300,000 people vied for the 50,000 tickets to the opening game on 15 May between Verdy and the Yokohama Marinos at Tokyo's National Stadium. Just in case they didn't quite get the idea, Mr Kawabuchi had recordings of wild cheering ready to play for the televised version. But he need not have worried. The opening game drew roughly a third of the entire television audience, almost double that for a baseball game in the same time slot. Football became the new craze. When people started painting their faces in team colours, Sony Creative rushed out tubes of washable 'game paint'. There was a J.League brand curry, J.League brand potato crisps, and Panasonic endorsed a ten-speed J.League bicycle. A J.League nightclub opened in Tokyo's Shibuya entertainment district, with cocktails in team colours and food from a 'J.grill'. 'J.League' was even voted 'word of the year' by a Japanese newspaper.

What the fans at the games found was a strange new world, inhabited by clubs with names selected, it seemed, almost at random from some crazed pick'n'mix basket of global culture, names which have subsequently given Japanese teams a degree of international recognition which has nothing to do with on-the-ball skills. Fans who had gamely supported Sumitomo Metals in the old Japan Soccer League now found themselves chanting for the Kashima Antlers. The Yamaha Motor Company had become Jubilo Iwata. Mazda FC became Sanfrecce (pronounced san-freh-chay) Hiroshima. Yomiuri FC became Verdy Kawasaki. Mitsubishi Motors became the Urawa Red Diamonds.

To add to the speedy and active charm of it all, there were the team mascots. Shimizu S-Pulse, of course, had its big fluffy yellow creature, known as Paru-chan. A *paru*, I was told by a woman who worked for the club, was some kind of mythical rabbit or hare, supposedly identified with the wooded slopes of Nihondaira; *chan* is a suffix attached to the names of objects of affection, such as children, or girlfriends, or big, fluffy, yellow, mythical rabbit-type things.

To go with the exotic and cute foreign names, like matching accessories on a new foreign car, came the exotic and cute foreign players to add even more glamour – Brazil's Zico at Kashima, England's Gary Lineker at Nagoya Grampus Eight, and former German international Pierre Littbarski, veteran of three World Cup finals, now playing at JEF United. Having bought the Rockefeller Center, Japan had now bought football.

Dutchman Dido Havenaar found himself swept up in the storm. Havenaar, built in the tradition of huge, blue-eyed Dutch goalkeepers, came to Japan in February 1985, long before the creation of the J.League, to play for Mazda FC in the old Japan Soccer League after seven years with the Dutch first-division team FC Den Haag. Despite planning to come for just a year or two, Havenaar stayed, and moved to Yomiuri FC, also in the JSL.

'At that time, soccer was playing before two to three thousand people,' he says. 'Most of the players worked for the company in the morning and came for practice in the afternoon. Only the foreigners were full professionals.' In those days, things were a little basic after the Dutch first division. 'I had to wash my own kit and clean my own boots, and carry a big bag with all my stuff for away games. The accommodation and the showers, they were like in shipping containers. The manager warned me. I was prepared for it.'

With the start of the J.League, Havenaar moved to Nagoya Grampus Eight, backed by the giant Toyota Motor Company and based in the vast industrial centre of Nagoya, some 300 miles from Tokyo.

'It was a very big change. Suddenly in 1993, there were fifteen or twenty thousand people at the games. If you played in Tokyo it was fifty thousand. And in the shops everything was J.League. Cups, toothbrushes, caps, everything was J.League.'

Havenaar, formerly a journeyman player for a company team, found himself a superstar.

'Before, I could go to the supermarket and pick up stuff without being recognised. Now if I go to a supermarket or a department store, everyone wants to have a picture or an autograph. It was difficult to go out of the house. Some people came to the house and asked for autographs. So we had to move, for security reasons. Our house used to be on the street, and it was always "ping-ping, ping-ping" on the door and, "Could you sign, please."

'I have two young boys. We'd go to the park to play football or something, but after maybe one minute all the people came saying "Sign! Sign!" and the boys would just be standing there, saying, "Papa! Papa! When can we start playing?" But I signed everything.'

Dido even had his own supporters group, or *oen-dan*, devoted to his cause.

'They were called Dido-dan. These people, they called my team in Holland to get information, and my family, and my brother, and asked, "How was he as a child?" and everything.'

For Mr Kawabuchi and Mr Monma and everyone in the big buildings in downtown Tokyo, this all seemed to be good news.

Sony Creative Products sold goods worth a massive 3.6 billion yen, while total sales of licensed products were estimated at 100 billion yen. Average crowds rose to 19,000 per game, double the J.League's initial forecasts. The following season, the J.League expanded with another two teams and Mr Kawabuchi doubled the fee for nationwide television broadcasts to 20 million yen.

But it couldn't last. The J.League turned out to be just another Japanese consumer boom.

'Japanese consumers are very fast to like something,' explained Mr Monma at Hakuhodo. 'They can also be very fast to stop liking it.'

Every year, the frenetic world of Japanese marketing is hit by a boom like this, usually driven by the vast army of fashion-conscious young consumers. In 1996, for example, it was the Nike sports-shoe boom, when young Japanese would pay up to $500 for a pair of rare second-hand running shoes. In 1997, it was the 'print club' photo-booths in video arcades, which produced photographs of the customer in sticker form, embellished with a selection of backgrounds and cute borders. In early 1999, it was anything to do with three cartoon characters called *dango san-kyodai*, or 'the three rice-ball brothers', who appeared in a popular children's TV show on NHK. In early March, hordes of housewives besieged stores in Tokyo in pursuit of the first *dango san-kyodai* CD, featuring their *dango*-tango theme tune. It sold out within hours.

All these booms can make companies very rich. They can also lead to disaster. In 1997, for example, Bandai, Japan's largest toy maker, had the idea of making small, plastic, hand-held games, the object of which was to feed and nurture a small egg (the *tamagotchi*) by bringing it food, clearing up its mess and generally keeping an eye on things. It may not sound like much fun, but during 1997 young Japanese schoolgirls were buying tamagotchi by the dozen. Bandai stepped up production in a desperate bid to feed demand. The eggs went global. Bandai was in overdrive. Then, in early 1998, the boom suddenly evaporated and Bandai was left with a mountain of unsold electronic eggs. The company recorded total losses of 14.5 billion yen.

The soccer boom did better than most. It lasted for three solid seasons. But in 1996, the J.League went the way of the tamagotchi virtual pet, the Nike sneaker and the print club. By 1996, the original ten-team league had been expanded to sixteen teams. Japan was chosen to co-host the 2002 World Cup with South Korea. The national team qualified for the Olympics for the first time since Mexico in 1968, and in Atlanta that summer managed to beat Brazil 1–0.

All this should have been good for football at home. But in the J.League, average attendance, which had been in the 18–19,000 region for the first three seasons, fell sharply to around 13,000. Sony Creative's sales of J.League merchandise fell by more than two-thirds. The temporary fans found that J.League potato crisps just weren't that tasty.

The sudden fall-off in support played havoc with the clubs' finances. Encouraged by the large crowds, and driven by the need to attract the popular individual stars the fans wanted to see, the clubs had allowed players' salaries to go through the roof. The losses began to mount.

As the J.League foundered, Japan itself had begun to change. After what Japanese call the bubble economy of the late 1980s, the country had slipped into a recession. The top banks were mired in debt. Unemployment was at record highs, although still far lower than anything seen in the West. In 1998, the number of suicides of people in their fifties and sixties jumped by 40 per cent – the generation that rebuilt Japan out of the rubble of World War Two. In Yoyogi Park and Shinjuku Station in Tokyo, homeless people, most of them men in their fifties or sixties, camped out forlornly under the trees and in the underpasses. In place of Japan's self-confidence there was now self-doubt.

'Nervous day,' said Perryman afterwards at the post-match press conference. 'Maybe with the expectancy. For two or three months, everyone has been speaking S-Pulse championship, S-Pulse chance. Now the talking was over. This was the day to do it.'

Mr Perryman – or Perryman-san to the Japanese – seemed to have taken up a kind of pidgin English, probably as a result of three years spent making himself understood to people whose grasp of the language is not always 110 per cent; or maybe this was the way they talked at Tottenham Hotspur, where he still holds the record for the greatest number of league appearances by any single player.

'But we didn't flow, we were not fluid in our play. The goal maybe helped us settle down. But we were never convincing, not even at 3–1. We weren't convincing.'

Perryman had changed out of his blue and yellow tracksuit into a smart grey suit. He was speaking to journalists in a neon-lit room, sitting at a desk on a podium before a board that carried the names of the main club sponsors. On his left sat the club's translator, Edmundo. In front, there were perhaps two dozen Japanese journalists, and me, all sitting quietly in neat rows below the podium, on chairs which had fold-down desk arms. It was rather like a particularly serious physics lesson. I noticed that the front line of chairs had been left empty, presumably to avoid any flying chalk or swinging rulers. For an English manager, it must be like dying and going to heaven.

After Perryman's opening remarks about the game, it was time for the questions. A reporter would put up his hand and wait to speak until invited to do so by the club press officer. The press officer was on hand to keep order, and I suspected he would be prepared to hand out detentions if things got out of hand. The questions were suitably polite, about whether S-Pulse had opted to play defensively, or why there had not been more shots. One was about an individual player, Yasunaga, who had been substituted after getting booked for a late tackle.

'Today he was late for the midday meal and he was late for everything else. As for the tackle, I haven't seen a tackle like this from an S-Pulse player for maybe two and a half years.

'When S-Pulse have been good in the past,' Perryman continued, 'it's always been from beneath the expectancies.'

'Wha?' said Edmundo, thrown temporarily off his game by Perryman's grammatical wizardry.

'From beneath the expectancy level. Today we were expected to do something.'

'Mmmm,' said Edmundo, pausing before delivering the latest analysis.

At the end of it, the journalists all clapped politely. Outside, the samba band was being loaded into a minibus. From the diehard fans in the stands came some high-pitched calls: 'Pellyman-san, Pellyman-san'. Pellyman-san paused and searched for the source, which turned out to be a couple of eight- or nine-year-old girls. He smiled and waved, and then walked back to the dressing room.

清水

2 PERRYMAN-SAN

Perryman-san was sitting behind his desk in the S-Pulse offices at the Hebizuka training ground. The training ground is set on a south-facing hillside, surrounded by woods, overlooking the coast road that runs from Shimizu to the bigger city of Shizuoka. It's all surprisingly verdant and lush, a pocket of greenery in the coastal urban sprawl. Sea eagles soar above the canopy of the trees. Birds sing. Phil Holder, S-Pulse assistant manager, had come in after training for a character-istically incomprehensible *tête-à-tête* with the boss.

'Didja 'ave a word, Stevie?' said Holder, sitting on the arm of a chair.

'I told him just now with Edmundo. I tell him before every fucking game. And after. For all the fucking use it does,' grumbled Perryman-san.

'The thing is he's got no fucking idea.'

'And he doesn't fucking listen.'

'He's just got to get out and hit it. BAM! Like you used to do.'

Perryman-san, dressed in blue shorts and a white tee-shirt, had his stockinged feet up on the desk, in contemplative position. I was wearing the blue and white plastic sandals that are part of Japanese

19

sporting culture; in clubhouses, as in domestic houses, you take off your shoes at the door and step up on to the raised, usually wooden, floor. Mine were too small for me which made it very hard to run. If there was a fire, I was certain to be the last out.

On the wall opposite, there was a white board with the match schedules, and a magnetic board with the line-up of players for the day's practice game. S-Pulse usually trained in the morning, starting with an early meeting in this office, attended by the coaching staff, everyone drinking coffee.

Phil Holder had arrived that season to take over as assistant manager. Now forty-seven, he had played with Perryman in the Tottenham youth team as a striker and the two had become close friends.

'When we played together, we didn't have to shout. Somehow I always knew where he'd be,' Perryman told me. 'It was kind of instinctive.'

The two of them together, Phil and Stevie, Stevie and Phil, were like a little bit of north London in Shizuoka Prefecture. The intuitive principle seemed to have been carried from the field into their conversations, usually delivered at maximum speed with minimum lip movement. This meant that following what exactly they were talking about with each other was tricky, even for a native English speaker.

Perryman, looking at a video of the previous game: 'This is shonky. Look at him. He's in fucking shonky-shonky land.'

Holder: 'He's like sort of hanging around.'

Perryman: 'Because that's where he fucking scored from last time. He's fucking lazy.'

While Perryman had continued to play for Tottenham, Holder had gone to Crystal Palace and then to America, where he'd played in the ill-fated American professional soccer league before eventually returning to play for Bournemouth. His coaching career had taken him back to Crystal Palace, and he'd met up again with Perryman at Brentford FC in 1987. Before Shimizu, Holder had been at Southend United and at Reading.

It struck me that Shimizu would be a bit of a shock after

Reading, but Holder seemed to be amused by Japan. I think the Japanese were intrigued by Holder, presumably because most of the time they couldn't work out what he was saying. Also, he's not the tallest former player, and he's perhaps not quite as skinny as he once was. After one game, I talked to Holder's partner, a glamorous blonde who stands about a foot and a half taller than her husband. We joked about who could play Holder if there was ever to be a Hollywood film about the J.League (after all, Tom Selleck portrayed a US baseball star playing in Japan in the movie *Mr Baseball*). I suggested Danny DeVito, she said Bob Hoskins.

The other key men in S-Pulse management were the Japanese assistant manager, Takeshi Oki, aka 'Oki'; the team doctor, Shigeo Fukuoka, aka 'the Doc', a former knee specialist at Shimizu hospital who was employed full time by the S-Pulse team; and the slightly diffident goalkeeping coach, Paulo Jose Valmorbida, aka, for some reason I could never quite understand, 'Fuka'. And there was Matsuba, whose official position I never quite understood but who was the fix-it-up-and-make-sure-it-happens man, aka 'Makka'. Makka, who was maybe around thirty, spoke pretty good English, enough to survive working with Ossie Ardiles and with the Perryman/Holder team. Understanding Ardiles was recognised as a bit of a challenge, even by sports reporters in England, owing to the unique combination of low-level and high-speed delivery, although it wasn't always hard to get the gist of things with Ossie. A video of Ardiles on the bench, watching S-Pulse lose to Kashima Antlers, includes his unique analysis of the game: 'Fuck, fuck, fuck, fuck, fuck, fuck, fuck, fuck.' That's the international language of football.

Edmundo Hanyu, S-Pulse's translator, claimed that Ardiles was hard to understand even in Spanish because of the way he talked, and Edmundo is Argentinian. He is one of hundreds of thousands of Brazilians, Peruvians and Argentinians descended from Japanese settlers in Latin America now working in Japan. He found his way over to S-Pulse from an electronics factory somewhere near the central city of Nagoya after the arrival of Ardiles. From translating Japanese into Spanish he'd graduated to Japanese into English, with a bit of Brazilian Portuguese on the side.

'There are words which the players understand directly from Steve, like "Shape!" or "Back!" or "Go!" But if the indication is more complicated, then I come forward to help during the games,' said Edmundo when I asked him about the rigours of the job. 'Of course, the word "fucking" doesn't mean anything in Japanese, but it's just to emphasise. So sometimes I find another Japanese word, or maybe I just say the right word more strongly. When they go out to the touch-line and shout at the referee, I don't translate. When the referee comes to see us, then I translate.'

It's a fine line. Two seasons previously, the Spanish translator at the Yokohama Marinos got sent off, along with his manager. Ardiles had been sent off twice during his three years, although Edmundo avoided the red card himself. Perryman-san, despite his fully committed touch-line style, has so far managed to stay inside the law. Most of the time, S-Pulse bounce along happily enough on a merry mixture of Japanese, Portuguese and Anglo-Saxon.

'Ossie was right about you,' said Perryman to goalkeeping coach Fuka, after Fuka had failed to pay up on a bet he claimed he'd never seriously made.

'Wha? Wha?' said Oki, trying hard to keep up.

'I was saying that Ossie was right about what he always said about Fuka.'

Fuka finally obliged. 'What did he say?'

'That you were a mean cunt. That's what he always said.'

'And he wasn't far wrong, was he?' said Holder.

'Fuka, you a mean cunt,' said Oki.

'Fuck off,' said Fuka.

The previous season, I'd visited Shimizu once and I'd seen Perryman working with Ardiles. The club and the fans loved

Ardiles. He was famous, which helped a lot. It was like buying a presentation bottle of Chivas Regal, or an Omega watch. He was foreign, and top quality, and he worked. Under Ardiles, S-Pulse had won the Nabisco Cup, the Japanese equivalent of the League Cup, in their very first season. The team had become one of the best in the J.League, but I'd always reckoned that without Perryman's communicative charm to ease relations, with Ardiles' Latin haughtiness, it could all have ended in tears. Phil Holder's role, on the other hand, seemed to be that of inner adviser, privy to the isolated manager's innermost thoughts and fears.

'I saw it as a bit of an adventure,' says Perryman-san about his original decision to follow Ardiles to Shimizu, giving up a job with the Norwegian team Start, where he'd gone after Tottenham. He and Ardiles had seen a few videos of S-Pulse playing, and Perryman had been to Japan with Bill Nicholson's Tottenham side, on tour. But neither man really knew what they were getting into.

'On the pitch,' assistant manager Oki told me one day, 'everything is good. But behind, it's very, very complicated.'

My own initial introduction came from the city's tourist department's *Guide to Shimizu.* 'Shimizu City was first inhabited about ten thousand years ago,' says the guide. 'A fact confirmed by the discovery of various ruins and relics in the area. The beautiful view of Mount Fuji is particularly famous and draws a staggering five million visitors annually.'

Five million seemed like a lot, but then every Japanese town, no matter how bland, has its special claims to fame. The totally awful steel town of Kashima, for example, home of Sumitomo Heavy Metals and the Kashima Antlers, has a visitors' map near the station which lists among its major attractions the Ibaraki Prefecture Fish Farming Centre. Who knows, maybe five million people a year go there, too. Each and every Japanese town has its own special delicacies and products that you just can't get anywhere else. According to the guide, Shimizu's 'typical goods' include early ripening strawberries grown on south-facing stone walls by the sea ('the season begins in the dead of winter, and you can come and eat as many as you like'), green tea ('much appreciated by people all over the country') and seafood ('Shimizu maintains the top position in the country for the landing and canning of tuna').

Shimizu has other special features, too, such as the port festival in early August when around 30,000 people take part in street dancing; and the shrine on the pine-tree lined beach of Miho that marks the site of a famous folk tale in which an angel comes down to earth to bathe and is caught naked by a local fisherman. Every November, a traditional Noh Play recounting the story is performed on the Miho beach by firelight, doubtless contributing to the city council's claims of tourist grandeur.

The myth of the angel and her robe, or *hagoromo*, explains a lot of things about Shimizu, such as why there are those bronze statues of naked women on the city's main street, along with the statues of footballers; and why the local canning company is called Hagoromo; and why the little family store that sells pornographic books and comics on the corner of S-Pulse Dori is called 'Angel'; and why Paru-chan, the S-Pulse mascot, has ears shaped like angel's wings. It is, you might say, the city's key mythic concept.

But what makes Shimizu really special, at least in the view of Shimizu-ites, is clearly football. 'Shimizu is known as a soccer city,' said my guidebook, 'and there are various unusual souvenirs, such as cookies, toys designed in the form of a soccer ball, and also green tea and candy named after soccer.'

'Now I don't understand all of it,' Perryman told me one day, 'but for some reason or other, this club has a particularly close relationship with the community. The community takes a lot of interest in what happens at the club. More than with the other J.League teams.'

So why did Shimizu choose soccer? Why not volleyball? Or water-skiing? What happened to transform this – let's be frank – totally nondescript Japanese port city into a cauldron of football madness? The answer eventually came from the city's mayor, Hiromasa Miyagashima, in an extremely serious meeting room in Shimizu City Hall. Mr Miyagashima is a tall, kindly looking man, a former head of the labour union at a local company that makes car parts for Toyota, and a member of Japan's dominant Liberal Democratic Party. His official meeting room in the city hall is suitably impressive. Lined with deep leather chairs, it has a showcase containing a rather weird collection of official gifts, including a vast wooden whale, a model of a ship and a big picture of Stockton, California, which happens to be Shimizu's sister city in the United States.

We drank local green tea and exchanged business cards appreciatively, although I suspect I got the best from the deal. Mayor Miyagashima may be the world's only mayor who hands out strawberry-scented scratch-'n'-sniff business cards with a coloured picture of snow-capped Mount Fuji. City officials are also equipped with mandarin orange scratch-'n'-sniff name cards. I ws told they were still working on green tea but experiencing some technical problems. 'It's rather difficult,' they said. I hoped they weren't also working on tuna.

We were on the fourth floor of the city hall, a building which stands like a concrete bunker in the midst of the small streets of one of the city's 'entertainment' areas (a collection of bars including one called 'Stomach'). The ground floor is full of people waiting to file applications for building permits, or to pay their local taxes, or to register this or that. On the front steps, there are flowers in concrete basins. The flower basins are shaped like footballs.

'Now Shimizu City is called "the city of soccer",' said the mayor, cutting straight to the point. 'And Shimizu provides a large number of the players in the J.League. There's at least one Shimizu player in every J.League team. And in the World Cup team in France, out of twenty-two players, nine were from Shimizu schools. That's really amazing when you consider there are six hundred other cities in Japan.'

The city has certainly done its bit to promote the game. Apart from the concrete flower basins and the bronze statues of players on the city's main street, Shimizu owns the Nihondaira Stadium. And it is spending 500 million yen, around $4.5 million, on building a nationally recognised training facility, with grass and artificial surfaces.

'Some people say we spend too much money on football,' Mr Miyagashima continued. I looked suitably shocked at the idea. 'But I think it's good recreation for the citizens, and for community building, and for developing the city's image.'

Sitting on the other side of the giant meeting table was Mrs Michiee Ayabe, the head of the city's 'Soccer Affairs Department', established in 1994. A former schoolteacher in her fifties, Mrs Ayabe had her own part to play in establishing the game in Shimizu. She is clearly not a woman to be trifled with. When we met, she looked me straight in the eye and thrust out her right hand to shake mine in an entirely and refreshingly un-Japanese kind of way. The two young men working in her department looked rather humbled. Mrs Ayabe is the only woman on the board of directors of the Japanese Football Association.

'Shimizu has a long history of football,' she told me earlier, producing a souvenir blue handkerchief from the previous year's national Under-12 boys soccer tournament, staged annually in Shimizu. The handkerchief showed a winged cartoon angel clutching a football. It came with a card, with the following explanation in English:

The story of the nymph who came down from heaven to Miho pine beach is well known among our old legends. If this legend had been written in modern times, the story might have been different, having instead the nymph attracted by the beat of a samba rhythm and coming down to earth to see a splendid soccer game.

In Shimizu, the game of soccer was kicked off by a young teacher in 1956 as an element in the education of children. Those children have grown up never forgetting the joy of playing soccer, and their enthusiasm has built the J.League.

That young teacher was a man called Mr Hotta. If Shimizu is a small soccer empire in Japan, Mr Hotta is the founder of the dynasty.

Interestingly though, during our interview the mayor never mentioned Mr Hotta by name, even when talking about the history of the city's soccer development. That's because, as Oki had pointed out to me, off the pitch in Shimizu, things get quite complicated.

Today, Mr Hotta has retired. He lives in a smart house in Shimizu, with a black Mercedes in the garage, and a head full of football. When I met him he was wearing a tee-shirt and orange S-Pulse shorts, and his house was filled with soccer memorabilia, from a collection of England's 1990 World Cup team miniatures to signed photographs of himself with Diego Maradona at a soccer school in Argentina. A year planner on the wall was marked with the dates of all the S-Pulse games.

In the early 1950s, when Japan was slowly picking itself up after the massive destruction of World War Two, Mr Hotta taught in a local elementary school. With two other teachers, Mr Hotta set about bringing football to the school. The young Mrs Ayabe was a pupil at the same school. Quite frankly, she was appalled.

'There was a rule that you weren't allowed to kick balls in the school yard,' said Mrs Ayabe. 'So we reported this new teacher to the principal for kicking the ball. And the principal said it was OK. It was soccer.' The young Mrs Ayabe's relations with the new teacher went through another rough spell soon after. 'I saw him throwing a ball at the head of a boy I liked, and I got really annoyed,' she says. But soccer caught on and Mrs Ayabe herself began to play. The game spread to the high schools, and home to parents. 'They realised that in soccer anyone can be a hero, anyone can make a goal,' said Mrs Ayabe.

Mr Hotta rose through the ranks of soccer administration, becoming head of the soccer department in the government of Shizuoka Prefecture. He presided over a steady growth in the popularity of the game across the prefecture. Captain Tsubasa, the young *manga* cartoon soccer player whose popularity in the early 1980s converted a whole generation of Japanese schoolboys to soccer, was a native of Shizuoka.

If it hadn't been for Mr Hotta, there would have been only one J.League team in Shizuoka Prefecture, and that would have been the Yamaha company team, Jubilo Iwata. But in the late 1980s, when plans for the new league were first discussed, Mr Hotta set out to make sure that Shimizu wasn't left out. Financially, things didn't look promising. Shimizu had no major national corporation to guarantee economic security. Jubilo Iwata, just fifty miles away, could play in the Yamaha Motor Company stadium, and Yamaha would cover the losses. But the proposed Shimizu team, based on a real Japanese soccer-playing community, fitted the new league's views on the future of the game perfectly. So in 1993, Shimizu S-Pulse became one of the ten founding teams of the J.League. The biggest corporate backer was a local television station and Shimizu City took a 3 per cent share. Ordinary Shimizu football fans and supporters owned 23.6 per cent of the club. In all, some 2,400 citizens paid at least 100,000 yen each (about $900) for shares in the club.

On the eve of the launch of the J.League, Mr Hotta had what might be called a bit of a setback. As head of the Shizuoka soccer department, he found himself accused of embezzling around $70,000 of official money to invest in the then-booming stock market on his own account. 'Embezzlement Scandal Rocks Japanese Soccer' read the headline in the *Japan Times* newspaper. Arrested and publicly disgraced, Mr Hotta had to step down as managing director of the new club. He was eventually sentenced to five years' probation.

In Japan, being publicly disgraced doesn't necessarily put you out of the picture – especially for only $70,000. There were suggestions that the whole thing was a political plot against Mr Hotta hatched by jealous representatives from the other areas of soccer-mad Shizuoka, who resented Shimizu's rise to pre-eminence. Recent Japanese political history has plenty of disgraced politicians who retain their political power through their personal connections. Former prime ministers such as Kakuei Tanaka and Yasuhiro Nakasone demonstrated that power could be wielded from offstage. The same was true of Mr Hotta, known to all in Shimizu as *sensei*, or teacher and master. After all, Mrs Ayabe, a former pupil of his, was running the city soccer department.

All this meant that the innocent foreigner, Perryman-san, had a lot more people interested in exactly what he was doing than some of the other J.League clubs.

'I was told by one of my friends on the coaching staff that I should be careful about talking about the club in public,' says Perryman-san. 'Even in English. Because they said you never know who's at the next table and who knows who, because everyone knows everyone else.'

In 1996, Ardiles and Perryman started off, strangely enough, with a clean-up exercise. You might think that Japanese football clubs are run with military efficiency. Japanese baseball clubs require of their players an almost total obedience to the rules. Joining the Tokyo Giants was compared by American baseball slugger Warren Cromartie in his biography, *Slugging it out in Japan*, to joining the Special Forces. Things at S-Pulse had taken rather a different turn. Before January 1996 when the Tottenham old boys team arrived, sixteen out of the club's seventeen foreign players were Brazilians, including Mirandinha, a former international who was signed for six months and never played, and Marcão, who was on the roster for three months and played just twice. The club's first manager was another Brazilian, Emerson Leão, who resigned in June 1994, followed by six months of former Brazilian international Rivelino. Despite spending the following year under a Japanese manager, when Ardiles and Perryman arrived the club had something of the atmosphere of a Brazilian beach party.

The new management duo decided that all this had to change. First, they banned non-players from the area around the pitch before matches. Then they moved against the casual style which had become part of the image of J.League players in their role as the nation's new pop idols. No more sloppy hip-hop tracksuits and tee-shirts at S-Pulse.

'Eventually we got the team travelling in collar and tie, which is correct, turning up at matches, collar and tie. It's a special day, you have to get your act together sooner. You have to get up and have a shave and focus as soon as you can. It's paying respect to the game.'

Despite the new respect, S-Pulse continued to play like crap. Halfway into the season, the new management team was called in for a meeting with the club. It looked like an early bath, but instead the club pulled out a sudden burst of understanding, of the type almost entirely unknown in English football.

'I feared the worst. But we walked in and they smiled. And their opening line was, "We know we've got problems. What can we do? What can we do to help?" '

From then on, according to Perryman-san, everything went right. Ardiles sacked the team's only non-Brazilian foreigner, Daniele Massaro, who drove off in a huff, and brought in a talented young Argentinian, Oliva, from his home-town, Cordoba. S-Pulse surprised themselves by finally winning a championship – in September, they beat Verdy Kawasaki to win the Japanese equivalent of the League Cup. The new management team was a success.

清水

3 I AM FAN

It was a Saturday afternoon in early May 1999, and I was back in Shimizu. The weather was perfect; sunny and bright with a cool breeze. It was in the middle of Japan's Golden Week holiday, which is in fact not a week at all but an extended weekend of leisure created by a group of early summer public holidays that fall together. During Golden Week, the trains and the airports are packed. The staff at Tokyo Station go on a kind of war footing, pouring men in uniform on to the teeming station concourses to direct and cajole old grannies and mothers laden down with children to the appropriate platform. All across Japan, festival banners are hung from houses and temples, long pastel-coloured flags shaped like swimming carp twisting in the sunshine.

Shimizu S-Pulse were about to play Urawa Red Diamonds, the team that started life as Mitsubishi Motors Football Club (Mitsubishi's company symbol is three red diamonds). Urawa is a Japanese version of Croydon, lying in the dull northern suburbs of Tokyo, forty minutes by subway from Tokyo Station. Urawa makes Shimizu look like Paris.

With a population of some 400,000, Urawa has quadrupled in

size since 1945. In 1994, the mayor, Soichi Aikawa, rather pathetically suggested that the arrival of the J.League had helped some of the city's new resident office-workers, the salarymen who are the foot soldiers of the Japanese economy, to recognise where they were actually living.

'I think there are salarymen whose only knowledge of the city is the station and the areas where they have their houses. In this connection,' said the mayor, 'it is helpful that the Red Diamonds have come to Urawa. As a symbol, the team has generated the citizens' consciousness of being Urawa residents.'

In a town where there is not much to be passionate about, the Reds command passionate support. While other J.League teams were struggling to half fill their stadiums, the Reds managed to make every game at the Urawa municipal Komaba Stadium a sell-out. It was the only place in the J.League where I'd seen ticket touts. All that, plus the good weather and the holiday, meant that for once the away stands at Nihondaira were almost full.

The game promised to be lively. The Reds fans started off proceedings fifteen minutes before kick-off with a sturdy rendering of some kind of team hymn by an all-male-voice choir. They then launched a series of vast and throaty 'Oi!s' at the yellow and orange Shimizu fans at the other end, followed by a series of heavy drum beats and a massive and perfectly choreographed 'UUU-RA-WARED-SUU'.

The Reds have always had Teutonic tendencies. They play in the dangerous colours of red and black, and they recruited German coaching staff and players in 1993 and 1994, including Guido Buchwald and Uwe Rahn. Apparently as a result, their supporters simultaneously developed a somewhat Germanic intensity, gaining a reputation for rowdiness and a tendency to chant 'Oi! Oi! Oi!' rather more often than is healthy. Urawa is the only team to have had anything close to crowd trouble; after some scuffling in the early 1990s visiting fans were confined to a separate stand.

The previous season, I'd been somewhat alarmed to see a sign reading ARYANS hanging over the side of the Urawa home stand, next to the Lufthansa advertising boards. What next, I thought, swastikas? But in Japan, of course, it's all part of the great global pick'n'mix approach to world culture, where signifiers float freely on the breeze of total miscomprehension. That afternoon at Nihondaira, I noticed that ARYANS had now mutated into ANIYANS. This struck me as a positive development. Perhaps, in a season or two, Urawa fans would be waving a big, red and black banner reading ONIONS.

Also on display at the Urawa end was a big picture of Che Guevara, presumably because it happened to be in red and black, and a sign saying IZGORETI PETRO, which I assumed was some sort of encouragement in Serb directed at their thirty-three-year-old Yugoslav midfielder, Zeljko Petrovic. This season, their other foreigners included a tall Italian defender, Guiseppe Zapella, previously from Monza in the Italian second division, and Aitor Beguiristain, now thirty-four, formerly a Spanish international who came to Urawa from Barcelona, which must have been something of a shock.

The Urawa supporters' opening gambit seemed a little heavy, and it provoked something like a rustle of disapproval from the other end of the stadium, as from an army awaiting the order to charge. But the S-Pulse fans refused to be provoked, as always maintaining the moral high ground and holding off the first Shimizu Ess-Pulses and the rattle of the samba until their team was on the field. From then on it was a no-holds-barred, high-volume shouting match, which was only partly related to the events on the pitch.

It had been a good enough season for Perryman-san and his boys so far. S-Pulse were third in the table when the game began, behind Jubilo Iwata and Verdy Kawasaki, and they needed a win to maintain their challenge at the top. The match became what I was beginning to realise was a typical S-Pulse kind of game – the team gave away two goals in the first twenty minutes, and eventually pulled them back in the last ten, keeping a crowd of about 18,000 in a state of high anxiety for most of the ninety minutes. With the score tied at full time, the stage was set for thirty minutes of golden-goal-wins-the-match extra time. Given that it was a nice day and an exciting game, this was not such a daunting prospect, but after thirty minutes of thrills and end-to-end drama, there were no golden goals and we were left with the draw.

'With regard to being two goals down at the end of the first half, I have to be happy with the result,' croaked a hoarse Steve Perryman-san at the post-game press conference. 'But in terms of pressure and shots on goal, then I'm not satisfied.'

For me, the main thrill off the pitch was being mistaken for some kind of foreign agent by one of the local reporters, who assumed I was on hand to assess the Reds' admittedly talented nineteen-year-old forward, Shinji Ono. Ono was a product of the Shimizu high-school system, but he'd been lured to the big-money Reds by the prospect of a larger salary than S-Pulse had been able to come up with. By all accounts, he was a player with international potential who had learned most of what the J.League could teach him and was rumoured to be heading to Europe.

'What do you think of Ono?' asked a rather unsporty-looking young man from the *Nikkan Sports* newspaper at half-time. Thinking fast, and eager not to be a complete disappointment, I said that in my expert opinion, Ono did seem pretty good, having cut the Shimizu defence to shreds with the pass that created the second goal (a pass that was so good that even I could tell it was good). But it wasn't going to be easy.

'Can he play in the Premier League?' asked the eager man from the *Nikkan*, who must have interviewed Ono before the game because he was holding a Reds' shirt with Ono's number 10 on it.

'Mmmm,' I said thoughtfully, aware that as an English person I was expected to have a view on this, and aware too that there was speculation that Ono would go to Manchester United. 'Maybe,' I said, and then paused significantly. 'But he seems a little small.'

The *Nikkan* man was either happy or he realised at this point that he was talking to an absolute idiot. He headed off, although in the second half he did offer me some of his crisps. I can only assume that the next day the front page of the *Nikkan Sports* was splashed with ' "ONO TOO SMALL" says British person.'

As the stadium emptied out, I decided it was finally time to introduce myself to the leader of the Shimizu S-Pulse samba band, and the *de facto* head of the S-Pulse supporters, Shuna Matsuda. After the rigours of the Urawa Reds game, I found the band members loading their shiny metal drums into the back of a small van in the parking lot.

Mr Matsuda is a formidable character. Early on he struck me as having about him something of the style of the Japanese gangster, the *yakuza*; the *yakuza* are a recognised social group who run reputable front offices, rather like Rotarians or the Masons, but with a tendency to extort money, run drugs and shoot people. They also have huge tattoos on their backs and they chop each other's fingers off. Matsuda was thick-set with swept-back black hair and rimless glasses. He looked rather like Elvis Presley. He also had the low centre of gravity stance of a man who can't easily be knocked over, even when kicked very hard in the head.

My suspicions on the gangster front were heightened when he told me that his principal sporting interests before football had been judo and the art of kendo, or traditional Japanese fencing, which are the sort of activities that the *yakuza* are reported to be particularly interested in, along with the Shinto religion and other traditional pastimes, such as emperor worship. Mr Matsuda is also an insurance agent.

I was to spend a lot of time over the coming weeks trying to see whether Mr Matsuda's back was in fact covered with large tattoos, and checking to see that he had all his finger joints. Other characteristics, such as gold chains, permed haircuts and sinister-looking handbags – assumed to hold guns, flick-knives, amphetamines and other accessories – are less definitive, since much of this paraphernalia is considered fashionable by quite a large proportion of the middle-aged male residents of Japan outside Tokyo.

Not surprisingly, it turned out that Mr Matsuda doesn't speak much English. I managed to get it across that I was interested in extending my familiarity with the samba band. Adding 'u' or 'o' to English words, and changing 'l's to 'r's can get you quite far in

Japan. Words such as 'hoorigan', 'goaru' and 'hafu timu' are part of the footballing vocabulary. But frankly this doesn't work so well when it comes to handling sophisticated transactions involving variables of time and space. We had been discussing the location of a forthcoming 'eventu' involving the samba band for about five minutes without making much real progress. I'd worked out that whatever the 'eventu' was, it had something to do with a stop on the railway line. After that things were beginning to go round in circles when Mr Matsuda suddenly remembered something.

'Yamada,' he shouted. 'Where's Yamada? Yamada speaks English.'

It turned out that Masatoshi Yamada doesn't just speak English, but is in fact an English teacher. You might have thought that someone would have remembered this earlier, but the Japanese are a very cautious and quite reserved people. Perhaps it was thought rude to draw my attention to the existence of a fan who spoke, by and large, excellent English.

When he's not playing the surdo bass drum in the samba band, Yamada-san teaches part time in private schools and in the after-school cramming classes which are considered essential for success in Japan's rigid examination system. Yamada, who's twenty-six, isn't a fan of rigidity. With his shoulder-length, dyed brown hair and his laid-back demeanour, I had thought he was probably the intellectual of the group even before he told me that his college degree was in international security relations with a special focus on the US–Japan defence arrangements. He is also a little bit of a techie dude. When not teaching, or playing the drums, Yamada runs the S-Pulse supporters web site, 'S-Pulse Supporters World – We Love S-Pulse'.

Unlike Mr Matsuda, Yamada-san is not of a martial disposition.

'Gary Lineker,' he remarked of the former England striker who spent two years in the J.League, 'was not such a success in Japan. He was often injured. And he scored only eight goals for Grampus Eight. But he had no yellow cards. I like that.'

Most of this I found out the next day. After the Reds' game, I decided to stay in Shimizu for the night to witness the 'eventu'. As a result of Yamada's timely intervention, I now knew that it was starting at 9.00 a.m. the next day, and that I would have to get to Kusanagi Station on the small, private Shizuoka Railway, three stops down from Shin-Shimizu Station. I was still a little confused about what exactly the 'eventu' was going to entail.

Because it was Golden Week, most of the hotels were booked. I found a room in a small family hotel, the E-Hotel, where the elderly owners seemed slightly alarmed by the arrival of a foreigner. The whole place had a sinister feel to it. There were too many doilies. They made me pay in advance. I scribbled down 'Japanese Gothic' in my notebook, evidently affected by the neurotic neatness of it all. I remembered the recent case of the Kobe curry murders, currently attracting massive interest in the Japanese media – a seemingly normal housewife had dumped arsenic into a communal pot of curry at a neighbourhood event. 'It's the quiet ones you have to watch,' a friend in Tokyo had warned me. Darkness fell.

Shimizu might be a port city but at night it is far from rowdy. I know this because the first time I went to a game there I ended up stuck at Nihondaira Stadium after the last buses had left, and decided to walk back to my hotel in the centre of town. It took about two and a half hours. I stopped once at a Seven-Eleven store to ask the way to the station and I came across a single reveller near the railway tracks at Shin-Shimizu and asked him the same question. I saw a few people in the distance at the end of Shimizu S-Pulse Street, but that was pretty much it. Even the 'entertainment' district behind the city hall was morgue-like.

So I sensibly opted for a low-key evening in, locking the door against any attempted weirdness from the nervous owners, and watched Grampus Eight play the Yokohama F Marinos on commercial television while eating a take-out dinner of rice and fish, accompanied by peanuts and a can of Asahi Super Dry beer. Lucky me.

The game, in front of 31,000 people in Yokohama's main stadium, was extremely dramatic. Grampus pulled back from 2–0 down to go 3–2 ahead in the last minute, only to give away an equaliser in the last seconds of regular time. Dragan Stojkovic, the former Yugoslav international who had been playing at Nagoya since 1994, was demonstrably not a happy camper, ripping his shirt off in despair and throwing it on the ground after the last-minute equaliser.

But the dramatic tension of it all was somewhat elusive, principally as a result of Asahi TV cutting away from the action for advertisements as the match was still going on. Stojkovic scored the first Grampus goal in the sixty-seventh minute with a spectacular free-kick, despite them being reduced to ten men a few moments before by the sending off of Nagoya's Brazilian defender, Torres.

As Stojkovic celebrated, Asahi TV cut to an advertisement for noodles. When the action resumed, an entire quarter of the screen was taken up with an inset of a charming young woman in a Japanese national team shirt, who seemed to be announcing the results of question three in some kind of phone-in competition.

Things on the pitch were heating up. The referee had his red card out again, this time for a Marinos defender; Stojkovic rattled the ball over the Marinos crossbar. Asahi TV cut instantly to an advert that involved a young man being chased by a rhinoceros, selling the new Nice One high-energy drink (slogan: 'Have a Nice One'), followed by the answer to question four of the phone-in quiz. Eventually, Grampus lost to a golden goal in extra time.

It was all very puzzling. After the football was over, I turned to NHK and watched the baseball. In general, the ads come between the action in the baseball – during the 1996 general election, which coincided with Orix Blue Wave playing the Tokyo Giants in the deciding game of the Japan Series, NTV opted to run the election results around the edge of the screen, thus demonstrating its priorities.

Given the fact that the pillow was of traditional Japanese construction, which means it was filled with what may have once traditionally been husks of rice but were now probably thermoplastic pellets, and given my fears about the odd couple downstairs, I slept rather well. With that pillow under my head, it was rather like sleeping on a sack of sand – bearable, but not very comfy. In the morning, I slipped into my shoes, which had been left by the front door, and headed out without saying anything to the owners on the grounds that a) it was quite early, b) I'd already paid and there was no mini-bar, and c) they clearly didn't understand a single word I said. I thought it would be better for everyone, but as I paused to do up my laces some fifty yards down the street, the lady owner was out after me, bowing low and issuing high-pitched 'at your service, thank you, please come again honoured guest' noises in Japanese. I bowed sheepishly back.

After that, naturally enough, I made for the Mr Donut by Shin-Shimizu Station in search of cultural familiarity. 'Donuts and Yumcha' said the sign. Inside, there was more smiling service and I selected something sugary, steering well clear of Mr Donut's special new tofu donuts and wondering about the Yumcha. They were playing old American records over the sound-system, introduced by Mr Donut's pre-recorded in-house DJ. As I left, he put on what seemed to be a song in Japanese all about donuts.

The dinky two-carriage train of the Shizuoka Railway took me to Kusanagi Station. On the road from the station, the first sign of the 'eventu' appeared – an elderly man wearing a white reflective bandoleer and a plastic crash helmet, with a wand, ready to direct pedestrians across the road. Crash helmets are big in Japan. In Yoyogi Park in Tokyo that spring, I'd seen municipal park gardeners wearing crash helmets while planting tulips. You can never be too careful.

I followed the men in helmets, who were liberally deployed in the area, on the prowl for pedestrians who might attempt to cross the road unaided, and headed for what was clearly the object of the 'eventu' – a huge, spanking new superstore run by the Jusco company. There was Matsuda-san, rallying the troops, there was Yamada-san, in his blue-tinted glasses, trying to stay out of the bright sunlight; and there was the expectant but impassive crowd of would-be customers, mostly the sort of people who would turn out at 9.00 a.m. on a Sunday morning to attend the opening of a superstore. These people, I thought, need a hobby.

The samba band, of course, already had one, although I have to admit that the band members assembled before me didn't really represent what you might regard as a cross-section of swinging Japanese urban youth, setting out to redefine the parameters of the nation. There was, to be honest, a strong hint of nerdiness in the air. Everyone was wearing white cotton zip-up jackets advertising something called J.Water; everyone except Mr Tanaka, a friendly faced, thick-set man whom I decided was probably Mr Matsuda's first lieutenant, probably in charge of chopping fingers. He was wearing a blue tracksuit and appeared to be handling logistics.

I decided to attempt some basic group analysis of the assembled band members. If there was a division, it was between the three or four men in their thirties or forties for whom this band had possibly become just a little too important, and the under-thirties and under-twenties, including a seemingly inexhaustible supply of quite serious-looking young girls. Among them, I came to realise, were some mother and daughter groupings. I wondered whether the mothers were along to keep an eye on their daughters, or if they too were in search of the high-rolling thrills of life with the band.

The S-Pulse samba band wasn't alone. Interestingly, there was a high schoolgirls cheerleaders group in yellow and blue leotards with the word SHARKS emblazoned on them, and heavy make-up. Yamada-san explained that they were from Shimizu's Tokai Dai-ichi private high school. There were also two teams of pre-school children in cute little cotton coats. Known as happi coats, these short, wrap-around, kimono-style coats were to be a recurrent feature of my time on the Japanese terraces. The happi coat is the equivalent of a team shirt for civilians at group events, such as shrine festivals, opening ceremonies, company functions and football matches.

I engaged Yamada-san in conversation. I couldn't work out whether he was pleased to see me or whether he thought the whole thing was just too embarrassing. But I had decided. He was the chosen one whether he liked it or not, my guide to the world of Japanese samba. We exchanged thoughts on the weather, which

Yamada thought was rather too hot. I got to asking about the band and when he'd joined. Ten months ago, it turned out, he'd gone to interview the band for his web site at one of their monthly practice sessions, held at the Crescendo Karaoke Club on the third Tuesday of every month.

'I went to interview them. They said . . . why don't you . . .' At this point he seemed to lose it.

'Join in?' I suggested.

'Join in,' he concurred. I asked him a bit about teaching. 'I don't like to work or study,' he said. 'I like all kinds of sport.' Warming to the subject, Yamada explained that before football, he used to be a fan of Formula One racing, and had travelled to Australia, Brazil, Britain, Mexico and France in pursuit of this somewhat expensive hobby. 'I used to be a fan of Ayrton Senna. But when he stopped racing, I lost some of my interest. Now I have a lot to do with S-Pulse.'

Since Ayrton Senna had stopped racing principally as a result of being killed in a catastrophic crash in the San Marino Grand Prix, I wondered at the time whether Yamada-san was being diplomatic; and whether the shock of seeing his hero's fatal accident had turned him into a football fan. In any case, here he was bright and early on a Sunday morning in Golden Week, opening a super-store. It was a crowded programme. First, at 9.00 a.m. exactly, the samba band moved into the roped-off area in front of the ribbon that was stretched in front of the closed doors of the store, playing one of their big all-hands-on-deck numbers. In front of the crowd, four young men, who in England would be called yobs, started dancing up and down like madmen, shouting 'ORE ORE ORE ORE, ESS-PULSE, ESS-PULSE!' at the appropriate moments. The crowd looked on politely and the samba team swung into a second number.

At this point, one of the four dancing madmen spotted the innocent waiting schoolchildren and decided to influence their young lives by dancing up and down in front of them shouting 'ESS-PULSE ESS-PULSE' while punching the air with his fists. Some of them joined in, somewhat cautiously, as if expecting the

ULTRA NIPPON

whole thing to end in tears at any moment. I noticed that at the back, one timid-looking group had decided to put their fingers in their ears.

And so it went on. After the samba band came the cheerleaders, who waved semaphore flags and danced around energetically. Then came the pre-school boys, who did a sort of synchronised (for four year olds) aerobic dance, followed by the girls, who started dancing disco-style to a Japanese song.

'This song,' said Yamada, almost getting lively, 'this song . . . uh . . . every summer in Shimizu . . . uh . . . everyone . . . uh . . . dances to it.'

'They dance to disco?'

'Yes. Disco.'

I realised that Yamada-san was probably talking about the Shimizu summer dancing festival. According to my Shimizu guidebook, the dancing is one of the main events of the Shimizu port festival and 'involves the people of the city in street dancing'. Up to this point, I'd thought that this was some kind of long-established, traditional dance, like English morris dancing, associated with the summer shrine festivals that proliferate across the country. But no. It was disco.

'It started . . . maybe ten years ago,' said Yamada-san, as the weeny boppers strutted their stuff in front of the superstore. So much for tradition. I decided then and there that I needed to be in Shimizu for the dancing festival.

After the teenies had finished, it was time for the ribbon-cutting ceremony, carried out by a selection of likely future customers. Then the waiting crowds trooped through the open doors, running the gauntlet of cheerleaders holding their sema-phore flags high, while the band played and the four madmen chanted 'ORÉ ORÉ ORÉ JUS-CO JUS-CO' which struck me as rather a nice touch.

I headed back to the parking lot with the band and on the way encountered one of the chorus of young women who had played the *tamborim*, a sort of small tambourine without the small metal cymbals which is hit with a flexible plastic stick at amazing speed. She had been giving me the sort of looks Japanese people give you when they are working up the courage to say something to you in English.

'Herro,' said the tambourine player, a smiley, round-faced and slightly plump young woman. She spoke very deliberately, her eyes darting about as she tried to remember the words. 'Are you from Engrand?' I said I was, and that my name was Jonathan.

'My name is Hori,' said Miss Hori. 'Tomita Hori. What team do you support?'

'West Ham United,' I said emphatically, although I am somewhat lapsed. Getting into this kind of conversation with a Japanese football fan can often become much more complicated than you might expect. When I told Izumi-san, a Yokohama Marinos supporter and also a passionate fan of Club Atletico del Rio Plata in Buenos Aires, that I was a West Ham fan, she said, 'Oh! Like the leader of Iron Maiden.' Miss Hori was equally up to speed.

'Ahhh,' she said. 'The Hammers.' I realised I was dealing with a professional. She paused, and then went on. 'I support Manchester United,' which wasn't so surprising. But Ms Hori had a rather more refined view of things than that. 'I like Eric Cantona,' she said, 'but now Eric Cantona has gone.' She looked a little crestfallen. 'You know who this is?' She produced from inside her purse a small picture of Eric the Great, playing for France.

'That's Eric Cantona,' I said authoritatively. Miss Hori beamed. I felt I was a hit.

On the roof, Matsuda-san was issuing instructions. He looked in my direction and I heard the word *gaijin*, which means outside person or foreigner, and then the word sushi, which means sushi. Yamada-san translated.

'Do you . . . uh . . . like . . . sushi?'

Sushi I liked. 'Mmmm, sushi,' I said, assuming that we were all off to eat sushi together for lunch, being already well aware that Shimizu is one of the main ports for landing tuna in Japan.

'Four o'clock,' said Yamada-san, 'Shimizu-no Ginza, near the station. Tekkamaki tuna roll. Big one.'

I had no idea what he was talking about. Shimizu-no Ginza

was the covered shopping street near the station plaza, but 'teppamaki tuna roll, big one' had me floored. Clearly it was going to be another 'eventu' and I was going to have to be there.

For the next few hours, I loitered around the port area, taking the opportunity to visit the very swish and modern port museum, officially called the Vehrkehr Shimizu Port Terminal Museum. 'Vehrkehr means "transportation" or "association" in German,' the official Shimizu guidebook told me, enigmatically. 'In this port museum, you can see the entire development of Shimizu Port, back to its origins and into the future.'

A nice lady, who seemed to be somewhat shocked by the arrival of a foreign tourist, sold me a ticket, and I wandered between the 'models of ships, goods and documents relating to shipping' that were on display, unable to make much sense of anything but generally appreciating the layout, plus the fabulous toilets. I noted from the official guide that I could in the future also visit the Tokai University Social Education Centre, which included 'a science museum with both live and mechanical fish on display'.

At 3.30, with the sky beginning to cloud over ominously, I headed for the Shimizu-no Ginza shopping street, stopping on the way to browse at the Angel porno shop. The store is fronted by a small street shrine to Shimizu S-Pulse. There's a screen with the silhouette of a player, and plates hanging on strings spelling out the letters S-P-U-L-S-E above neat flowerpots of bright red and purple geraniums and pansies. Other hanging ornaments dangling in the wind include small footballs, shiny compact discs and silver stars. Inside, a nice-looking old lady with a feather duster stands guard over piles of hard-core sado-masochistic *manga* comics and copies of Japanese *Playboy*.

When I arrived at Shimizu-no Ginza, the purpose of the sushi-big-one-eventu rapidly became clear. A line of wooden trestle tables had been laid out down the middle of the pedestrian walkway. There were numbered cards on sticks marking out distances in metres along the line of tables, which disappeared into the distance ahead of me. From 0 metres near the station, I walked on one side of the tables all the way up to 110 metres, where some kind of command post had been established on a small stage, and from there carried on to 250 metres. The citizens of Shimizu were going to make a 250 metre long tekkamaki tuna roll; if they succeeded, it would be not only a new Japanese all-comers record, but indeed a new world record. Shimizu would finally be placed firmly on the map. The previous Japanese record was a mere 236 metres, set by a place called Kesennuma in Miyagi Prefecture.

The hard core of the samba band was being distracted from the task in hand by some cut-price sports goods. Matsuda had been joined by some other fairly thick-set people, including Mr Tanaka and a rather bleary-eyed fan in a black and white tracksuit. This was Mr Sakura, who I'd met earlier in the season when S-Pulse played Bellmare Hiratsuka. 'Call me Mr Cherry Blossom,' he'd said, which is what Sakura means in Japanese.

Matsuda soon had the situation in hand, going off to the central command post to get our instructions. First he sent us all off to wash our hands; then we were deployed from around 185 metres to 190 metres, standing on one side of the table. Along the middle were the special rolling mats made of bamboo, rice steamers were on standby and boxes of chilled, raw tuna were being handed out. There must have been wasabe sauce somewhere but it became a bit of a blur. Diligent old ladies handed out disposable plastic gloves and we eyed the task in hand.

'This . . . uh,' said Yamada, who was on my right, 'is organised by the shopkeepers here. They are . . . uh . . . concerned about the new store. There are supposed to be six hundred people here to help roll it. I don't think they have enough.'

A man who Yamada-san said was the member of parliament for the town wandered by in a smart black suit, accompanied by his personal secretary.

'That is the main job of Japanese law makers,' said Mr Yamada, in satirical mode, 'to attend events like this one. Not to make law. That's why I will not vote for them. Because they do not do their job.'

Some thick-set people with permed hair, gold necklaces and

handbags stopped by to talk to Mr Matsuda. The boyfriend of one of the sixteen-year-old tambourine players turned up, looking shifty and slightly embarrassed as he was introduced to the samba team. The mayor, Mr Miyagishima, dropped by. I decided to take his photo and as I did so he walked towards me, the only foreigner in the line-up. I bowed politely. He said something in Japanese. I smiled politely. The mayor headed off and was next seen talking to Matsuda-san.

'He said, "Thank you for coming to help," ' said Yamada-san.

'That's very nice,' I said.

And then before we knew it, there was a commotion down around the 85-metre mark.

'It's coming,' said Yamada-san, seriously. 'The *nori*. The seaweed roll. It's coming.'

It's worth remembering, if you ever do try to make a 250-metre-long sushi roll, that the important thing is the paper-thin seaweed *nori* which holds it all together. Get that right and the rest is easy. Down the line, we could see two worthy citizens rolling a vast wheel of dark green seaweed down the centre of the bamboo mats. It was a huge roll, a vast roll, the thickness of a large Gouda cheese, about eight inches wide.

'They have three of these rolls to make the distance,' said Yamada, obviously slightly in awe of the sheer technical brilliance of it all.

'Mmm,' I said.

The whole operation was being coordinated from the grandstand at 110 metres, which was linked via walkie-talkie to various sushi sub-commanders deployed along the length of the tables, wearing happi coats of course, and carrying big orange and gold S-Pulse flags; presumably as back-up in case radio communications broke down.

The command went out – deploy the rice. The old ladies on the other side of the table plonked down a lump of vinegared rice in front of each roller and we started squashing it flat, in line with the printed instructions that had been handed to each of us in advance. We put the raw tuna, cut into sticks, down the middle, and then the rolling began. This was clearly the critical stage, requiring split-second coordination. If someone wasn't ready to roll, the seaweed could tear, and the people of Kesennuma, Miyagi Prefecture, would sleep safe in their beds.

'Careful,' said Yamada-san.

'Careful,' I said.

And we rolled, three-quarters of the way over. Then we went for the full roll. There it was – an admittedly slightly uneven, deep green, sushi roll, about two inches thick, sitting in front of me and snaking off on either side as far as the eye could see. It had a kind of beauty.

But it wasn't over. Next we placed our hands palm upwards in their disposable plastic gloves under the roll, and then we lifted, slowly and steadily, demonstrating that we had created a self-supporting structure which would not fall apart as soon as it was moved from the table.

The television cameras rolled. The cameras flashed. Yamada-san smiled. I smiled. Beers were handed out. The old ladies, who had of course secretly organised the whole thing, produced sharp knives and cut the roll up into ten-inch portions, producing handy plastic bags to allow people to take home their handiwork, and started packing up. We were all given a small certificate; mine stands on my mantelpiece to this day. Two days later, there was a picture in one of the Tokyo English language dailies, saying that in all 200kg of tuna had been used to create a tekkamaki which was 241.5 metres long.

It had been a very big day. I felt it was time to go.

'I'm going home,' I said to Yamada-san.

'Goodbye,' he said.

'Bye-bye,' I said to the sushi-rolling samba band.

'Bye-bye, Jonasan-san,' they said, and waved. I felt I'd almost made it. But not quite.

I took the late-afternoon train back to Tokyo from Shimizu Station. On the way, I picked up a copy of the *Japan Times*. Coincidentally, it had a long article all about the *yakuza*. It had emerged that the head of a *yakuza* crime gang had acquired one million shares in Japan Airlines, the biggest airline not only in

Japan but in Asia. Interestingly enough, JAL is one of the main sponsors of S-Pulse because of its close links to Suzuyo, the privately owned distribution and shipping company which took control of S-Pulse in 1994. Was S-Pulse controlled by the mob? Was Mr Matsuda the enforcer? Would I live to find out? Did anyone care? I fell asleep speeding towards Tokyo at 150 miles an hour, as train maidens wandered up and down the aisles offering souvenir cakes from Shizuoka, hot coffee and beer, whiskey and water and ice cream.

清水

4 NOBLE BARBARIANS

Three days later, when Shimizu S-Pulse played Nagoya Grampus Eight in the Nagaragawa Memorial Stadium in Gifu, I decided it was time to get serious.

The Gifu match was on a Wednesday afternoon. In theory, the holidays would end the next day, although Japan wouldn't be back at anything close to full speed until the following week. I'd arrived in Gifu the night before, travelling for the first time with the S-Pulse team from Shizuoka Station, although I was confined to the normal seats while the team travelled in the first-class compartments which, for some reason, are known as 'Green Cars'. It was pouring with rain, a steady heavy downpour that lasted all day and reminded you that Japan is after all, a collection of islands on the edge of the Pacific, from where typhoons sweep in, dumping vast quantities of rain on the pachinko parlours and the end-of-spring cherry blossom. At Shin-Gifu Station, one stop beyond Nagoya, the team boarded the big orange S-Pulse team bus. During the journey of almost an hour through the rain, the team watched a recording of the recent Brazil versus Barcelona match on the coach video.

This was definitely a very polite travelling group. I'd expected some rowdiness, or noise at least, from around twenty-five males travelling together. On the train they went to sleep (having completed training earlier that afternoon), and on the bus they watched the video in a respectful silence. It struck me that it would be a very bad idea for Paul Gascoigne ever to contemplate playing in Japan.

Oki-san, the Japanese assistant manager and a Shimizu boy born and bred, had told us that Gifu is 'in the country'. We did pass some rice fields before we plunged once again into urban Japan – pachinko parlours, convenience stores, rows of car showrooms and drive-in opticians.

There were more videos later after we'd dined at our plush five-star Gifu Renaissance Hotel; the team and staff ate together in a banqueting room on the top floor, with Perryman-san, Oki, Phil Holder, the doctor, Fuka the Brazilian goalkeeping coach and Edmundo the translator sitting together. After seeing the end of the Brazil–Barcelona game, most of the players drifted off. Perryman and the management team watched the video of the last game against the Urawa Reds.

'Look at him,' says Perryman-san to no one in particular, referring to the positioning of one of their forwards. 'Where is he? He's in SS land.'

'SS land?' I ask cautiously of Phil Holder.

'He's up in the seats.'

'Oh.'

'The SS seats. The expensive ones. At the top of the centre stand.'

'Oh.'

'This is shonky,' says Perryman.

'I reckon you're goin' to have to lay the law down,' said Holder.

'I've told him three thousand times I've fuckin' told him.'

Then they go back to the video. Fabinho, the talented but often slightly out-to-lunch Brazilian forward, was still in the room, listening and quietly finishing his ice cream. Perryman-san pounces on him.

'Fabi, Fabi, come over here,' and he physically demonstrates how Fabi should be positioning himself near a defender. Edmundo throws in translations into Brazilian. Fabi nods, looks a little dazed and confused, and wanders off. Holder mutters something about getting out of bed. Eventually, everyone except Perryman-san begins to show signs of weariness. Holder drifts off to make a phone call and then comes back.

'Are we winning yet?' he says.

The next day the rain had gone and after eating breakfast in the hotel with Perryman-san, Oki and a rather fragile-looking Phil Holder, I went out for a stroll. The hotel is near the stadium and I found the members of the samba band already sitting in the sunshine waiting for the gates to open, some four hours before kick-off, surrounded by their shiny metal drums and tambourines. They'd come down by road from Shimizu, a good five or six hours driving, getting up at four o'clock in the morning. Yamada-san was among them, bleary-eyed behind his blue-tinted John Lennon spectacles.

'I am,' he said in the slow but exact way he has of talking, making sure that every word is correct, 'not so well. I am, in fact, a little tired.'

After registering my presence, I wandered off to take a look around. The stadium itself is part of a sports park built on the banks of the Nagara River, probably in the late 1980s – those heady days of economic expansion – along with the adjacent conference centre and the hotel. Aside from taking in the occasional video-watching, buffet-munching football team, the hotel clearly did a good line in weddings, particularly in early May. A sign outside announced the availability of a 'mini-bridal' special. Inside, on one side of the vast marble lobby, there was a ceremonial staircase with large displays of white and yellow flowers, leading down to a lectern. This was the lobby chapel, available, so the sign said, for just 250,000 yen, around £1,300, allowing the lucky couple to make their most solemn and enduring vows in full view of the reception desk.

I wandered over to the concrete-reinforced banks of the river, which flowed at the foot of a low hill topped by Gifu castle. The castle is a modern reconstruction, the original having gone up in smoke, along with the rest of the town, during the war under heavy American bombing directed at the city's metal works. According to my guidebook, Gifu is famous not just for weddings but also as a centre for traditional Japanese swordsmiths, for the production of lacquered parasols, and for its Oku cormorant fishing, a sort of underwater version of hawking. From the end of May, fishermen take groups of tourists out in wooden boats on the river, and ply them with alcohol and food while demonstrating the traditional art of using diving cormorants on strings to catch fish. The birds are unable to swallow the fish they catch because of a tight band wrapped around their throats. This somewhat brutal activity, presumably sanctioned by the Japanese society for the prevention of cruelty to cormorants, explains the bronze cormorants deployed around the fountain in the lobby of the hotel, adjacent to the lobby chapel steps.

Underneath all this pseudo-rustic flimflam, Gifu is about as rural as Wolverhampton; over the years it has gradually become joined to the urban sprawl of Nagoya, possibly the most non-descript city in all of Japan, which is saying something. Football has made Nagoya famous. Nagoya Grampus Eight is probably the best-known Japanese football team in Britain, firstly because Gary Lineker played there when he went to Japan at the end of his playing career; secondly because the French manager Arsène Wenger ran the club in 1995 and 1996, before moving to Arsenal and winning the English League and FA Cup double in his first full season; and thirdly because Nagoya Grampus Eight rivals Kyoto Purple Sanga as the most absurd of all the J.League team names.

Why Grampus? Why Eight? Sometime in the Middle Ages, when Japan was divided into warring fiefdoms, Nagoya castle was besieged by a wicked foe who succeeded in setting the castle alight, causing much consternation among the citizenry. But, so the story goes, a school of whales appeared in the sea off the city. They used their water spouts to shower water on to the burning castle, extinguishing the fires and saving the city. So the whale was a natural choice, and 'grampus' as we all know is another name for a killer whale or orca. It's assumed that there were eight of them, although when I asked team officials about this, they became confused and said they weren't themselves entirely sure.

So why not Nagoya Whales Eight? Possibly because whales, though regarded in Japan as cute and edible, are just not speedy or active enough; or perhaps because of the existence of a baseball team called the Taiho Whales, based in Yokohama. However, in the mid 1990s, the Taiho Whales were beginning to flounder and lose support, and changed their name to the Yokohama Bay Stars, presumably because the word 'grampus' had already been taken.

The Grampus Eight mascot is a fluffy simulacrum of a killer whale called Grampus-kun. In fact, the club has a Mr and a Mrs Grampus, Grampus-kun and Grampako-chan. Grampako-chan, like Minnie Mouse, has a small red bow just ahead of her dorsal fin. An hour or so before kick-off, when I wandered back to the ground, groups of young children were being lined up for unspeakably cute photographs with the two six-foot tall, black and white cuddly beasts, who waddled around and flapped their flippers for maximum effect.

At the Grampus end, the red hordes had laid out their banners, including the usual handful written in English. I decided my favourite was the infinitely polite SHOW US PLEASE YOUR BEST PERFORMANCE, which hung along with ULTRA NAGOYA, ROSSO BRILLIANTE and the imperative GET THE GLORY. More perplexing was NOBLE BARBARIAN, which I suspected was a reference to Nagoya's brooding, angry and often brilliant Yugoslav star, Dragan Stojkovic. Stojkovic, whose nickname even before he came to Japan was, for some reason, 'Pixie', was on the pitch with Nagoya's new French manager, Daniel Sanchez, both wearing smart European-style suits.

As Sanchez wandered around, Stojkovic sat down on a trainer's seat on the touch-line, leaning forward, staring into space and looking moody. He had a lot to brood about; his hometown in Yugoslavia, Nis, was one of the targets of the current NATO bombing campaign over Kosovo. Earlier in the season, Stojkovic had participated in a 'stop the bombing' protest with Petrovic at Urawa Red Diamonds. When they scored, which they both did, they pulled up their shirts to reveal 'stop the bombing' slogans on their tee-shirts. Politically, it wasn't so successful because it didn't stop the bombing. In footballing terms, it wasn't hugely successful either. Petrovic got booked. Stojkovic, who wisely kept his shirt on, survived unscathed, although his team lost. Now, as he sat there on the side-line, a Japanese photographer was creeping cautiously up from behind, trying for a shot to capture the broody loneliness of it all with the sort of stealthy approach work normally associated with safaris.

Meanwhile, at the other end of the stadium, the S-Pulse fans were their usual mass of festive yellow and orange in the bright sunshine, and the samba band was in position in the centre behind the goal, preparing for action but not yet playing. I thought it was time to join them.

I wandered through the ticket barriers into the away end of the stadium, heading for the samba crew. As I worked my way around the stand, the first person I saw wasn't Yamada, but the charming and boisterous 'call me Mr Cherry Blossom' Sakura-san. Sakura-san is a man who believes that communication is not so much a matter of language as of the will.

'Ahhh, Jonasan-san,' he roared as he spotted me. 'S-Pulse supporter group number one. Number one in Nippon, des-ne?' Jonasan-san agreed, and was slapped on the back by Mr Sakura who was clearly not overly affected by the 4.00 a.m. start. 'This is Mr Oba,' he said, swinging around to indicate a young fan whom I recognised from the Bellmare game. 'He is lovely boy.'

Mr Oba disagreed with what was apparently a suggestion about his sexual orientation.

'Noooh. No lovely boy. Sakura-san is alcohol-boy.'

'Wha?' said Mr Sakura. 'Wha?' playfully grabbing Lovely Boy around the neck.

The two of them were wearing short, pink Japanese happi coats, marked on the back with the words K's Club. I had already seen how organised the Shimizu fans are in full samba rhythm, and I was beginning to find out more and more about how it all worked. I now knew that the K's Club jackets meant that Mr Sakura and Mr Oba belonged to a sub-group of fans who were particularly devoted to Shimizu's thirty-three-year-old mid-fielder and local-boy-made-good, Kenta Hasegawa.

At Gifu, it was Sakura-san who, his breath heavy with the smell of beer, led me to the front rows and got Oba-san to give me a red-orange S-Pulse K's Club supporters shirt. We stood with Mr and Mrs Koike and their ten-year-old daughter Arisa, who was wearing a shirt like mine and holding a tambourine. They handed me a pair of yellow S-Pulse plastic clappers. This was it. I was ready.

So were the S-Pulse fan commanders. In central position, at the head of the samba band by the cymbals, stood Mr Tanaka; it was his job today to direct the band and decide how, what and when we should be chanting. Mr Matsuda was the musical director of the band, strapped about with a vast surdo drum. Below him there were two rows of women wielding *tamborims*, tin bell things called *agogos* and rattling tins, and all the paraphernalia of the well-equipped samba unit. Behind Mr Matsuda sat the heavy rhythm section including Yamada-san, sheltering behind his sunglasses.

In front of me, on the rail overlooking the pitch, was Mr Oba, whose job it was to ensure that the members of K's Club were kept fully informed of Mr Tanaka's chanting decisions. Along the rail, four or five other sub-lieutenants were poised to perform a similar task for their sections of the crowd. It's not easy being one of these guys. They have to be able to watch the game, keep an eye on Mr Tanaka and relay the chanting and waving to the crowd behind them. It's a full-time job.

K's Club is in fact just one of a series of eighteen small supporting sub-groups, all of whom defer to Mr Matsuda. Some, as Yamada later explained, are devoted to particular players, such as K's Club. The Nobori Support Club, on the other hand, rallies for midfielder Masaaki Sawanobori; S-Keepers backs goalkeeper Masanori Sanada. Other groups, such as Chapeu Laranja (which means orange hat in Brazilian Portuguese) and the Shimizu Citizens are, well, just team supporters.

All of these groups follow Matsuda's judgement on pretty much all key matters. I asked Yamada about it, wondering how this was organised. Did they have meetings? Did they have elections? He became possibly even more thoughtful than usual, searching for the right words.

'Mr Matsuda is leader because . . . because . . . he is the best . . . at leading when we supporters are in the stands . . . and he does many things, like organising the samba band.'

'So he takes more responsibility?' I suggested, putting words into Yamada-san's mouth.

'Yes. He takes more responsibility. So he is leader. And because he is an insurance sales agent, he has enough free time to organise things.'

A few minutes after I took up position, the two teams filed on to the pitch. The stadium was close to capacity; the two ends were packed. The appearance of the players provoked the beginnings of applause from the S-Pulse supporters. This was hastily suppressed by the crowd commanders, who clearly regarded this kind of overly spontaneous crowd reaction as bad discipline. Instead, Mr Tanaka gestured to each of his front-line sub-lieutenants to make sure they were ready, mouthing the words 'Shimizu S-Pulse', and when he'd got the nod, he turned back to the band and stretched out his two arms.

'SHIMIZU ESS-PULSE,' we shouted all together very loudly, arms outstretched. The band banged out the rhythm and paused. 'SHIMIZU ESS-PULSE,' we shouted again, and paused. And then once more, 'SHIMIZU ESS-PULSE.' It was the challenge thrown down, silencing the red masses at the other end of the pitch with the sheer exuberance of it all. Here we are. Now Mr Tanaka had his arms held up, crossed in front of him – the Japanese gesture for stop which was mimicked by his sub-lieutenants down the line. On the field, Shimizu were about to kick off. Tanaka turned to the band and they started to play the syncopated, bouncing beat of what I always consider to be the happy 'we're in possession and playing very nicely' song. We sang, twirling scarves and plastic clappers above our heads, 'Oh o OOOOH o o o o ooooh, Oh o OOOOH o o o o ooooh. SHIMIZU ESS-PULSE!' again and again, until the crossed arms instructed us to stop.

After ten minutes, I was sweating and hoarse. It seemed to me that a lot of the chanting was pitched just slightly too high, so that some of my o-o-o-o-ohs had come close to screaming. This was either a musical issue related to the pitch of the samba band, or it was because Japanese football chants are written for women, which is entirely possible.

Now a wail went up, spontaneously, mostly it seemed from young women. Yes, indeed, Daisuke Ichikawa, our nineteen-year-old attacking left-back and the pride of Tokai Dai-ichi high school, who had played for the national team against Korea the previous year, had been brutally brought down by a thigh-high tackle. Tanaka was on the case.

'ICHIKAWA!' he shouted to the band and the lieutenants.

'ICHIKAWA!' we shouted back, smashing our plastic clappers together.

The free-kick was taken, and we were off into one of the more complex manoeuvres. I have still not quite worked this one out. It involves standing right side forward and waving your right arm up and down while chanting 'UM DOIS TRES QUATRO' and then turning around to put your left side forward chanting 'UM DOIS TRES QUATRO' again while waving your left arm up and down. I have to admit that at Gifu I thought everyone was chanting 'ESS-PULSE MUSCLE, ESS-PULSE MUSCLE' so that's what I chanted. No one seemed to mind.

At some clubs, the supporters take steps to avoid this sort of confusion. At Bellmare Hiratsuka, for instance, a club struggling on the brink of bankruptcy at the start of the 1999 season, the supporters' group was engaged in a fund-raising effort for the club at the gate. More unusually, in a bid to develop the support base, they were also handing out leaflets headed 'Bellmare Superwave!' which spelt out the chants for the uninitiated. Since the chants were written in Japanese *katakana* script which is phonetic, unlike the *kanji* pictograms, I could work out a number of them, ranging from the somewhat limited 'BELLMARE, OLE OLE OLE' to the more ambitious 'BELLMARE LEZ GO, RA-RA RA-RA RA-RA-RA, RA-RA RA-RA RA-RA [loud! times four], BELLMARE LEZ GO!' My favourite was 'OO OOOOOH OOOOOOOOOH, OO OOOOOH OOOOOO BELLMARE!'.

I could have done with this kind of assistance at the Gifu game. Now, we were going into an even more complicated arm-waving routine, which involved shouting 'ORE ORE ORE ORE' while crossing your arms above your head. I was trying to follow Oba-san's gestures while turning from time to time to Tanaka-san to see what was next. It was not easy to watch the game at the same time. All of a sudden, Mr Koike behind me grabbed my two arms and started waving them from side to side for me, obviously concerned about the possible implications for the ensemble of having a dysfunctional foreigner with no sense of rhythm cavorting in the front rows.

As if to confirm his worst fears, Grampus Eight then scored, their twenty-one-year-old forward, Kenji Fukuda, blasting the ball past our keeper, Sanada, right in front of the rhythm section. It was a shock. But Mr Tanaka didn't blink an eye. Within seconds he was up again.

'SHIMIZU ESS-PULSE,' he shouted.

'SHIMIZU ESS-PULSE,' we bellowed back. For good measure we followed up with a round of 'SANADAs' just in case our goalkeeper thought that we didn't love him any more. We did. We were supporters. Ours was definitely not to reason why; or to reason at all.

For Japanese fans, I had begun to realise, or for most of them, support isn't conditional. It's what you do, no matter what your team does. You try as hard to support as they try to play. This lack of critical attitude creates absurdities. If a player stands in front of an open goal and blasts the ball over the crossbar, the crowd will still chant his name, presumably on the assumption that he was, in fact, trying. Booing their own team, or any member of that team, happens very rarely (although the following week, when S-Pulse played struggling JEF United, the JEF fans deliberately sat on their hands for the entire first half, to show their growing disappointment with the string of defeats. I assumed their argument was that if the team didn't do its job, which was to win football games, they weren't going to do their job, which was to support.)

'Japanese supporter es um tipo unico,' Carlos Alberto Santos, Shimizu's veteran thirty-eight-year-old Brazilian midfielder told me later, communicating in the mix of Brazilian-Spanish-Italian which we had developed. 'Si um jugador, a player, fa bene, does well, los supportores sono molto contenti, very happy. And if you don't do well, they say good. This is nice. It's very nice. But it can be a problema.'

'A problema?' I asked.

'Si,' he said. 'If they are not critical, some players they come here from Brazil, where the crowds are very, very critical, and they play too relaxed.'

Scotsman Eddie Thomson, managing that season at Sanfrecce Hiroshima, had found it altogether too strange when he'd arrived for his first game at Hiroshima's Big Arch Stadium. Sanfrecce, which sounds like a beach resort in southern Italy, is one of the stranger J.League team name creations. You have to know that during the seventeenth century, when the mighty Shogun Ieyasu was waging war to unify Japan, he was opposed by the Mori clan who were based in Hiroshima. According to the legend, one of the Mori chiefs had warned his three sons about the risks of disunity by taking three arrows and snapping them one by one. Together, they were unbreakable. San in Japanese means three; frecce, if you take into account the continuing Japanese problem with the pronunciation of 'r', becomes flecce, which is Italian for arrows. It's easy when you know how. (It's less easy to work out why supporters from a city with the troubled history of Hiroshima should opt for the team slogan 'Pour on the Heat'.)

In early 1997 Eddie Thomson's new club had been struggling at the bottom of the J.League in early 1997, and his first game for them ended in a 3–1 defeat.

'We'd lost 3–1 and they were dancing and cheering. In Scotland I would have been creeping out of the stadium. I rang one of my friends in Scotland. "You're no going to believe this," I said. "We just lost 3–1, and they think we're wonderful." ' After another loss, the crowd started calling the team to go back on to the pitch. 'I wouldnae go,' said Thomson. 'I thought they were winding us up.'

Halfway through the first half, one of the S-Pulse strikers blasted the ball past the Nagoya right post. Tanaka-san, who already had his hands full, what with conducting the band with his back to the pitch, and keeping us chanting, looked anxiously over his shoulder to his lieutenants as he heard the gasps of appreciation.

'Who?' he mouthed over his shoulder to the front-line men, crossing his arms to bring the current chant to a rapid conclusion.

'Nobori,' came the reply from one.

'No. Hattori,' shouted two more, off to the left. Mr Tanaka made a snap decision.

'NOBORI,' he shouted.

'BOOM BOOM BOOM,' went the band.

'NOBORI,' we screamed.

By half-time, Shimizu were still one goal down. I was frankly knackered, as well as hoarse. Everyone else was too, and the band slumped over their samba drums. Ten-year-old Arisa went for the orange juice in the cooler box under the seats. Mr Sakura extracted a can of beer.

'Holding the big drums up for the whole game is very tiring,' Yamada said as I passed him, looking like a man in need of performance-enhancing drugs. I set off, a red-faced foreigner, searching for the kindly beer maidens.

Hurrah for social order. Hurrah for a self-policing polite people with a well-developed sense of group responsibility. How else is it possible to have vending machines in public places dispensing cans of beer, and in some cases, half-bottles of whiskey? How else is it possible for young women to wander through the stands at a soccer match, shouting *'irraishaimasse,'* 'at your service', and attract attention by waving a handful of fanned 1,000 yen notes?

At the back of the stadium I found a young woman dispensing

cold cans of beer into plastic cups for 450 yen, or about £2.50. It seemed a bargain at the time.

There was a sudden stirring down at the front of the stand. Grampus-kun, that lovable furry old killer whale, was heading our way! Now Grampus-kun was just below us, within what some English fans might regard as spitting distance. 'Grampus-kun, Grampus-kun,' pleaded the Shimizu fans, reaching out to stroke the very symbol of the foe. Cameras clicked. Grampus-kun waddled off.

It is not always sweetness and light with the Shimizu fans. In 1997 during a game against Kashiwa Reysol, what the Japanese call a regrettable incident occurred, involving the Brazilian forward Edilson, who was at the time the J.League's leading scorer. The game had gone into extra time when Edilson, who had already been booked, committed an egregious foul on a Shimizu defender and then collapsed himself, feigning injury and successfully avoiding the notice of the referee. Shimizu counterattacked. Then Kashiwa counter-counterattacked. Edilson miraculously recovered as the ball came back towards him, sprang to his feet and scored the golden goal, winning the match for the visitors.

In Europe, there would certainly have been trouble, if not a full-scale riot. In Shimizu, the hardline fans took what, for them, was appropriately drastic action, sitting down in front of the visiting team's bus after the game, blockading the exit from the stadium and demanding an apology from Edilson for his dishonourable act. Being a fairly easygoing Brazilian, not ordinarily given to foul play, Edilson was personally prepared to admit remorse. But Kashiwa's team managers, representatives of the giant Hitachi Corporation, were having none of it and they refused to allow the apology. The fans laid siege until two in the morning, when, having made their point, they went home. Kashiwa eventually went home, too, and Shimizu S-Pulse were fined by the league authorities for failing to keep order at their ground.

At a normal J.League game, the two year olds are usually the only ones making trouble, although there have been other incidents. In 1995, the J.League president, Saburo Kawabuchi, held an emergency press conference in response to violent incidents blamed on 'over exuberant' fans who were threatening security at J.League games. At a televised game between the Urawa Reds and Jubilo Iwata later that season, the Urawa crowd started lobbing plastic water bottles on to the pitch after the referee missed what they thought was a deliberate hand-ball inside Jubilo's penalty area. The day before, the press had reported that anonymous warnings had been received that there would be trouble from the Urawa fans if their team didn't play better against Jubilo, after a steady stream of dismal performances.

If Japanese fans ever do get rough, I would prefer not to be there. Despite the overall placid nature of the terraces, you have to bear in mind that there may be a lot of martial arts expertise behind those cheerful faces. That smiling eight year old, for instance, is probably breaking bricks with her forehead in PE lessons at school.

For the moment, though, things seem pretty safe. 'Me S-Pulse fans' number one bad boy,' the jovial Mr Sakura told me one day, during an in-depth discussion of the social implications of football violence. 'But England, Deutsch bad boy, no. Me up-tempo bad boy! S-Pulse up-tempo supporters number one J.League.'

And so to the second half. 'SHIMIZU ESS-PULSE,' we bellowed again, as the team came back on to the pitch. We were 1–0 down, and it was clear that only through the total commitment of all concerned, including us, was this match to be saved, and possibly won.

Much of the second half is a blur of oohs and ahs and olés. Reading the official report on the game, some of it comes back. Six minutes into the second half, the excellent and gentlemanly Carlos Alberto Santos slotted a shot into the Grampus net from right of centre just outside the goal area – one all. Six minutes later, S-Pulse's Toshihide Saito, a defender, made it 2–1, causing scenes of unparalleled jubilation among our ranks, and justifying all the hard work we had put in so far. For the first time I heard the crowd unaccompanied by the band – 'UMA MAS, UMA MAS,' which apparently means 'one more, one more' in Portuguese. This happy state of affairs lasted for approximately seven minutes before one more goal came, unfortunately for the wrong side. Grampus had equalised. We redoubled our efforts, particularly at corner kicks and free-kicks near the Grampus goal, shouting 'Ooooooaaaaah GO! GO!, Oooooaaah GO! GO!' or something very similar.

It was to no avail. Despite the relentless pressure from S-Pulse, or perhaps because of it, Grampus scored again. They were ahead – 3–2 with just nine minutes left. It didn't look good. We were tired. Ten-year-old Arisa, beside me, had stopped banging her tambourine. There was a stunned silence. It was all too much. But then Tanaka-san shouted 'SHIMIZU ESS-PULSE' and the band thundered into action, and we shouted back, 'SHIMIZU ESS-PULSE', prepared to give our all for the lost cause. It was heroic. It was noble. No one started filing out of the stadium in despair. We could win this one. After all, just three days ago, Grampus had given away an equaliser in the last minute and lost in extra time to the Marinos.

'ESS-PULSE ESS-PULSE,' we chanted, standing up and stretching out our arms. We squatted down again shouting 'OOOOORE OOOOORE!' then, standing up, 'ESS-PULSE ESS-PULSE.' So busy were we in our total support that we almost didn't notice the S-Pulse equaliser, from Hattori this time, in the eighty-ninth minute. More jubilation, but then the game was off again. Grampus has the ball in the midfield. They lose possession. Shimizu's Ando takes the ball down the right wing for S-Pulse, lobbing it over the defence for Kuboyama, who crosses in front of the goalmouth. In the last minute of regular time, Hattori blasts it in.

We go crazy. Lovely Boy Oba-san comes and gives me a hug. So does Sakura-san. The band launches into a series of victory choruses, with our favourite happy tune, 'OREEH ... ORE ORE ORE ... ESS-PULSE ESS-PULSE, OREEH ... ORE ORE ORE ... ESS-PULSE ESS-PULSE.' The whistle goes. S-Pulse 4, Grampus 3. It's a famous victory, but highly, highly stressful.

'It is not so good for my corazón, for my heart,' says Carlos Alberto Santos afterwards.

清水

5 THE DUNGA DEBATE

I'd hoped to meet Dragan Stojkovic after the Gifu game, but
somehow, it didn't seem the best time to approach the man who
gave every appearance of being the grumpiest player in all of
J.League soccer. Firstly, there was the trauma of the team's second
last-minute loss in less than a week; and secondly, the war in
Kosovo meant NATO was still bombing his hometown.

In the toing-and-froing of players, reporters and officials after
the Grampus–S-Pulse game, the Nagoya press assistant, Mr Izumi,
and his colleagues encouraged me to ask Stojkovic for an
interview. 'There he is. Ask him,' they said, timidly indicating with
eye movements the presence of the man they too call 'Pixie'. I
decided Mr Izumi was just trying to stir things up. Instead, I
accosted Daniel Sanchez, the smart, besuited Nagoya manager, a
big man possibly over six feet tall, with a striking resemblance to
Gerard Depardieu, and arranged to visit the Grampus training
ground next day.

I spent the night in a characteristically faceless business hotel
near Nagoya Station, complete with sinister old receptionist and
one of those total-plastic-unit bathrooms that can be hosed down

to cope with any eventuality (when top Japanese executives want to kill themselves, they generally choose a business hotel). The next day, I located my traditional Japanese breakfast of non-tofu donuts and coffee at a Mr Donut shop adjacent to the station, and took the subway to the Toyota company sports ground in the suburbs.

It was a long journey, taking about an hour and ending up in the sort of non-countryside that fills in between the cities in Japan, a mixture of light industry and clumps of trees interspersed with rice paddies and car parks in almost equal numbers. From the station, I walked along a road dodging fast-moving, brightly polished trucks. It was nice to know that if I ever did get hit by a truck in Japan, at least I would be able to see my screaming face in the radiator. In Osaka once, I encountered a convoy of small but perfectly formed and very shiny cement-mixing trucks. If you can keep a cement mixer shiny, you really do have an edge in life.

The Toyota company sports ground is located opposite a gravel works and adjacent to high-tension powerlines. This backdrop is typical of a lot of J.League training grounds in a country where space is in short supply – the Kashima Antlers train next to Sumitomo's Kashima steel works; JEF United work out by a rubbish incineration plant; and the Japan Football Federation's national team training ground is downwind from a nuclear power plant.

Apart from its location, the Toyota ground is a well-appointed place. Near the gateway stands a group of institutional-looking brick buildings, and, more bizarrely, a croquet green where a group of old people were pottering about. These, I assumed as I walked cheerily past, must be retired Toyota employees, enjoying the calm of their twilight years after a hard life spent seeking world automotive domination. As I approached the soccer field, several mysterious platoon-sized squads of young men jogged past, like young recruits at an army boot camp, each group following a leader holding a small pennant. They seemed to be chanting something about 'good game'. These were clearly new Toyota employees, undergoing the sort of traditional semi-military indoctrination into the essence of the company which is still *de rigueur* for Japan's biggest corporations, aimed at creating dedicated middle managers who will sacrifice domestic happiness and personal health for the greater good of the organisation.

The Grampus team, meanwhile, was just finishing a practice session in the bright spring sunshine, watched by a dozen or so young women fans – wives of Toyota's dedicated middle managers, perhaps – who were sitting in a specially covered spectators' seating area.

Grampus is rumoured to receive some $8 million annually from Toyota's subsidiaries, making it one of the richest clubs in the J.League. Inside the clubhouse, small team pictures on the walls showed how some of the money had been spent, In the 1993 and 1994 pictures, there was the innocent smile of England's very own Gary Lineker. In 1995 and 1996, there was Arsène Wenger.

After Wenger left, in 1997 Grampus went into something of a confused spell, managerially speaking. Wenger's initial replacement was Carlos Queiroz, a Portuguese who had coached Saudi Arabia to the 1994 World Cup in the USA but who lasted at Nagoya for just three games. Sanchez himself had taken over from a Japanese coach just shortly after the start of the current season.

Daniel Sanchez, talking at the side of the training field and wearing a blue and white Le Coq Sportif tracksuit, wasn't at all happy about the previous two last-minute defeats.

'Incroyable,' he said. 'Unbelievable. Can you imagine this happening in Europe? Or in Latin America? No. Not at all.

'They don't know how to change tempo. At 3–2 up, they continue to play in exactly the same way, they don't think tactically to fall back, not to give the ball away. They were giving the ball away in the midfield. It's a big problem.'

Pretty big, it seemed; and it was getting bigger.

'They need to be more aggressive, more competitive, but you can't change that in two or three months. The most important thing for Japanese football right now is to develop this competitive spirit.'

The Japanese? Not competitive? But surely Japan is the supreme competitor, with those high-tech products and lengthy working practices and all that do-or-die kamikaze spirit. What about all those platoons of young salarymen, marching up and down outside in the sun? What about the very principle of so-called 'fighting spirit', words which the Japanese have adopted into their language, the sort of willingness to suffer for the cause exemplified in those TV game shows in which the competitors eat hairy spiders, or immerse themselves in slime?

Not according to Mr Sanchez, and to most of the other foreign coaches who work in Japan. Things are not always what they seem. The problem, meanwhile, was continuing to expand in a satisfactorily Gallic, philosophical sort of way.

'The football, it is a little against the spirit of Japan,' said Sanchez. 'Of course it is a collective sport, but it is a collection of individualities. [This sounds even better in French.] There's no hierarchy in football. In football, a young player is just as good or even better than an older player.'

For Japan, this is still a revolutionary concept, as evidenced by the fuss which erupted in the corporate world when car makers Mazda, owners of Sanfrecce Hiroshima, appointed a thirty-eight-year-old executive to its board of directors. Toyota itself had announced that the next month it intended to move towards the Sanchez doctrine of individual ability, with news that the company was planning to abolish seniority-based pay for its 20,000 middle managers. But Sanchez had already moved on.

'And football requires leaders on the field,' Sanchez explained, in magisterial mode, 'but here, when you want a player to be a leader, they don't like it. They all want to be equal.'

Was there a contradiction here? If Japan was hierarchical, surely there would be leaders? Everyone couldn't be equal. But Sanchez, it seemed, was arguing that the hierarchy which emerges on the football field is a product, not of pre-ordained social rankings, but of individuals choosing to assert themselves. (In the West, these individuals are often technically known by other members of the team as 'noisy wankers', but that's another cultural question.) The Japanese, to generalise wildly, are not a people who are culturally encouraged to express their individuality forcefully. Japanese football teams are not full of people yelling, 'Pull your finger out.'

I'd been struck by this from the first time I saw a Japanese team play. With most of the teams, there's very little shouting between the players. The first time I went to S-Pulse's Hebizuka ground, when Ardiles was still in charge, Perryman-san spent a lot of time on the side-lines just shouting, 'Speak! Speak! Speak! Speak!'

'It's taken us two seasons to get this lot to shout for the ball,' he said. 'There's a tendency to sit back and watch. Maybe they think shouting shows a lack of respect for the player with the ball, as if you're suggesting the player who's got it doesn't know what to do with it. I tell them that, as I see it, it shows more respect to the player to warn him that he's about to be tackled than it does if you let him get tackled.'

Dido Havenaar, the Dutch goalkeeper who has been in Japan since 1985, reckons it's not so much respect, as fear.

'They're afraid of making mistakes. They don't want to take responsibility,' he says. 'I have played in Japan for five different teams, and with every team it was the same. If I get the ball, as the goalkeeper, I want to throw quickly to go for a counterattack. But I'd look to the right-back or the left-back, and they'd make like, "No, no, no, no, no, not to me. I'm a little bit tired." Or sometimes they would be standing just behind an opponent to make sure you couldn't reach them. So that's a problem, the fact that they are afraid to take responsibility and to make decisions.'

At Sanfrecce Hiroshima, the Scots-born manager Eddie Thomson had even started fining his new players and threatening them with suspension if they didn't talk to each other during practices and during the games. 'We had huge problems,' he said. Grampus Eight's Sanchez obviously found this reticence equally perplexing.

'No one shouts for the ball. And no one encourages each other, or gets angry when someone makes a mistake. They just carry on.' I pointed out that this was not the case with Stojkovic. 'Ah, mais Stojkovic, il n'est pas japonais.'

'They've got the technique. They work hard,' he continued.

'They're a hard-working people, so there's no problem there, and they're learning. But it's their mentality that you have to change. They must be more competitive, meaner, more aggressive. These are things that count a lot in football now, being a bit meaner than your opponents. Now it's the one who wants to win the most who will generally win. Who has the mentality to win, will win. You often see that happen. And that's important here.'

Some two weeks later, on a rainy day, I came back to the Toyota ground for my interview with the apparently surly Slav, Mr Stojkovic. Grampus had improved since the two traumatic defeats. It seemed worth the risk. Phil Holder and Steve Perryman at Shimizu had suggested that I say hello; apparently, in 1990 before the World Cup in Italy, Perryman and Holder had taken Brentford FC to Zagreb in Croatia on a training camp, where they had played against the Yugoslav national eleven including Stojkovic, who was being heralded as one of the stars of the forthcoming World Cup. 'He seemed a nice enough sort of bloke,' said Holder. 'I doubt if he remembers us.'

Les Mottram, a Scottish referee who had been working for the past two seasons with the JFA, also suggested I say hello, having sent Stojkovic off on a number of occasions. 'He gets a wee bit steamed up,' said Mottram. 'But you couldn't find a nicer man when he's not playing.'

According to Sanchez, it wasn't just me and the entire front-office staff at Grampus who were likely to treat Stojkovic with a deference bordering on abject fear. 'The players respect him a lot and that's normal. But, on the pitch, that kind of respect shouldn't stop you talking to him, even shouting at him if he needs it; that should be part of the game, and afterwards it's all over. But here, non! Here they think that even on the pitch, to Pixie, to Stojkovic, they should not say anything at all.'

By 1999, Stojkovic, at thirty-four, was the J.League's leading foreign star, and one of its longest serving. He'd joined Grampus in the summer of 1994, after the US World Cup, and he'd played again in the Yugoslav team in France in 1998. He had three children in school in Nagoya. Compared to the mayhem unleashed in his home country over the previous four years, Japan seemed like a good bet.

I ended up doing the interview with the two of us sitting on plastic chairs in the stairwell of the Nagoya clubhouse. Mr Izumi had told me that I had only fifteen minutes. Pixie was a man on a tight schedule (why he's called Pixie I still don't know, I didn't have time to ask). When he arrived, he gave me a big, open smile. As they said, you wouldn't find a nicer man. When he's not playing.

I asked him how it had been, adjusting to Japanese soccer when he first arrived in 1994. He spoke in heavily accented English, choosing his words carefully, and pausing from time to time while he thought of how to say what he wanted.

'It was very hard,' he said. 'I don't know nothing about Japanese soccer before. This is the first opportunity . . . to know something about Japanese soccer. So I was excited to go to Japan. And today I am sure that I don't make a mistake. I was right to come here. Because this a good experience for me. A good life experience, but also for the soccer.

'Their football is really, well, you know, a little bit different,' he continued with charming understatement. 'You know I play in Europe, and for me soccer number one is European soccer. So here it is something different. It was very frustrating. But I tried to do my best, I tried to give a good example for the Japanese players. And after six months all the things are going up, positively.'

But perhaps things could not have got much worse than they were at the beginning.

At the beginning they made really, really . . . un-be-liev-able mistakes. Especially in defence. So for me, I cannot, I was not able to accept this kind of mistake. I can say stupid mistakes. Yeah. You lose a game like children. And on the other side this is a professional league, with professional players, so I was frustrated. But especially in the tactical work.'

Humbly, I suggested that from my recent observations, he seemed to have adopted what might be considered a forthright style of play, which was perhaps at odds with the traditional politeness displayed by his Japanese team-mates.

'All the players, you know they are really kind, they are good friends. But if you want to be a good professional soccer player, when you miss a goal, or you miss a big chance, you cannot smile. You cannot be happy. You must be angry. It is normal reaction.' He shook his head in disbelief. Even after five years in Japan you could tell he couldn't quite accept all this nervous grinning. 'They miss a chance . . . and they smile. When I miss a good opportunity, I never smile. Never. You must be angry. You must be ready to try again. To score. So . . . this kind of reaction was very, very different from where I played before, you know?'

'What's the funniest thing that's ever happened to you?' I asked, hopefully. He looked perplexed.

'I don't know,' he said. Ooops. Obviously football is not a particularly funny activity. I hurriedly got back to tactics.

'Physically they are good. Technically, also good. Their problem is tactical. They must repeat, repeat, a million times just to put it in the memory. This is an important thing for them. But the problem, maybe, is lack of experience, especially international experience. They pay the price for this. They lose three games in the World Cup. And of course, they were a little bit naive. They paid the price for that, too. Today in world soccer you must be angry, you must keep playing until the end, you must be a little bit clever, and never give up.'

He paused, as if struggling with something. It was the old question which drives the Europeans slightly mad in Japan, the flashback to the horror of the last-minute defeats by the Marinos and by S-Pulse, the hard-won victory snatched from your grasp in the final minutes because of the lack of some intangible something or other in your own team.

'It's always the same thing, always the same mistakes,' said Stojkovic. 'This is really a question for analysis, for deep analysis. Why in the last three or four minutes, they lose the game? Why? Why? Why? I don't know. Maybe they don't believe in themselves. Maybe they're scared. But I don't understand. Because it's not normal to lose 4–3 after 3–2 in the last three minutes.'

'Are they frightened of you?' I asked.

'They respect a lot. For me, I'm very happy because I'm here in Japan and I've learned a lot about Japan, their culture and so on. And they're a great people. They have a lot of respect. I have especially a lot of respect here.'

There may be a fine line between respect and terror. But it was true. Far away from the agonies of his troubled homeland, Stojkovic was a local hero in Nagoya.

'And tomorrow, when I leave Japan, I can be very proud about everything that I do here, because my name will be well known, and tomorrow I can come back. So this is a big, big experience, an enormous experience. Security for kids. It's great, it's great. For my kids also it's a good experience to live in Japan.'

Then his mobile phone rang. The fifteen minutes were up. I asked him where he was from in Yugoslavia and he told me he came from the town of Nis, 200km south of Belgrade. I remarked I'd passed through it once when driving to Greece in 1974.

'Now you can't use the road,' he said. 'They just bombed the bridge.'

'Mmm,' I said.

'Let's hope all this stops soon,' he said.

Now he was heading across the car park, followed by the PR man, Mr Izumi, who was holding an umbrella over his head.

'Pixie, Pixie,' shouted a group of supporters eager for autographs. He waved, got into his black Toyota without signing any autographs and swept off. I'd forgotten to mention Brentford. I'm sure he would have remembered because when he's not playing, he's a really nice bloke.

In 1999, during the first part of the season, Stojkovic was joined briefly on the top shelf of Japan's foreign acquisitions by Bulgaria's

Hristo Stoichkov, once regarded as one of the best players in Europe, but now older and not so fast. Stoichkov, also thirty-four, was signed up by Kashiwa Reysol, formerly Hitachi FC, at the end of 1998 direct from Barcelona. Reysol are another of those J.League teams based in the populous urban sprawl around Tokyo, and they still had money to spend.

I saw Stoichkov play once at the National Stadium in Tokyo, against Kashima Antlers. It wasn't an uplifting experience. The Kashima Antlers were playing their home games at the National Stadium during the first half of the two-part J.League season because their own stadium was being enlarged so that it can be used as a venue for the 2002 World Cup. Playing at the National Stadium can attract large crowds, but that night there were only about 7,000 fans in the 57,000 capacity stadium. Kashima's fans, according to the Japanese media, include alleged ex-motorcycle gang members, saved from a pointless life of crime by the arrival of the J.League team in their dull hometown. The former bike boys were doing their best for the atmosphere, waving huge maroon flags behind the goal. There were perhaps 800 Reysol fans, in yellow and black, singing 'We Are Reysol, We Are Reysol', and chanting 'KASHIWA REYSOL, KASHIWA REYSOL'. That game, Kashima versus Kashiwa, would be an English language sub-editor's nightmare, paralleled in recent history only by the war between Iran and Iraq.

The boys from Kashima had won the 1998 championship, supported by Brazilian international Jorginho in midfield and coached by Brazil's Ze Mario. But Jorginho had been shipped home in the cut-backs, and it was clear that this season the Antlers had lost their edge. But if Kashima had lost direction, so had Reysol. Nevertheless, they eventually won 2–1, more or less by accident. Hristo Stoichkov certainly wasn't much help.

Stoichkov has something of a hair-loss problem so he doesn't look particularly young. The impression of a man who really needed to sit down and have a bit of a nap was intensified by suggestions that he had probably been a lot thinner when he was the rapier in the Bulgarian attack which so famously beat the

Germans in the quarter-finals of the 1994 USA World Cup. Stoichkov was now the epitome of the ugly foreigner – bad-tempered, knackered and hugely overpaid.

To everyone's great surprise, including his own club's, the game that night against the Antlers turned out to be his last in Japan. Stoichkov went back to Barcelona for the club's 100th birthday celebration match against Brazil. He went on to play for Bulgaria against England and then he retired from football. So I'd seen his last club appearance. It was a historic moment in the annals of world football. The highlights included Stoichkov shouting at his own manager, physically pushing one of his own players and stomping on the Antlers' Brazilian midfielder, Bismark. In between, there was a large amount of gesturing and some dives in the penalty area, one of which was followed up by an aggressive run at the referee in order to give him full-on, 100 per cent, eyeball to eyeball contact. In Japan, that's the cultural equivalent of pulling a large gun and shooting the referee in the stomach. But Stoichkov didn't get booked, despite several clear attempts to intimidate the referee physically, stopping just short of taking hostages. As the match went on, the Bulgarian was getting away with murder. The referee seemed completely cowed. But then, the relationship between the superstar players – foreign and home-grown – and Japanese referees is a troubled one.

One of the men in the forefront of efforts to sort it all out is a no-nonsense Scottish PE teacher from the village of Shotts in Lanarkshire outside Glasgow, also home to a maximum-security prison.

'We like to say we train them for the prison,' says big Les Mottram, who is well over six feet tall and dangerously fit, ideally sized to take the role of the implacable law giver. We met in a Starbucks coffee shop just a few minutes walk away from the National Stadium. Mottram is a serious coffee drinker.

Mottram's arrival in Tokyo straight from Euro 96 was more evidence of Japan's efforts to acquire the best the world had to offer. He had what he thought was a four-month contract and, aged forty-five, it seemed a good way to round off his refereeing career. His brief was to beef up the local referees.

'The Japanese referees, you know, were fairly inexperienced,' said Mottram over a tall cappuccino, talking against a background of Japanese pop music and clattering coffee cups, 'because football doesn't have a great history here.'

His career in Japan had got off to a flying start.

'My first yellow card after I arrived in Japan was Dunga,' Mottram told me, with evident satisfaction. Carlos Caetano Bledorn Verri, also known as Dunga, was until the end of 1998 captain of Jubilo Iwata, the pride of Japan, and also, as it happens, captain of the national team of Brazil. Not Dunga?

'Yeah, Dunga. It was Marinos and Jubilo. I mean, he committed a very rough tackle. I don't care who commits the foul, I just go for the yellow card. And he says, "Ohhh, referee, this is not a foul in Japan." And I say, "I'm new, I'm from Scotland, and it's a foul in Scotland."

'Dunga was very bad to referees. He was insolent, arrogant, abusive. Not with foreign referees. With a foreign referee, he was a different man. But with Japanese referees. Great player. Great player. Fantastic skills. Fantastic vision. I was glad to see the back of him.'

Mottram had been in the country for just five weeks when he refereed the 1996 Nabisco League Cup final between S-Pulse and Verdy. The following day he was invited to lunch with the chairman of the J.League, Mr Kawabuchi. That led to an offer of a two-year refereeing contract. Rather than going back to teach criminally inclined youths in Scotland, Mottram was now teaching Japanese referees the finer points of the game – and reminding them who's boss.

'I try to tell them. Look, this is a yellow card, I say, and it doesn't matter who it is. I try to tell them, when you're on the field, it doesn't matter how much money they're being paid because the class system is the players down here and the referee up here. But they go on to the field thinking referee down here, superstar up there and not the other way round. The problem is that because of the class system here, it's taking a long time to get through.'

Mottram has his fair share of stories of times when the local referees haven't been quite up to the challenge. At the end of the 1998 season, he went to watch Kashima Antlers play Jubilo Iwata in the first of a two-stage championship decider.

'João Carlos, who was the Kashima manager at that time, wasn't too happy with one decision, so he ran on to the field to chase the referee. Now this is a packed stadium. He ran on to the field and began to chase the referee. He got maybe fifteen or twenty yards on the field, and the play is carrying on, and then he stops and he thinks, "What am I doing here?" and he goes back.

'I'm sitting next to the official match inspector and he's looking at me, so I say, "Look, we'd better get a seat up here for Mr Carlos. He's coming up here, you know." But the referee went over and just says, "Don't do it again." I mean, where else in the world will you get a coach or a manager who runs on to the field to complain to the referee, staying in the dug-out? That's the sort of thing we're talking about. They think Carlos is the coach, he's the boss of Antlers, so you can't send him off. But those are the first ones you want to send off. I enjoy it.'

I asked Mottram what was the worst thing that had happened to him during his time in Japan. Mottram paused. He really couldn't think of anything at all, although he has been attacked a few times, most recently at the local derby in Osaka between Gamba and Cerezo.

'I do the match, Cerezo wins 2–1, no problems in the game. We come out . . . and I'm mobbed . . . mobbed by Cerezo fans. You know, wanting photographs, wanting my autograph. When I go to a train station and someone sees me, they want a photograph or they want an autograph. And you know, I feel very awkward about the whole thing. I mean, I don't have – like Stojkovic – this superstar mentality. I'm only a referee.

'If someone in Scotland came up and said, "Les, can I have your autograph?" I would say, "Why?" When I first came here people used to come up and ask, and I'd think, "Is this a joke? Is someone winding me up?" '

Earlier in the season, Mottram sent off Stojkovic's Yugoslav friend Petrovic, of the Urawa Reds, after the 'Stop the NATO Bombing' tee-shirts incident in a game against Sanfrecce Hiroshima. After the booking for taking his shirt off, Petrovic started giving one of the assistant referees the benefit of his match analysis. Mottram gave him a second yellow card and off he went, an early bath for Petrovic-san.

'The next day,' said Mottram, 'I arrived back in Tokyo from Hiroshima, and at the airport there were some Urawa Reds fans.' Sounds dangerous. Would there be 'Scottish Ref Bashed at Airport' headlines? 'And they came up and they apologised to me for his conduct. "We are sorry for Petrovic-san. He was bad. He was wrong. Please accept our apologies." Absolutely fantastic. Fantastic.'

'The foreigners are treated with a lot of respect in Japan,' said Steve Perryman one day, when the subject came up. 'But too much respect can be negative for the game.' As far as he was concerned, the presence of foreign players could intimidate not only the referees, but sometimes the Japanese players. Shimizu were playing the Kashima Antlers one time when Jorginho the Brazilian midfielder and former national player, was still with them.

'Jorginho committed a quite appalling foul on one of our players, and the referee blew for a free-kick,' Perryman recalled. 'One of our Japanese players started off running aggressively towards Jorginho and I thought, "Great, he's riled up, he's going to tell him where to get off." By this time Jorginho was making innocent "Who, me?" gestures. As our player got closer, I could see him slowing down and slowing down, and I thought, "Oh no. Oh no. Here it comes." He arrives at the spot, and what does he do? He shakes hands with Jorginho.'

It was the same when other teams played Jubilo and Dunga.

'If I was the Japanese national coach, I'd have watched the games against Jubilo,' said Perryman, 'and any Japanese player who came within two metres of Dunga, I'd have put him in the national side. They don't dare go near him. When Dunga plays, he owns the opposition, he owns his own team, he owns the referee and he owns the two linesmen.'

Les Mottram reckoned the culture of fear of Dunga was even more widespread.

'I found he was very insulting to his own players, too, during the game. If a player made a bad pass, he would go up and remonstrate with them on the field, in front of everyone and show them what they were doing wrong. Terrible. Terrible. But he's a hero over here. A hero.'

Dunga's intensity was clearly recognised by the Japanese. After he ended his 160 million yen ($1.5 million) per year contract with Jubilo, Dunga moved into advertising a new canned coffee, called Black, thrusting it towards the viewer under the slogan 'Get tension'.

At Sanfrecce Hiroshima, Eddie Thomson had a more positive view of Dunga's influence on Jubilo.

'Good overseas players are the ones who organise the Japanese players, help them and organise them, who virtually coach them on the park. Dunga was a perfect example. Dunga was worth his weight in gold. Now Jubilo is the finest team in the league, they play the best football, and they play like Brazil play. Dunga has turned his team around. Now they've got five or six younger players in the national team, and they've all come through because of Dunga. He's paid his way a hundred times.'

But Perryman-san, the subject of Dunga could get him seriously steamed up. Honest, straightforward, Anglo-Saxon Perryman saw Dunga, when it comes down to it, as the archetypal dodgy Latin American. He argued that the pernicious influence of Dunga had in particular blighted S-Pulse's great rivals, Jubilo

Iwata, while threatening the future of football as a whole in Japan, and possibly world civilisation as we know it. I have to say I am tempted to agree.

The Dunga/Jubilo/Evil Empire question came to a head in S-Pulse's game against Jubilo early that season. The match turned out to be the defining moment of S-Pulse's performance in the first half of the two-stage league championship. Before the match got under way, S-Pulse were lying second in the league. After the opening games against Verdy and Bellmare, they'd lost two games, going down 1–0 to Cerezo Osaka, and 3–2 at home to the Yokohama F Marinos. This left them four points behind Jubilo. If S-Pulse won the home game against them, the gap would close to just one point.

The Nihondaira Stadium was almost full to capacity with more than 19,000 people there. The away end was packed with the blue flags of Jubilo. S-Pulse had the better of the first half. Roughly twenty-five minutes into the game, Alex was brought down just inside the Jubilo penalty area. Now Alex, being Brazilian, has been known to fall over spontaneously from time to time, but this was a clear penalty. The Jubilo players, maintaining the Brazilian theme, started to crowd the Japanese referee after the decision. They continued to argue for three minutes in total, delaying the penalty. No one was sent off. S-Pulse scored. The first half ended with the home side still one goal up. The second half promised to be interesting.

When the game restarted, it turned out to be interesting for all the wrong reasons. Jubilo came out and threw themselves into attack, equalising after fifteen minutes. And then Alex, the star S-Pulse forward, was elbowed in the face; and then he was hacked. There was a lot of niggle. It looked as if Jubilo had set out to provoke Alex. If so, they succeeded. Both Alex and Santos ended up in the book, although with just over fifteen minutes left, it was still 1–1. Things were about to go badly wrong for S-Pulse.

It began with a dubious penalty award to Jubilo. Two minutes later, Jubilo went two goals ahead with a legitimate goal. As S-Pulse players tried to restart the game quickly, a Jubilo player ran to pick up the ball and threw it away. Ten minutes later, Jubilo scored again, making it 4–1. The game was as good as over. But with just three minutes to go, S-Pulse's attacking left-back, Ando, drove a left-footed shot into the right of the Jubilo net, making it 4–2. Another Shimizu player, Hattori, ran to pick up the ball from the back of the net to get things moving again. Two Jubilo players, Suzuki and Fukunishi, followed him in. A scuffle developed over the ball. Hattori eventually threw a weak punch and one of the Jubilo players ended up on the ground, claiming grievous injury. Hattori was sent off. The Jubilo players walked free.

At this point, the S-Pulse crowd began what by local standards could be classed as a major riot. They started throwing plastic bottles, outraged by what they'd seen just in front of their noses. Jubilo's captain, Nakayama, was seen supposedly trying to calm the crowd down, making things worse. When the game eventually restarted, Jubilo scored again to make it 5–2.

'I was so upset, not with the fact that they beat us,' said Perryman-san later, in a retrospective moment in his office, 'but with the manner in which they beat us. You bring in your foreign influences, your Dunga and whoever, and, of course, in comes the good and in comes the bad.

'Dunga . . . in terms of football playing . . . is magnificent for young players to look at but because he comes from a nation where the game has been going on for so long, he's got all the trick side.'

Dunga, for Perryman, was the dark side of the footballing force. In fact, Perryman-san even thought that Dunga had written a book about being devious that had been translated into Japanese. (I managed to find one book by Dunga in a Japanese book store, but it seemed to be just an autobiography. Of course, that may amount to the same thing.)

'And I'm saying,' said Perryman-san, 'that this is a short-term view. From twenty years of intense football thinking and discipline, Phil and me know how to cheat and waste time, we know all that. But we don't think the Japanese crowds or Japanese players deserve it. We think we'd be selling them short. Now that may cost us a result along the line. But when we leave, I think we can leave clean.'

The local journalists shared Perryman-san's view of the evil Jubilo Iwata. Many were of the opinion that everyone knows that Jubilo cheat, and that Jubilo had laid a trap for S-Pulse into which S-Pulse had naively fallen. In another Jubilo game, against the Urawa Reds, I saw Urawa's big Italian defender, Zappella, get sent off after a Jubilo player jumped on him from behind, off the ball, and then pretended he'd been punched.

'There's enough to teach them without teaching them the extra, extra, extra cheating deviousness,' continued Perryman. 'Well, I've seen it all at Jubilo. I've seen the ballboys at their stadium not give us the ball back, and Jubilo are winning. I've seen it. With my own eyes. But if that's how they think they can win games . . . I'd have more belief in myself, in my players, to be able to defend a situation.'

Perryman-san was so agitated by the Jubilo defeat that he was extensively quoted that month in one of Japan's major football magazines, *Soccer Weekly*, on the threat to the future of the Japanese game. S-Pulse, at Perryman's prompting, wrote to the JFA to query why Hattori had been sent off, while the Jubilo players who waylaid him in the net had escaped unpunished. About three months later, the JFA wrote back saying that this was one of a number of queries about refereeing decisions that they were looking into.

'There has to be a quality of football,' Perryman continued, in full soliloquy mode, 'and I believe in fair play, to keep that crowd coming, and especially the young people. If there becomes a hint of hooliganism, violence here, I think it could absolutely devastate this game.

'In Europe, we know about fences, TV surveillance cameras, police with dogs. In South America, we know about supporters being shot, players being shot, referees being hit with bottles. Japan does not need that. They don't want it. If a lot of developed football countries could turn the clock back, I think they would have been a lot harsher, quicker, on events on the pitch. Bad tackles, acting, diving, gamesmanship, and generally bad conduct.

'Japan, as a new football nation, has got the ability to stop the rot before it happens.'

6 PIRATES

I was sitting in the corner of a Denny's twenty-four-hour restaurant somewhere in Shinagawa in the south-west of Tokyo, beneath a lurid pink picture of a strawberry dessert. I had always imagined my quest for the true meaning of Japanese football would lead me into small, atmospheric Japanese bars to drink beer and sake at the counter while eating strange shellfish and having drunken discussions with the owner about the merits of Manchester United. Instead, I was drinking too much coffee in Denny's surrounded by people eating meat loaf.

I was with supporters of the Yokohama Marinos. There was Izumi-san, a woman in her early thirties who worked as an editorial assistant on a women's magazine. Izumi-san is a self-confessed enthusiast for all things Argentinian and for Club Atletico del Rio Plata in particular. That night, Izumi was wearing a red and white CARP scarf, and carrying a red and white handbag. Izumi-san was learning Spanish. When her mobile phone rang, she'd answer, 'Si?'

We'd met at Shinagawa Station, on the Yamanote Line which circles Tokyo. It was rush hour; crowds of office workers slid through Shinagawa Station's new high-tech hallway, all gently muffled noise and reflected white light. The station loudspeakers were playing a perpetual, periodic dong-ding noise, which is a constant feature of all Japanese stations, unnoticed by most people. Once you notice it, you start to go a little mad.

Across the table was Naohisa Kikuchi, a broad-faced, smiling character with a long black pigtail, who works as a building surveyor. Mr Kikuchi had picked us up at the station in a big white Nissan recreational vehicle with a mini-television on the dashboard and a serious stereo. He was wearing a blue and white Yokohama Marinos sweat top, and carrying a blue and white Marinos sports bag.

We'd eaten. I'd ordered the Japanese grilled salmon set, complete with miso soup. Someone else had a plate of chips. I was the only one drinking beer. Everyone else was drinking coffee. In Denny's, you can drink as much coffee as you like. We were talking about the differences between being a baseball supporter and a football supporter in Japan.

'Baseball supporters' groups are very . . . very . . . oh. Mmmm . . .' said Izumi-san, searching for the word. 'Koh-shi. Mmm. Koh-shi nan-des-ka? What's koh-shi?' she asked, turning to Kikuchi-san. 'It's popular in Japan and in Korea and in China,' she told me, over her shoulder.

I was perplexed. Quite a lot of things are popular in Japan, Korea and China – chopsticks, rice, zither-like musical instruments that go plink plonk. But Kikuchi-san was on the case. Fiddling in the pocket of the blue and white Marinos sports bag, he produced a palm-sized Sharp electronic translation device, and used a stylus to tap in the word 'Koh-shi'.

'Con-few-shin,' said Izumi-san, reading over his shoulder. 'Baseball supporters' groups are very Confucian. They are very organised and strictly arranged with old people above young people. But football is more free.'

After my time with the S-Pulse fans, I had gradually been coming to the conclusion that this wasn't always the case, but Izumi-san and her friends had been football fans since before the start of the J.League. They were serious fans. They spoke with the authority of time served for the cause, in the years before the football boom.

'When Japan took the bronze medal for football at the Mexico Olympics, I was in primary school in Fukuoka Prefecture,' said Izumi-san. 'I went to my first game in the mid 1980s, because a friend gave me a ticket.'

'How many people used to watch?' I asked.

'Two hundred, three hundred,' said Izumi-san. And everyone laughed.

'Two thousand people in the National Stadium,' said Kikuchi, still laughing. The National Stadium seats 57,000.

'Football was a minority sport,' said Izumi-san.

This was also a group with very definite views on the nature of being a fan.

'Every team has an official fan club,' said Izumi, meaningfully, 'but a fan club doesn't always mean supporters. In Europe and America, those who go to the stadium seem to enjoy football itself. But in Japan, it seems to us, many of the people at the stadium don't know how to enjoy football. They just dance and sing and shout when a goal is scored. Our group is different. When a goal is scored it makes us very, very happy. But when our team loses, it makes us very, very angry.'

I kept quiet about my sorties with the samba band. Then Kazu Miyazaki turned up, and he had things on his mind.

I had first met Kazu Miyazaki, Izumi-san and the others a year before, at the start of the 1998 season. We met outside the main railway station in Yokohama in what I didn't realise at the time were fairly exceptional circumstances. Every time I met them after that, the more exceptional they became.

The Yokohama Marinos had just beaten Consadole Sapporo 4–0 at the Mitsuzawa municipal stadium. It had been an easy victory for the Marinos, a team backed by Nissan, Japan's largest motor company. Nissan had started life in the vast port city of Yokohama. It's a big place, spreading out to the south-west of Tokyo. The economic output of Yokohama is allegedly equal to or greater than the combined gross national product of Holland, Belgium and Luxembourg.

The Sapporo team may have been feeling a little homesick; based on the northern island of Hokkaido, their home city is prone to snow and ice even in April, and so the club is obliged to play all its home games in the vicinity of Tokyo for the first month or so of the season. In Yokohama, on the other hand, snow seemed unimaginable; it had been a beautiful sunny afternoon, the walkways approaching the Mitsuzawa Stadium were lined with neat flowerbeds filled with red and yellow tulips. A flowering cherry tree could be seen at one corner of the stadium.

Not surprisingly, the Consadole fans were heavily outnumbered in the stadium. About three hundred of them were behind the goal to the right, waving red and black flags and singing 'Ohhh Sap-po-ro, Sap-po-ro, Sa-po-rooohhh' or chanting 'Con-sa-do-le, Con-sa-do-le' to the beat of a big bass drum.

Apart from its latitude and its snow problems, there were two other interesting facts about Consadole that season. The first was the identity of their goalkeeper, Dido Havenaar, once the idol of the Dido-dan at Nagoya Grampus Eight. Two years earlier, Dido and his Dutch wife had successfully applied for Japanese nationality. He explained after the game that this made it easier for him to keep on playing, although the story, as we shall see, was a little more complicated than that. The second was the signing of Hugo Maradona, younger brother of Diego. Watching young Hugo play that afternoon was a very strange experience. It was clear that while no slouch with the ball, he definitely wasn't in the same class as his more famous brother. But Hugo does look disturbingly like Diego. He has the same dark hair, the same barrel-chest and the same arm gestures. He wears number 10. Every time he got the ball it was fascinating and vaguely disconcerting, all of which I am sure more than justified his transfer fee, even if it didn't actually win games.

It didn't win that one. The Marinos that season were a strong team, including four players who went to France for the World Cup that summer – goalkeeper Yoshikatsu Kawaguchi, defenders

Masami Ihara and Norio Omura, and the diminutive long-haired striker, Shoji Jo. That afternoon, Jo scored twice, executing a full body-flip after the first before blowing a kiss to the home bench, while the home crowd unfurled red, white and blue banners that ran from top to bottom of the home stand (the *bandeiras*, Izumi-san helpfully explained later).

After the goals, the Marinos mascot, a huge Donald Duck lookalike in a sailor suit which was in fact a seagull, performed exuberant forward rolls on the touch-line. With the start of the J.League in 1993, the Marinos had opted for a Spanish Latin American flavour, in contrast to the samba style of Shimizu S-Pulse or the Teutons over at Urawa. A team brochure helpfully explained: 'Marinos is the Spanish word for sailors. It perfectly reflects our international stance, and the spirit of the international port city of Yokohama, our hometown.' There were also some rather less Hispanic thoughts on the team colours, chosen not so much because blue, white and red looks good, but for reasons of deep symbolism: 'Blue represents composure and the sea in the port of Yokohama. Red represents sudden bursts of power and passion. White represents concentration and integrity.' Blue, white and red also happen to be the colours of the club's owners, Nissan, although this wasn't mentioned.

Beyond the name, the club had recruited a series of Spanish and Spanish Latin American players and managers, with varying degrees of success and regular degrees of drama. At post-game press conferences, the manager always outlined his thoughts in front of a board emblazoned with the sponsors' names and what I assumed to be another Marinos' corporate mission statement, this time in Spanish: 'Aqui empiezan 90 minutos de emocion. Hagamos Goles. El Yokohama Marinos.' (Here begins ninety minutes of emotion. Let's score goals.)

That season, 1998, the hombre in charge of making goals was Francisco Javier Azcargorta, a balding, rather portly Spaniard with a walrus moustache who reminded me of a bank manager. Azcargorta had taken over the Marinos in early 1997, coming from Athletic Bilbao, and he had brought in three more Spanish speakers, including two former Spanish internationals – a stooping thirty-five-year-old forward, Julio Salinas, and, recently acquired from Athletic Bilbao, Jon Andoni Goicoechea. The third Spanish speaker was a Paraguayan midfielder, Julio Cesar Baldivieso.

Goicoechea's debut had presented the Marinos' fans with a truly terrible pronunciation challenge. They sensibly solved this by reducing him to 'Goi-ko', just as the former German international, Pierre Littbarski found himself reduced to 'Litti' or 'Ritti' when he first played in Japan for JEF United. Goicoechea hadn't done much on his debut, coming on briefly at the end. He didn't do much for the rest of the season, despite having cost the Marinos a substantial amount of money. This, and the equally unthrilling performance of Salinas, led to Señor Azcargorta's replacement by his Spanish assistant coach, Jesus Antonio de la Cruz, halfway through the 1998 playing year. The Spanish-speaking trinity of Goicoechea, Salinas and Baldivieso soon followed. De la Cruz found himself speaking Spanish on his own.

But on that Saturday in April in Yokohama, that was all in the future. Things were going well for the Marinos. Their supporters' end was packed to capacity, opening up before the game started with the rendition of a serious-sounding anthem. I now know the words. I found out later that it was written by Kazu Miyazaki, the man who was now about to down his first cup of Denny's coffee. The anthem, which begins in Japanese, 'Yokohama-ni umarette yokatta', goes like this:

> I was very lucky to be born in Yokohama
> There is love in this town
> I am very happy to be raised in Yokohama
> There are dreams in this town
> Yokohama, Yokohama, never changing pride
> Yokohama, Yokohama, we have new dreams
> I am very happy to live in Yokohama
> In this place we are proud
> In this place we have dreams.

After that, the Marinos fans settled down to regular chanting. They have a high-energy directness about them, spending most of the time singing 'Ma-ri-nos, Ma-ri-nos, Yuki Ma-ri-nos' over and over again. When they scored, the usual vast roar and flag-waving was accompanied, à la Buenos Aires, by clouds of white ticker tape made by the fans from cut-up newspaper, which fluttered dramatically across the stands.

After the game, I was walking back towards the station in the dusk in a contemplative and satisfied mood, along a narrow and crowded pedestrianised street lined with noodle shops, a McDonald's and a few video arcades. Dusk was falling. People were hurrying home, or hurrying out. It was just another Saturday night in Yokohama. Then, behind me, I heard the sound of a crowd, chanting 'Ma-ri-nos, Ma-ri-nos, Yuki Ma-ri-nos'. This was extremely unusual.

A group of fans was coming up the road, out on their own and entirely unsupervised. There were twenty to thirty of them in a long crocodile, most of them in blue and white Marinos shirts, a few waving small Marinos flags. The sound of the chanting was amplified by the narrowness of the street. They were led by some tough-looking guys in sunglasses with long hair, who looked a bit like bikers. Japanese biker gangs can be rough, particularly in a place like Yokohama. 'Trouble,' I thought, noticing that the evening shoppers also looked a little alarmed.

Of course, it wasn't like that. There wasn't any trouble. There weren't any riot police. It was more like bumping into a group of Hari Krishna disciples on Oxford Street, or perhaps guitar-playing evangelical Christians. The same combination of almost manic cheeriness and dangerously bright eyes was drawing the same kindly and slightly embarrassed smiles from the passers-by, who were all desperately avoiding eye contact.

But I was impressed, and started snapping photographs as the procession advanced. This was revolutionary. Neither before nor since at a J.League game have I seen fans celebrating in public. Normal etiquette calls for all stupid fan behaviour to be confined entirely within the stadium walls. There are individual exceptions

– for instance, I once saw with my own eyes a Shimizu S-Pulse supporter wearing a yellow Paru-chan hat while boarding the bullet train for Tokyo at Shizuoka Station. But he wasn't jumping up and down and shouting 'S-Pulse, S-Pulse'. Normally, there is strictly no dancing in the streets, no forcing cars to slow down and asking them whether they support Arsenal, no drunken conga-lines around the city fountain, and definitely no throwing bricks at policemen.

The crocodile snaked on towards the station, drawing to a halt outside it by a modern bronze statue, the sort of civic art which litters Japanese public spaces. One of the sunglassed, long-haired citizens climbed up the fountain (thereby probably violating numerous warnings against the dangers inherent in climbing fountains), waving a big Yokohama Marinos banner and leading the singing, as the others gathered around in a group. Then they stopped. I looked around. Roughly half of the group were women, and they included a young man with a white stick, apparently sight impaired, being led by someone who could have been his sister. To enjoy being a football fan in Japan, you don't necessarily have to be able to see the game. Another fan with dark shoulder-length hair climbed up the fountain and shouted something in Japanese. Everyone fell silent, then they sang the Yokohama anthem one more time very solemnly. At the end of the song, the man in the sunglasses shouted something again, everyone raised both their arms in a Japanese salute and shouted, 'Banzai! Banzai! Banzai!' (Banzai, a thousand years, got rather a bad press in the West on account of its wartime associations. It means little more than 'Hurrah!')

I didn't know it then, but the man in the sunglasses was Kazu Miyazaki. A thirty-three-year-old butcher, father of one, com-poser of the Yokohama anthem, tribune of the people and head of a supporters' sub-group known as the Yokohama Pirates. It later turned out that the march out of the stadium was a deliberate consciousness-building exercise, part of Kazu Miyazaki's grand plan to change Japan through football.

But that was last year. Now Kazu Miyazaki was not a happy

man. Things had changed this season in Yokohama; and things had changed at his beloved Marinos.

At the start of the J.League, the Marinos' main rivals had naturally been the other Yokohama-based J.League team, the exquisitely named Yokohama Flugels. More than 50,000 people turned out in 1998 to see a local derby between the two sides in the newly opened Yokohama International Stadium, a vast concrete structure capable of holding 70,000 people, which will host the 2002 World Cup final. When the two teams met, scuffling between their rival fans was not unknown. By J.League standards, the two teams were doing well.

Japan's second biggest airline, All Nippon Airways, or ANA, used to hold a controlling share in the Flugels, along with a locally based construction company, Sato Kogyo. The team played in ANA's colours of sky blue, dark blue and white. Their mascot was a bird with a flying helmet and goggles. But with the economy sliding into recession, the Flugels' management had suddenly announced in October 1998 that the Sato Kogyo construction company planned to withdraw its support for the club. ANA, which had its own share of financial problems, had decided it couldn't continue alone. The decision came as a complete surprise to the fans, to the players and to the Flugels' German manager, Gert Engels. Collectively, they felt the full force of Japan's 'Do you ask the frogs when you drain the pond?' management style.

'It was in the papers before the players and the staff heard about it,' said Gert Engels, who went on to take the job of head coach at JEF United. 'Some players had phone calls in the night from journalists asking if it was true, but nobody knew.'

The proposed solution managed to upset even more people, including Kazu Miyazaki – the absorption of the Flugels into the Marinos, to create the rather unattractively named Yokohama F Marinos.

'The reactions when we found out were shock and anger,' said Engels when I met him at JEF United's training ground one day. 'We thought maybe there was some way to change it. But the decision was already made. We heard later that the decision had been made very early in either June or July. Made and finished.'

The players may have been upset, but at the next match they still beat Cerezo Osaka 7–0 at the brand-new International Stadium. The Flugels' last game of all was that New Year's Day final of the Emperor's Cup, when they'd beaten S-Pulse in front of a capacity crowd. After the club folded, the J.League, in a rather cynical move, produced a video called *Legend of the Flugels*, celebrating their brief history.

After the merger announcement, the Marinos were playing an away game in the old Japanese imperial capital, Kyoto, against Kyoto Purple Sanga. (Purple is associated with the imperial house. Sanga is the Buddhist community of monks and nuns. Figure that one out.) Things got a little rough. When the Marinos' charming and mild-mannered managing director, Takehiko Taniguchi, tried to explain things to the Marinos fans he was given a rowdy reception. According to press reports the next day, Mr Taniguchi was hit on the head by a 'microphone' thrown by one of the crowd, and suffered a small cut above the eye. I was puzzled about why a fan would have a microphone at a football match; it seemed very Japanese. (This is the news. Angry fans rioted today in Central Yokohama, throwing calculators and digital watches at the police . . .) It turned out that the missile in question had been a megaphone. Emotions were nevertheless running high.

At the Flugels' last league game, 13,000 fans turned up at Mitsuzawa Stadium. The Flugels won 2–1, and came back on to the pitch after the end of the game to say farewell to the supporters. Gert Engels told the crowd he hoped they would be able to meet again next season, and said he still hoped ANA and the J.League would save the club. One of the Flugels' players, Koji Maeda, announced that he was 'boiling with anger' over the way the players and fans had been treated. Then they all went on a lap of honour, throwing their shirts into the crowd. The club's national team stars, goalkeeper Seigo Narazaki and Motohiro Yamaguchi, broke down and wept.

Marinos' fan Kazu Miyazaki was outraged.

'This merger is a very big problem for us,' he began, fixing me in the eye across his second cup of coffee. 'We used to be the Marinos and now we're the F Marinos. The Flugels' fans have lost the team they used to support.

'I asked some foreigners whether something like this would happen in Brazil or Europe and they said no. What I can't put up with is that they have completely ignored the supporters of the two teams.'

I had to agree that he seemed to have a point. The others were listening and nodding as Kazu talked. The man was a natural leader, and he had a programme.

The young Kazu had watched the 1974 World Cup in Germany on TV and been impressed by the crowds chanting 'Deutschland, Deutschland'. He'd seen the Liverpool fans at Anfield, who he says sang 'all sorts of things'. He'd watched the 1978 Argentinian World Cup; and he decided that something was wrong with Japan, where people didn't sing and shout and get upset about football, or about anything very much.

'For example, there is a thought in Japanese culture that making a conflict or making a fight isn't so great,' he said, in one of the greater understatements of the evening. 'And not fighting for a long time makes people forget how to. We are not used to having real discussions about things. We want people to think through this merger thing and reconsider it. The problem is, people don't know how to fight.'

Now at this point I have to say that I began to wonder where exactly we were going. I had to admit that I agreed with Kazu. Japanese people do by and large avoid conflict. As a nation, they have, well, rather given up on fighting for the past fifty years, but there are some rather persuasive historical reasons for that. But Kazu was still going, and he was going for the really, really big picture.

'In a word,' he said, and he did say this – I know, because I wrote it down, 'I'd like to change Japan through football.'

'Ah ha,' I said.

'Well, that's the final destination. I'm Japanese and I'm naturally proud of Japan. But the Japanese nowadays, they're apt to give up when things get difficult. People are weak in the face of authority.

So people have to take time to think if a decision is right or wrong. Both in politics and in the case of this merger, people don't take the time to think whether things are right or wrong.'

I took another sip of coffee (by now, I'd switched from beer). I noticed that as he became more animated, Kazu's eyes were beginning to water with emotion. Now, though, we were back to the Flugels–Marinos affair.

'Elsewhere in the world,' said Kazu, reaching for the broad global vision, 'you had football first, and then you had business. But in Japan in the J.League, the companies come first and football is always second. I don't think football can really be popular in Japan in its true sense until it's in the hands of the people rather than in the hands of the companies.

'In Japan,' he continued, 'politics is controlled by politicians and by bureaucrats and unless people get politics back in their hands, Japan cannot be a truly good country.'

'Mmmm,' I said again.

'And it's the same with football. When football is in the hands of those who really love football rather than in the hands of business, then it will be good. We have to be prepared to fight. How to fight, that's the problem.'

What was I to make of Kazu Miyazaki? He was clearly someone who thought about things, and who wasn't prepared to suck his teeth and shake his head from side to side and say that things were difficult or sensitive or complicated or any of the other things that people in Japan say when they really don't want to think about something difficult. The guy was a thinker. But was he a nut?

Here I was, in a strange Denny's in a strange land, talking to a charismatic individual. But I was out of my cultural depth. Had I met the leader of the Aum Shinrikyo Cult, which was responsible for releasing poisonous gas into the Tokyo subway, I might have thought he was a very good bloke, too. Was Mr Miyazaki a dangerous rightist, dedicated to re-arming Japan? Was he a maniac? Or was he just an enthusiast? Would we be letting off explosives? Assassinating Shoji Jo? Abducting the Marinos fluffy seagull mascot, Marinos-kun? Telling the management to take the F out of the Marinos, or the seagull in the sailor suit gets it?

I had no idea. The conversation continued. It transpired that Kazu wanted the help of foreigners like myself to explain to Japanese people about differing footballing cultures around the world, and to tell them that if they tried to amalgamate Manchester United and Manchester City, the fans wouldn't stand for it. There'd be trouble.

So how to fight? The first step was clear. Until the merger, Kazu Miyazaki had been the supreme leader of all the fan clubs of the Yokohama Marinos. Later I saw the newspaper picture of Kazu in 1995, after the Marinos had won the league for the first time, with the team captain, Ihara, on his shoulders, after the fans had invaded the pitch. 'The supporters are the base of the team,' the caption read.

Members of Kazu's own sub-group of fans, the Pirates, used to fly their skull and cross-bones flag in the prime position behind the Yokohama Marinos goal. In 1995, it was Kazu who had organised the fifty-metre long and nine-metre wide *bandeiras* that had graced the National Stadium for the championship play-offs. It was Kazu who had organised the North Korean-style crowd display at the testimonial match that same year for Kimoura, a retiring former Nissan player – fans held cards above their heads to produce the red and white Japanese flag on one side, and the player's name and number on the other. Kazu loved the Marinos. The Marinos had let him down.

Kazu had tried to fight the merger. He'd been ejected from a fan committee set up to coordinate with the management because of his unwavering opposition to the whole idea. He'd been black-listed by the club for handing out anti-merger leaflets at a meet-the-players open day at the start of the season. He was regarded as dangerous. I'd asked a friend who is a sports reporter about it all. 'Oh, you met Miyazaki?' she'd said. 'He's like a terrorist. He's like the IRA.'

The merger went ahead. So Kazu had given it all up. He'd

stepped down as leader of the fans. He had withdrawn with a loyal group of supporters. Confronted with moral decay in the heart of his empire, he'd withdrawn into the wilderness, accompanied by his loyal retainers, bearing witness that all was not right in the brave new world of the Yokohama F Marinos. As a result, Kazu's position as legitimate leader had been usurped by, of all people, the man who had thrown the megaphone that day in Kyoto, Okayama-san, leader of the fan group known as Yokohama Big Shout. After the incident, he'd apologised and gone along with the merger. Now the Big Shout drum team were manning the *bandeiras*.

But Kazu Miyazaki had not abandoned his people altogether. He was still bearing witness to the disorder of the world by attending home matches.

'I go to the games, but I don't support the F Marinos,' he said. 'I go because I want to appeal to as many supporters as possible to think about the merger.' The others nodded. It was a supporters' strike.

'We want them to take the F out of Marinos,' said Izumi-san, emphatically.

I sympathised, but at this point I'd drunk so much coffee I could hardly speak. It was time to go, before the trains stopped at around midnight. Someone ordered another coffee to go. We went down to the car park. Kazu climbed into his little Japanese-style butcher's van and drove off into the Shinagawa night, planning a revolution.

清水

7 FULIES MUST DIE

A few weeks later, I called Izumi-san on her mobile phone.

'Izumi-san?' I said.

'Si,' she said.

I asked how things were going and whether Kazu was still going to watch the Marinos, not mentioning the F to avoid offence.

'Of course,' she said. 'But he has decided to make a move against the supporters of Yokohama F Marinos,' she continued, in her sing-song voice. This sounded worrying, I thought. What kind of move? Self-immolation? A small explosion?

'OK,' I said, warily.

'Call me on my mobile phone at the stadium. We will meet after the game.'

The newly merged Yokohama F Marinos had been having an average season. The team had abandoned the old Mitsuzawa municipal stadium in the city centre where I'd first seen the non-F Marinos play Consadole. Instead, home games were now being played at the 70,000 seat Yokohama International Stadium. This is fine if you have 70,000 people for a World Cup final. It's less fine when you have 11,670 for an evening game against JEF United. The new stadium was harder to get to, involving a ride on the city's subway from Yokohama Station, and then a trudge through the spacious and boring streets of Shin-Yokohama, or New Yokohama, walking between faceless apartment blocks towards the stadium which sits on a raised podium like a cross between an alien spaceship and a multi-storey car park.

Perhaps it's unfair to dismiss Shin-Yokohama as entirely boring. It does have the Dream House, a seventy-room, multi-storey karaoke parlour, complete with a green, six-storey tall model of a brontosaurus. And the traffic lights play a lovely tune when it's time to cross.

As I wandered towards the stadium for the 7.00 p.m. kick-off, I passed some old people sitting on benches and looking a little lost in the gathering dusk. I also saw a neatly dressed, fat boy on a bicycle, aged perhaps ten or eleven, who was concentrating hard on spitting at pigeons. Another sign of a society in decay, I thought to myself. The Japanese were getting increasingly worried about youth of all ages, even the very young ones. It didn't help that just over a year ago, an eleven-year-old boy in the city of Kobe had murdered and decapitated one of his younger schoolmates, and left his head in a bag outside the gates of their primary school.

1999 had also turned into the year of the 'collapsed classroom'. According to the media, unruly seven and eight year olds across the nation were turning classrooms into battlefields. The junior and senior high schools weren't much better, with flick-knives being the current boom item among young males. On the Tokyo subways, a sinister poster warned people to 'Watch Our Children' – in the picture, a young boy stares at his thumb, which has turned into the blade of a knife. Then there's the continuing media-obsession with the high-schoolgirls who are supposedly turning to a life of prostitution in order to finance purchases of designer handbags, which have obsessed Japanese television and newspapers for at least three years.

In an effort to stem the imminent collapse of normality, the Japanese government had just launched a series of posters and television advertisements, aimed at encouraging fathers — traditionally absent from the Japanese family because they're forced to spend absurd amounts of time in the office — to spend more time with their children. 'A man who does not help in child-rearing cannot be a proper father', says one poster featuring a male dancer called Sam. He is the husband of J.Pop super-idol Namie Amuro and father of their recently born baby.

So I thought about saying to the fat kid, 'Don't spit at that pigeon,' and doing my bit to preserve social order in Japan. But I'd spat at a few pigeons myself as a lad.

After walking for what seemed like an age, I arrived at the monolith of the Yokohama International Stadium, circling round it for another age to find the press entrance. Eventually, after going up and down stairs and getting lost inside, I looked out on to the pitch. The players were already warming up. Over to the right, a long, long way away, was the blue and white mass of F Marinos flags, led by a man with a megaphone, and the pounding of a big drum. I assumed this was Mr Okayama and his Big Shout boys. Over to the right, huddled together on the first tier of the stadium, there was a group of perhaps 200 JEF fans, doing their best to make a loud noise. Between the two stretched vast tracts of soul-destroying emptiness.

Still, it must have seemed like a big day out for the JEF fans. JEF United's training ground might be located next to a rubbish incinerator, giving the players a healthy daily dose of dioxins, but their stadium at Ichihara further round Tokyo Bay is far, far worse; from the main stand you can see the refraction towers of the adjacent oil refineries. Ichihara is probably the equivalent of Tilbury, or Dartford. Compared with Yokohama, it's not a nice place.

JEF United have never been favoured by their location, but in the early days they were one of the star teams of the J.League. The former German international, Pierre Littbarski, played for JEF, brought in to give the people of Chiba Prefecture something to live for beyond the Chiba Lotte Lions baseball team. But now JEF had fallen on hard times. They were second from bottom of the league. They had financial troubles. There was talk of relegation.

Today's game wasn't inspiring. JEF United were unlucky not to score early on when their only foreign player, a Brazilian called Baron, broke through Yokohama's nervous defence. The JEF crowd had settled into a persistent, 'GO JEF UNITED, GO JEF UNITED'. The Marinos' megaphone and drum men were sticking with the chants I'd heard the previous season – 'Oooooh Yuki Ma-ri-nos, Ma-ri-nos, Mari-nos, Yuki Ma-ri-nos. Oi! Oi! Oi-oi-oi!' and so on, to an underlying, rapid 4/4 beat. I couldn't catch any Fs. It looked very much like the old Marinos, unless you noticed the very small F on the team badge.

When Yokohama scored, there was the same snow of confetti at the home end, while the man in the blue and white Marinos-kun seagull suit did his usual forward roll on the side-lines. When JEF equalised a few minutes later, a giant cartoon seagull with a clenched fist appeared on the massive electronic scoreboard with the words 'FIGHT ON!' It was the sort of thing which could give a small child nightmares.

At half-time I set off for the home end, in search of Izumi-san and Kazu and the Pirates, trekking round past the Kentucky Fried Chicken outlet and the tables selling blue, white and red F Marinos shirts. I found them down behind the goal, together with Kikuchi and a number of other people I hadn't met before. I noticed that no one was wearing F Marinos colours. Izumi and Kikuchi were wearing dark and light blue Argentinian national team shirts. Kazu was sitting down, wearing a white sweatshirt. He was also wearing wrap-around dark sunglasses. It was 7.30 at night. There was a battery-operated loudspeaker at his feet.

'Have you seen our protest banners?' said Izumi. She pointed up to the second tier. I could make out two banners. One said in a mixture of roman and Japanese script: 'M plus F equals what?' The other said in Japanese: 'How many fans does a team need?'

'Meet us afterwards at the north gate,' whispered Kazu, after saying hello. 'We are going to make a protest.'

It had taken so long to get there that by this time the second half had got under way. Kazu looked distracted. JEF added to their troubles by scoring an own goal. The F Marinos fans behind us erupted into a frenzy of drumming, and the newspaper confetti rained down. I headed back to my seat.

Despite their early promise, JEF lost 3–1. I rushed off in search of Kazu Miyazaki. This involved completing another circuit of the stadium, complicated by the fact that the stadium signs appeared to have got confused over which way was north. By this time, the vast esplanade running round the stadium was emptying of fans; only a hardcore of teenage-girls still hung over the railings, hoping for a glimpse of their team heroes. Across the vast, empty spaces of the stadium concourse drifted strange ethereal sounds, broadcast on a hidden loudspeaker system. It was spooky.

Now, when I'd heard about the fans protest, I'd expected something rowdy; maybe shouting slogans at the top management as they climbed into their air-conditioned limousines; perhaps some scuffling with the security guards; maybe some burning of effigies. I found Kazu Miyazaki surrounded by a crowd of around 100 people, most of them sitting on the ground in front of him, some standing in small groups, listening to him talk. He wasn't even using the red battery-powered megaphone which I'd seen earlier.

'The building over there is a hospital,' explained Izumi-san, who stood up to greet me, 'and of course the patients would be disturbed if we used the loudspeaker.'

Kazu was speaking about the merger and outlining his views on the likely impact on the football club of the recent developments on the business pages. Nissan, the club's main owner, he reminded them, had huge debts and had gone looking for foreign help. In March, the French car maker Renault had bought around a third of Nissan's shares and was taking management control of Japan's largest car maker. Nissan had been rescued by foreigners, who were going to take a very close look at their finances, including the costs of running the Yokohama F Marinos.

'Monsieur Carlos Ghosn has been named as the new head of Nissan by Renault,' said Kazu. 'They call him le cost-killer. He will want to cut costs, and he will want to cut spending on the football club. And then how will we survive? Currently the management of the club ignores the ordinary people. They have not tried to develop a relationship with the community or with the ordinary people who love football.'

The crowd was a mixed group, both men and women, some of them looking sceptical, some of them looking impressed. All of them looked interested, drawn in by Kazu Miyazaki's intensity and by his humour and by, well, his charismatic personality. Not everything he said made total sense, but at least he was thinking about things, in a society where that kind of behaviour is hardly encouraged.

There were a few questions from the floor. One woman said that it was all a waste of time. The merger had happened and that was the way things were in Japan.

'I used to be a Nissan FC fan,' she argued, 'and then I changed my support to the Marinos. So why shouldn't I change to the Yokohama F Marinos? What's the big difference?'

A young man said he'd always been a Marinos supporter and he didn't like the merger, but he was worried that protests would distract the players.

Kazu started handing out reading materials – photocopied, handwritten sheets in neat Japanese script, with facts and figures on the Renault–Nissan merger, complete with graphs.

'Nissan is planning to cut five thousand jobs,' said Izumi-san, 'and those workers will ask why the company should be spending money on a football team when it can't afford to give them jobs. We are very worried about the future.'

The struggle session had begun at around 9.00 p.m. At 10.30 p.m., Kazu announced that he wanted to set up a group, or a society, that would seek to develop sports culture. Everyone who wanted to join the Kazu campaign for radical change and pure Marinos signed up. At 10.45 p.m. we went in search of food – and more coffee. This time it wasn't Denny's. It was a twenty-four-hour Japanese diner chain called Skylark, but the principle is the same. It included, yes, constant free refills of coffee.

As we wolfed down plates of noodles and cutlets, conversation in the booth was wide-ranging. There were new faces, too – a young woman with long, dyed-blonde hair who turned up in a red Honda sportscar; a couple of slightly nondescript youths, one of whom produced for our entertainment a wind-up model of the Urawa Reds mascot, a green and red fox, which vibrated interestingly across the table and kept us amused for at least five minutes; and Mr Shimada, a biker who was probably in his forties. Mr Shimada also had shoulder-length, dyed-blond hair which he sometimes wore with a big coloured bow as a headband, and he always wore aviator sunglasses.

Izumi-san and I were given a lift by a young woman called Miyuki who works as a sales representative for Nissan, but drives a claret-coloured, lightweight Mitsubishi Minica Toppo because Nissan don't make lightweight cars. She also drives at great speed. Miyuki was wearing an Argentinian national team shirt. She looked like a classically slightly ditzy Japanese woman. She had shoulder-length, dyed-brown hair, wire-rimmed glasses and a husky voice that spoke of sustained consumption of both cigarettes and coffee. She asked me what I thought about the atmosphere at the stadium. I said it was intense in patches, and asked her what she thought. Often, this sort of question gets a stock reply – 'It was amazing' or 'It was really boring'. But Miyuki had been thinking:

'Before, when Miyazaki-san was at the front, we used to support, and at the same time he would help us to understand what was going on on the field. Now, with the fans led by Okayama and the Big Shout group, all they do is shout and chant whatever happens on the pitch.

'Also, there is a split. Miyazaki and Okayama used to be friends. Now they are far from being friends.

'There is no *wa* at the stadium,' she said, using the word for a sense of group togetherness, which is so important in Japan.

'Miyazaki-san says we need to have pride,' she continued. 'Pride in our team, and pride in our country. But what does that mean?'

I was floored. This was not a question I had been expecting, or knew how to answer. What does it mean? In Japan, the question of national pride also touches on the question of national guilt – or lack of it – for Japanese atrocities during the war. I mumbled something about pride being conditional. For instance, I am sometimes proud of West Ham – when they play well – and sometimes I'm ashamed – when there is racist behaviour on the terraces. It's the same with Britain, I continued. Sometimes I'm proud – of parliamentary democracy and the protection of individual rights – and sometimes I'm not proud – of brutal British colonialism and conditions on the Northern Line. I thought I'd done well, but I lost her along the way.

'I think we've been spoiled by peace,' she said with determination. 'Because of that, we don't think about problems ahead, like the environment. We just think it will be OK, and we'll see it through.'

I suggested that being spoiled by peace was probably better than being spoiled by war, and she nodded, but I'm not sure she was convinced. It was all very disconcerting. The conversation returned to fan behaviour and I mentioned the Shimizu samba thing. Izumi-san was scathing.

'I watched the S-Pulse crowd once,' she said with barely concealed disdain, 'and it was like watching a religion. I don't like it. If they want to do something on their own, as individuals, then that's OK. But not all together. And all at the same time. I don't like it. When they first started, I heard they even took lessons in samba.'

I felt a bit awkward. By the time I got home, wired beyond all possibility of sleep by coffee, it was 3.00 a.m., but that's football. Mr Shimada, the biker, had left clutching a small black can of the new Dunga-endorsed Black coffee. 'He says it helps him to relax his heart,' said Izumi-san, 'but he is not normal.'

Kazu Miyazaki's 'Stop the F' dissident movement was not the only grassroots response to the demise of the Flugels. The next day I dragged myself out of bed at around 11.00 a.m. and set off again for Yokohama. My destination this time was a much smaller local stadium in a leafy park in the city's suburbs, home – at least for this Sunday afternoon – of an entirely new football club. The new team, Yokohama FC was less than two months old and played in the Japanese Football League, the country's third division. At Yokohama FC, the spirit of the vanquished Flugels lived on.

I missed the kick-off. As my taxi pulled up outside the ground, I could hear chanting. 'GO-OOH! GO-OOH! GO-GO! YOKO-HAMA EFF-CEE!' The tiny ground was packed. There was only one small stand, running along the length of the pitch and it was full. At one end, arrayed on a grassy embankment behind the goal, there stood perhaps a thousand Yokohama FC fans. Some were wearing team shirts, white with light blue and dark blue flame patterns, advertising Citibank on the front and something called 'Socio Fuliesta' on the back.

'OUR TEAM, OUR DREAM' read one banner. 'FLY HIGH FEARLESS' read another. The club's symbol was a phoenix rising from the flames. There were sky blue and dark blue flags and a drumming team that was opting for a syncopated swing. At the other end, perhaps twenty or thirty opposition fans supporting the visiting Yokogawa Electric company were making the best of things, chanting away and stressing that all important 'g'.

The Yokohama fans had plenty to cheer about. Their team was walking all over the boys from Yokogawa; and there on the bench, watching it happen, dressed in stylish black, was their new coach, Pierre Littbarski. Pierre Littbarski who played for Germany in three World Cups was now coaching Yokohama FC in the Japanese third division.

Not surprisingly, after the Flugels–Marinos merger had been announced, the Flugels fans themselves were possibly even more unhappy than Kazu Miyazaki and the Marinos supporters. Stunned by the news, the three main Flugels' supporters groups – the A-Azurri, Olé Yokohama and a group called 'Tifosi' – had started a 'Save the Flugels' campaign. More or less by default, an unlikely leader emerged from the ranks, a thirty-eight-year-old scriptwriter called Tomio Tsujino, a serious-looking man with thick black glasses.

'I used to be just an ordinary supporter,' said Tsujino when I met him later, 'but then I went to the meetings with the fans and I proposed that all three groups unify. They agreed, and said that it was such a good idea that I should take over the campaign.'

Things then became increasingly interesting. The 'Save the Flugels' campaign gathered 350,000 signatures on a petition calling on the largest shareholder, ANA, to save the troubled club. In three days, 10,000 people contributed 67 million yen, more than half a million dollars, to the campaign fund. But none of this made any difference. The corporate decision had been made. The Flugels were finished. At this point, the system expected the complaining fans to sit down and shut up, having elicited widespread public sympathy for their worthy, but doomed, struggle against authority. What happened next shows that Japan isn't what it used to be.

The angry frustrations of the Flugels fans happened to coincide with larger changes under way in the way that Japan does business. The vociferous 'Save the Flugels' campaign, and the press coverage, eventually attracted the attention of the giant international sports marketing agency, IMG. Founded by Mark McCormack, an American, IMG is one of the biggest marketing agencies in world sport, representing some of the world's best golfers and tennis players. Now they were trying to get involved in football in Japan. IMG is hardly a philanthropic organisation, but its view of the way business is done is very different from the world of ANA and Nissan, the two companies that had agreed to merge the Flugels into the Marinos. IMG's local soccer specialist was a Belgian former professional, Robert Maes. Mr Tsujino, the campaign leader, was invited to a meeting.

'They said they wanted to bring this team back,' Maes told me in his office in central Tokyo. 'We said we were willing to help, but they would have to forget about bringing this team back. It was impossible. The team was gone. But I told them that we could help them make a new team, if that's what they wanted.'

It was a marriage of convenience. IMG wanted to get a

foothold in Japanese football and the disconsolate supporters didn't have anywhere else to go. No reputable Japanese company would risk antagonising the corporate might of ANA and Nissan by supporting this ragtag bunch of whining former Flugels fans. All the companies that had backed the old Flugels team were linked in some way to ANA, just as most of S-Pulse's sponsors have some kind of link with the Suzuyo company. Like samurai whose lord has perished, the Flugels fans were now the ronin, the outcast bandits of Japanese football. Having failed to transfer their allegiances to the Yokohama F Marinos, the Flugels fans were clearly regarded as renegades.

The F Marinos managing director, Mr Taniguchi, is a kindly looking man. As general manager of the unmerged Marinos, it was Mr Taniguchi who had felt the full force of the fans' anger over the merger when he'd been hit on the head by the famous flying megaphone the previous season. He seemed rather perplexed by it all. This was not something he was used to, having been drafted in to run the Marinos from his former position as director of vehicle sales for Nissan in south-east Asia. He viewed things through the startlingly different perspective of corporate Japan.

The whole Nissan complex sits on a hill overlooking the port of Yokohama, one of the world's great industrial views. In Britain, we tend to associate heavy industry with decay, rusting warehouses and crumbling brick. Yokohama Port, spanned by the swoop of the Yokohama Bay Bridge is conversely a vast panorama of endeavour, of aluminium works, oil tankers, trucks and bulk carriers, shipping in iron ore and bauxite and shipping out JVC video cameras and Nissan cars.

I met Mr Taniguchi at Nissan's sports club in their Yokohama headquarters. Outside on the astro-turf training pitches, forty or fifty elementary schoolchildren in blue F Marinos shirts were dribbling balls around traffic cones, watched by a crowd of young mothers. The sports club is next to Nissan's customer service development department.

Mr Taniguchi's misreading of the fans' situation was impressive. 'The players and staff members are the ones who loved the

Flugels the most,' Mr Taniguchi told me, with evident sincerity and an equally evident profound lack of understanding of the passionate relationship between fans and their clubs. The players and staff moved their allegiances to the F Marinos or to their new clubs, accepting the new era. I think the players and the staff must be the ones who loved the Flugels the most.'

To an English person, Mr Taniguchi sounded a little crazy. In Europe, the players are the professionals, the mercenaries who play for money, whose allegiances can be transferred if the price is right. The fans are the poor victims of a passionate obsession which ties them to their club for life, or at least until the club goes bankrupt.

I realised that Mr Taniguchi thought of the players as the salarymen of a Japanese company, entirely committed to the organisation, like those squads of dedicated young recruits at the Toyota sports ground. The fans, on the other hand, were the fickle consumers, and as such could pick and chose at will between competing brands. Don't like Kyoto Purple Sanga? Why not try Cerezo Osaka? Rangers make you unhappy? Why not try Celtic? And as Mr Taniguchi and his colleagues would have to dilute their love of Nissan as a result of the forthcoming merger with France's Renault car company, whether they liked it or not, so the fans should accept the merger of the two competing teams.

'Then this other group of people, superficially seeing themselves as former Flugels supporters, came along,' he said, warming to the theme, and colouring slightly as he struggled to suppress his emotions. 'But these voices are not accepted by us. The city and Chamber of Commerce of Yokohama have accepted that the Yokohama F Marinos is the only team in Yokohama. And now this other team is set up. We are very . . . we are very embarrassed. Everyone is embarrassed. I personally am totally unhappy with the situation.' By Japanese standards, that meant that Mr Taniguchi was really, really steaming.

'No one was going to touch this team except us,' said Robert Maes at IMG. 'We said we have to make a team the European way. You make a company to set up a club, you employ us as your marketing agents, and we do the rest. Basically, these were people who had been waving a flag the week before and didn't know too much about football. So we said, "You will take all the decisions, but we will make all the suggestions." '

And so Yokohama FC sprang to life from the ashes of the Yokohama Flugels. While corporate Japan didn't like the idea, ordinary people and the Japanese media loved it. Maes and IMG set out to turn all that into a football team.

A couple of weeks later, I was on a bus heading out for the remotest outskirts of Yokohama, for another supposedly home game. Having been set up in April, the new club hadn't managed to secure a regular stadium to play in; it was planning to appear at seven different 'home' grounds across the area. Aikawa was the remotest, forty minutes by bus from the nearest train station, a residential suburb where the urban sprawl of Tokyo gradually gives way to the wooded hills which climb up to Mount Fuji.

I arrived at the Aikawa municipal sports ground during half-time, having seriously misjudged how far away the place was. But two thousand two hundred other people had made the journey to see Yokohama FC play Kokoshikan University First Eleven. Twelve or thirteen of them seemed to be supporting Kokoshikan.

At the entrance to the main stand, behind a trestle table, I found Mr Tsujino, now the president of the Yokohama Fulies Sports Club Ltd, owners of Yokohama FC (Fulies being what comes out if a Japanese person says 'Flugels' over and over again). He was wearing a dark suit and tie, as befitted his new role as club president. After the game, he got straight into the big themes. In Japan, when you start talking about football, before you know it you're talking about society, the education system and the political economy.

'For an English person, Japanese sport must seem pretty weird,' he said, 'because soccer teams are associated with companies. But you have to understand that Japan didn't even have the concept of sport until the Meiji era [from 1868] and then we had school sports and professional sport. In England, you had community-based grassroots sport from the beginning. In Japan, it's always top down, instead.

'When soccer started, people moved outside the existing system, and then they saw that the situation of sport in Japan is rather strange. They concluded that corporate sport is not the way forward. The merger of the Marinos and the Flugels had nothing to do with the supporters. It was a company decision. We're trying to develop a real community-based team.'

Mr Tsujino was one of the many fans who put up their own money to set up the new sports club. Subsequently, under IMG's direction, the club had founded a social club, the 'Socio Fuliesta' whose logo appeared on the shirts. It was modelled on the Spanish and southern European 'socio' concept, as seen at Barcelona; 5,000 fans paid 30,000 or 50,000 yen ($300 or $500) for three- or five-year season tickets to watch third-division soccer. Of course, the fans were hoping that Yokohama FC wouldn't spend the next five years in the third division.

There were some twenty professionals on the team's roster, the majority of them former players with J.League teams. They included Rehak Pavel, a thirty-five-year-old Czech on loan from Sparta Praha, who had previously played in Japan for JEF United, Littbarski's old club. The problems of the J.League and the move to cut club rosters at the end of the previous season meant that players were available on the cheap. They weren't the best, but they were better than everyone else in the JFL.

The biggest star was on the bench. The great Pierre Littbarski had signed up with IMG Japan a few months before the first meeting with the 'Save the Flugels' committee, having ended his playing career with the Japanese second-division team, Sendai. He'd been looking for a job training a J.League team, having become the first foreigner in Japan to secure a J.League coaching licence. Now he was jumping up and down on the bench, shouting at his players in a mix of German, Japanese and English, in the Japanese Football League. Robert Maes had told him, 'Pierre, if you train a J.League team you're going to be in that Japanese structure which is very hard to work with, because you don't have the freedom you need as a coach to make decisions. But here, we're making the team, and you can do it the way you like it.'

Littbarski proposed Yasuhiko Okudera as the new club's general manager, a former player who had been involved at JEF United in the early 1990s and also at Sendai. Okudera is virtually a household name in Japan. In 1987, he was the first Japanese ever to play football professionally in Europe, where he spent nine years at top German clubs, including Hertha Berlin.

All of this star talent wasn't paid for by the fans alone. Just five months after the ignominious collapse of the Yokohama Flugels, the new Yokohama FC had a developing list of sponsors, including Citibank and the German tool company Bosch. IMG even managed to sell television rights to the Yokohama FC games to Sky Perfect TV, partly owned by Rupert Murdoch, which was re-broadcasting them on one of its local sports channels. All the sponsors were foreign companies.

'We started going to foreign companies with the idea that it would give them an opportunity to show their interest in Japanese society,' said Robert Maes. 'By sponsoring the club they could demonstrate their belief in the country. It worked well.'

At the same time, with the media interest in the new club continuing to build, IMG started putting pressure on the Japanese Football Association. Technically, as a new team, the club would have to start off in the local Kanagawa League and work up to the Kanto League, before getting into the national Japanese Football League, and from there into the second division of the J.League. This was not an attractive proposition for a club that needed to succeed in order to support its finances. The Fulies wanted to get directly into the third division, the JFL. According to Maes, the J.League and the JFA initially said no. Yokohama FC would have to start at the bottom and work up.

'The Yokohama FC people, they were crying,' recalls Maes. 'President Tsujino was saying, "We want this team," and we said, "You heard them, we cannot play." But we also said the Japanese Football Association had to announce it, knowing very well that they would get killed if they said that. I mean, the first person to say that would get shot. At that time people were very upset.'

So the JFA caved in, offering Yokohama FC the chance to play in the eight-strong third division, the JFL. There were conditions; in theory, the new team was only affiliated to the JFL and wouldn't be eligible for promotion to the second division of the J.League itself, known as J2, for two seasons. It was enough. After all, at that time, in February 1999, Yokohama FC didn't have any players, and the league was due to start in April. Things were still difficult.

'This is a revolution in Japanese sport,' said the former national heart-throb, Okudera, 'but there are financial problems. And we still need to sort out our home grounds.'

Training was a problem. By May, training was being arranged on a day-to-day basis. Eventually, the team seemed to have found a training ground at a US Army depot at Sagami, home of the 35th Supply and Service Battalion, whose motto, appropriately, is 'Support the Orient'. I tried to get in to see the team training there once, having been promised a meeting with Littbarski by the club's front-office manager, Mr Tanabe. I failed to get past the notice on the fence, 'Caution, this area patrolled by military working dogs'.

Yokohama FC was in theory an entirely new team, but the fans obviously didn't think so. 'We're Back' read one of the tee-shirts issued to celebrate the opening game in May, at the old Mitsuzawa Stadium, which brought in a capacity 20,000 crowd. The fans, said Maes, had wanted to keep the name Flugels but couldn't because the name had been signed over to the F Marinos. Fulies was their second choice, also registered by ANA as a patented name. The old colours of light blue, dark blue and white survived – the same colours as ANA's planes – as did the flying motif.

I bought a light blue and white tee-shirt at the first game (I opted not to sign up for a copy of the forthcoming club song, to be released by The Alfee, a sort of middle-of-the-road Japanese rock band). 'Reach for the Sky' my tee-shirt says on the front, in English, beneath a dark blue phoenix. 'With Wings of Freedom' it says on the back.

As Mr Taniguchi had made clear, ANA and Nissan and possibly the entire city government of Yokohama were extremely unamused by all this. Suggestions that ANA might be interested in minimal sponsorship of the new team, to show its sympathy for what had happened, went unheeded. The word on the street was that ANA and Nissan had even warned the local commercial television network, TV Kanagawa, to stay away from Yokohama FC or risk losing advertising. Despite the plans to host the World Cup final in Yokohama, ANA was also rumoured to have asked the mayor of Yokohama not to cooperate with the new team, adding to their problems in finding suitable training grounds.

'Their team went bankrupt, and they didn't want to see anything new,' says Maes of ANA, 'because they thought it was not possible. They feel that it was their failure, and that we are rubbing their noses in it, saying, look, we could save the team, why couldn't you?'

The team did have one fan in the corporate élite, though. Saburo Kawabuchi, the J.League chairman, had gone along with the merger, and he'd joined the Socio Fuliesta, the perfect expression of his big idea of community-based football, even if it hadn't worked out exactly the way it was planned.

'Had the Antlers or the Reds gone bankrupt, it would have been a big problem because their supporters are very strong,' Mr Kawabuchi said about the merger, 'but no one expected a problem over the merger of the Flugels because they weren't so popular. But it was a big mess.'

清水

8 BIG ARCH

It was now almost the end of May and the first half of Japan's two-stage season was moving to its close. The evil Jubilo Iwata, to the dismay of all right-thinking people, had continued to play consistently well. S-Pulse had remained in second place throughout May. For S-Pulse to stand a chance of catching them, Jubilo had to lose. They didn't.

In between J.League games, Jubilo even found time to win the Asian Clubs Championship, the Asian equivalent of the European Cup but with much more travelling. They beat the top Iranian team, Istiqlal, in front of a crowd of 100,000 in Iran. It was hard to imagine the well-coiffeured and elegant Jubilo boys managing to beat the hard men of the Islamic Republic of Iran, but it happened. And they escaped to tell the tale.

Jubilo's regional commitments meant the club played a number of midweek games to make up the league schedule. On Tuesday, 26 May Jubilo played Avispa Fukuoka from the southern island of Kyushu, who at the time were near the bottom in the league. Jubilo managed to win only 1–0, with a golden goal in extra time, but it was enough to clinch the first-stage title. The house that

Dunga built was still solid. To add to it all, following the triumph in Tehran, Jubilo had been voted Asian Club Team of the Year the week before; and their manager, Takashi Kuwabara, had been voted Club Coach of the Year, although the rather colourless Kuwabara showed no signs of actually enjoying his job very much.

'In this game, you should enjoy the good times when things are going well,' observed Perryman-san sagely. 'There's certainly more than enough bad times.'

Jubilo's win put them four points clear of S-Pulse, who had one game left to play. Even if S-Pulse won, they would still be one point short. For the S-Pulse fans, it was a bitter blow. Once again they were second.

'S-Pulse is a very good team, but we're always coming second,' Yamada-san complained. 'The team that comes first changes – maybe the Flugels one year, or Antlers, or Jubilo. But we're always second.' It was getting annoying.

To make sure of second place, S-Pulse still had to beat Sanfrecce Hiroshima, managed by Eddie Thomson, a man who could never be accused of being short on colour. Sanfrecce were lying in a very creditable sixth position; creditable because Sanfrecce, even more than S-Pulse, had had their share of cutbacks in recent years. In 1997, the club's biggest shareholder, Mazda, had almost gone broke. Just as Nissan would eventually seek assistance from Renault, Mazda had been rescued by Ford, who brought in a Scottish CEO to get things organised. Eddie Thomson turned up on the scene in the same year. Thomson arrived from Australia, where he'd gone from coaching Sydney City to becoming the national team coach, taking Australia to the Atlanta Olympics and building up the team that almost made it to the 1998 French World Cup under Terry Venables. Before that, Thomson had played for Hearts and Dundee United. Despite the Scottish accent, Thomson was now an Australian citizen. It was a challenging combination.

'Eddie's a good friend of mine and we talk all the time,' says Les Mottram, the J.League's super-ref. 'But he's got himself a reputation. Eddie – typical Scotsman – gets a bit het up at some of the decisions, and he goes out there and he starts remonstrating. That's the way he is. If you take that away from him, he probably won't be as effective. Before the match, I always say to him, "Eddie, sit on your arse because the last thing I want to do is send you up to the stand and then have to go out to dinner with you afterwards." '

Hiroshima, despite having been destroyed by an atom bomb on 6 August 1945, is a very pleasant place. Visiting for the first time is disturbing and sobering. There's the damaged A-bomb dome and the peace park, and there's the landscape of low hills by the river which seems familiar from old photographs and newsreels of the levelled city. After a while, you get used to it. Just around the corner from the A-bomb dome, which was undergoing renovation when I walked past, is the home stadium of the Hiroshima Carps baseball team, and then there's the Diodora multi-storey electronics shop and the Sogo department store. And you can eat Hiroshima's famous pancakes.

'I like Hiroshima,' said Eddie Thomson one sunny day, adding with unintended irony, 'there's not as many people as there are in Tokyo.' Not that the big man is averse to crowds. After a game in Tokyo, he'd demanded to be allowed to travel on the Maranouchi subway line in the rush-hour so he could have the experience of being jammed into the carriage by powerful station officials in white gloves and green uniform jackets. (In fact, this most abiding image of modern Japan is not that common – you really have to know when and where to go if you want that carriage-jamming experience.)

Hiroshima is much quieter. There are indeed fewer people, and not because of the bomb, but because Hiroshima is a provincial city, where people have a bit more time. The city has wide main streets. Wooden trams rattle up and down, running all the way to the port area where huge car-carriers load Mazda cars *en route* to Europe and the United States. You can sit there and watch Japan's trade surplus with the rest of the world taking shape before your eyes.

The day before the S-Pulse game, I travelled out to Sanfrecce's home stadium, the 50,000 capacity Hiroshima Big Arch track and field stadium, a spectacular and elegant athletics stadium built in the wooded hills above the city in the Hiroshima Prefectural Park. The Big Arch and the surrounding sports complex had been built for the Asian Games in 1994. An ultra-modern driverless light railway, the ASRAM line, runs out of the city centre and takes about forty minutes to get to the sports complex. The carriage I was in carried the season's Sanfrecce poster, produced in the team's shocking purple colour with the English slogan 'Run for Wins'. It had photos of three players, including the leading goalscorer, Tatsuhiko Kubo, and the big Australian defender, Tony Popovic, in action with cartoon speech bubbles: 'BAM!', 'SHWAM!' and 'YAAAAAY!'

From the station, I trudged uphill on a stone pathway through the park towards the curve of the big stadium, walking beside an ornamental stream through neatly tended gardens. Classical music wafted faintly through unseen loudspeakers.

At the stadium itself, the players were out on the pitch for a light training session. Eddie Thomson is a tall, grey-haired and extremely fit-looking character now in his early fifties, with blue eyes that it has to be said twinkle mischievously. On the other hand, I wouldn't fancy a punch-up with him. Like Perryman-san, he had an English assistant coach, Michael Hickman, aka Hickey, who had played for Brighton, Grimsby, Blackburn Rovers and Torquay. Hickey had met Eddie at Sydney City, where he was his assistant coach. Then he'd gone to the national team, followed by time at Reading, Leicester and Wolverhampton Wanderers. Then Hiroshima. Play football. See the world.

The other foreigner on the staff was the Spanish doctor, Pedro, and there was the English-speaking assistant manager in his thirties, Nobuhiro Ueno, known as Nobu. After the training, Thomson went into the mandatory pre-game meet-the-press session, talking to the handful of local newspaper and television reporters assigned to cover every possible aspect of Sanfrecce's daily existence and performance. This time, the focus was on the performance so far.

'We've scored a lot of goals, much more goals than we've scored in previous years,' said Thomson. 'So the first part of the season's been good. The year before I took over, the team only won ten times in the whole season. Now we've won eight in the first half.'

'What in your opinion is the difference with last season?' asked one of the reporters, an earnest young man in glasses, holding his notebook at the ready. He spoke quietly and displayed the sort of respectful deference that characterises even the most hard-bitten Japanese hacks. Nobu translated into English.

'Scoring goals,' said Thomson-san. Nobu translated this back for the young reporter, who nodded enthusiastically. 'That's been the big difference this year. We've taken our chances. We're one of the highest scoring teams this year, and that's unusual for us.' But the big man wasn't getting out of it that easily.

'But why did we score the goals?' asked the reporter again, displaying a rare and plucky persistence in his search for the ultimate truth. Thomson-san patiently outlined a theory about why Sanfrecce had scored more goals. The basic premise was that the team had played better. The reporter wrote it down, and followed up. 'But what can we do to make it better in the second half of the season?'

'There's nothing really. It's just general playing. Sometimes we make bad decisions, sometimes we pressurise when we should fall off. Decision-making is our biggest problem. Any more questions? There's always one more.'

It struck me that both Thomson and Perryman had a knack with the Japanese footballing press. They were always patient. They would always take the questions seriously and try to explain the game. Other managers were not always so patient. The new national coach, for example, a sulky Frenchman called Philippe Troussier, was famous for a streak of Gallic sarcasm that the Japanese took very personally. For many of the reporters, as for many of the fans, football is a new game.

Earlier that season, after Sanfrecce had lost 3–2 to the F Marinos despite being two goals up, I had seen a downcast Eddie Thomson face repeated questions about a decision to substitute a midfielder, made when Sanfrecce were still 2–1 ahead. The

Japanese reporters clearly thought the substitution must be directly related to the fact that Sanfrecce had then more or less given away the two additional goals. Thomson patiently answered the same question three times, explaining that the substitution had nothing to do with the goals because one was scored directly from a free-kick, and was essentially a goalkeeping error, while the other followed a mistake by a defender. The Japanese reporters didn't seem convinced. In baseball, which most of them would have grown up playing, the manager's decision to change a pitcher or to adjust his batting order will often have a direct influence on the outcome of the game.

The Japanese footballing press loves to talk about playing systems; the pages of the weekly soccer magazines are heavy with incredibly complex diagrams explaining who went where and how in each game, as if the game is a creation in the manager's mind and is something that can be measured, studied and reproduced, if only enough effort is expended in the process. 'They love to talk about playing systems,' said Perryman-san.

This season the wise ways of Thomson-san had indeed produced a creditable performance from Sanfrecce. But before he arrived at the start of the 1997 season, Sanfrecce had not been doing too well. In fact, Sanfrecce had been in what might be called a state of disarray. In 1996, the club had finished third from bottom under Dutch coach Wim Jansen, despite the fact that the team had three national squad players and a South Korean international midfielder, Noh Jung-Yoon. Like Perryman and Ardiles at S-Pulse, Eddie Thomson's first season was a clean-up job which included the three national team players, Takagi, Moriyasu and Michiki, who were all paid around 80 million yen, $700,000, a year.

'They weren't working out during the two hours of practice,' Thomson told me in the dressing room after the training session. 'And then they'd stay behind afterwards, to show that national team players trained harder. Come matchday, they'd be tired. Or they'd come in at eight o'clock at night to see the physiotherapist, even though the staff had worked all day. They'd come in

Tominori Endo (foreground), the leader of Chapéu Laranja, demonstrates how to play samba and watch football at the same time as S-Pulse play Grampus.

Left Get the Victory: S-Pulse fans rejoice after the dramatic victory against Grampus at Gifu. Mr 'call me Mr Cherry Blossom' Sakura stands to the right in the black shirt. Below him, Mr Oba of K's Club makes the V for victory sign.
Right Consciousness raising in Yokohama. Kazu Miyazaki speaks out against Nissan, All Nippon Airlines and the 'F' Marinos merger after the game against Sanfrecce Hiroshima.

Left Hidetoshi Nakata, superstar: Twice Asian Footballer of the Year, and the first Japanese player to make a success in Italy's Serie A. (Allsport)
Right S-Pulse's goalscoring Brazilian forward Alex, helped by Paru-chan and translator Edmundo Hanyu, tells local TV how it feels to be man-of-the-match.

Daisuke Ichikawa, Shimizu's 19-year-old home-grown star, deals with some fans at a national team training camp at the J. Village in Fukushima in May 1999.

On a clear day you can see Mount Fuji: the view from the Nihondaira plateau overlooking the S-Pulse ground and Shimizu City. (Yumiko Nagae)

Welcome to Shimizu, home of Mr Average. The traditional port industries are struggling, the population is declining, but the town is proud to be Japan's 'city of soccer'.

It's a record: S-Pulse samba band leader, Shunya Matsuda (in the white coat), and his first lieutenant, Mr Tanaka, prepare to produce the longest sushi roll in the world in Shimizu-no Ginza shopping precinct during Golden Week, 1999.

Tomita Hori (left), loyal supporter of S-Pulse and Eric Cantona, with her husband and two fully equipped Nagoya Grampus Eight fans before the away game in Gifu in May.

Dancing in the street: Seiji Naya, president of the S-Pulse fans, in front of the Chapéu Laranja float at the August port festival in Shimizu.

Paru-chan greets a budding young S-Pulse supporter at the opening of Shimizu's new Jusco super-store in May.

The Yokohama F Marinos' mascot, Marinos-kun, and friends before the game against Sanfrecce Hiroshima.

Fill this space: 'Print Club' photo booth technology allowed the author to get in to the frame with Paru-chan. Floppy-eared Paru-chan hats are also available at the S-Pulse shop.

Shimizu's gifted Brazilian striker, Alex, feels the heat from Jubilo's No. 10, Toshiya Fujita, during the first stage championship clash at the Yamaha stadium in Iwata on December 4th.

Victory night: Kenta Hasegawa (right) leads the celebrations at the traditional beer shower ceremony in the gardens of the Nihondaira hotel. To his right stand Fabinho and Sawanobori, with Brazilian goal-keeper coach Fuka in the middle. (Yumiko Nagae)

Yugoslav international Dragan Stojkovic, of Nagoya Grampus Eight, launches a characteristically emotional on-field appeal for justice. Japanese football, he says, is 'really a little bit different'. (Michi Ishijima)

Mottram the law-giver: Scotsman Leslie Mottram presided at the 1994 World Cup and Euro 96 before coming to Japan to work with the Japan Football Association. (Yumiko Nagae)

A long way from White Hart Lane: Steve Perryman, armed with ceremonial mallet, white gloves and yellow rosette, installs a brass plate carrying his footprints and signature on Shimizu's S-Pulse street. Assistant manager, Takeshi Oki, stands behind.

Perryman-san and translator Edmundo Hanyu field questions at a post-game news conference. Japanese journalists traditionally give the winning manager a round of polite applause. (Yumiko Nagae)

just for a massage. The thing about it was that the people who were working their arses off on the park were getting less than half the money.'

Left largely to their own devices by the previous management, the players had started to act according to traditional Japanese behavioural patterns, recreating in the team the senior–junior relationships which are all-pervasive in Japanese corporate life. As Nagoya Grampus coach Daniel Sanchez had earlier observed, Japanese traditional culture is not necessarily conducive to good football.

'There was no team spirit,' said Thomson, getting a bit exasperated just thinking about it. 'Takagi would have his group of younger players, who'd carry his boots and his bag out to his car. Michiki would have his, and Moriyasu his.' Clearly this state of affairs was not likely to appeal to a canny, hard-working Scot. 'I put up with this for about two weeks and then I said, "Right. This has got to fuckin' stop." I mean, they'd be deciding when we could train and when we couldn't, depending on their own schedules and so on. So I said, "We train from 10 to 12 and then we're finished. And if I see anyone still on the training pitch when I'm driving home, I'm going to fine you." And it stopped.'

For the first season, things didn't improve much. Sanfrecce finished tenth in the first stage and eleventh in the second stage. In the middle of the year, Thomson got rid of Antonio Carlos Santos – 'a Brazilian who was being paid a million dollars a year for doing absolutely fucking nothing' – and he brought in two Australians, one of whom, Tony Popovic, was to form the backbone of the defence. The new discipline was causing some friction.

'People came up to me and said, "The players think it's like a prison camp around here." And I said, "If you want it to be easy, we'll be relegated next year." '

At the end of the season, Eddie Thomson staged his coup. Takagi, Moriyasu and Michiki were sold, despite the fact that Takagi had scored a third of the club's goals that season. The team's South Korean international, Noh Jung-Yoon, was sent to play for Breda in Holland on loan. The purge turned out to be a triumph.

'We got rid of the four highest players and replaced them with four of the youngest players. Everyone was telling me I shouldn't do it. But it proved successful. The younger players have come through and now two of them are in the national team themselves. Everyone thought we would struggle, but we climbed the league. We won more games than we'd won before and we improved. We made a lot of decisions, we made a lot of money on the transfer market, and it worked out good.'

Sanfrecce had finished ninth in the second stage of the newly expanded eighteen-team league the previous season, despite the absence of their old stars. Now they were in sixth place, which, in Eddie Thomson's opinion, is at least one of the reasons why Japanese teams still need overseas managers.

'I don't think Japanese coaches have the confidence to make big changes like that. I don't think they're tough enough to do it, to get rid of five, seven or eight players just because they're not good enough, and drop this one from the first team when he's an ex-international, and drop the next one, and be able to look ahead and plan for the future.'

In Hiroshima, Eddie Thomson has become something of a local personality. He's accosted by fans for autographs.

'You see them following you along the street sometimes, but they're too shy to come up and ask for an autograph. If you stop, they stop. Eventually, I say, "Do you want an autograph, or what?" '

At the start of the season he'd been paraded in a smart suit at the Yoshida Shrine, dedicated to a hero of the warrior clan which had ruled Hiroshima in the sixteenth century, where he'd been presented with the three symbolic arrows (the san frecce) of the clan by a Shinto priest in white robes, while two men in full samurai armour looked on.

'The reporters asked me if I thought the arrows would bring us luck. I said, "If you think they're lucky, they're lucky." '

In April, he'd spent an afternoon behind the counter at the newly opened Hiroshima Post Office, one of the club's sponsors, selling stamps – 'I told them when I got there, "Right. Take the day off." '

Sanfrecce was now a no-nonsense outfit. Unlike S-Pulse, Thomson didn't have many options if anyone was injured. The defence was built around the two substantial Australians, Tony Popovic, now aged twenty-five, and twenty-one-year-old Hayden Foxe, a ginger-haired, straight-up bloke, the sort of Aussie who could be relied upon to charge machine guns when asked without asking too many questions. That year, Foxey was challenging for a place in the Australian national team. Up front, goalscoring was the principal responsibility of twenty-two-year-old Tatsuhiko Kubo, one of Thomson's local success stories. But in general, at Sanfrecce solid team organisation had to compensate for lack of individual quality.

There had been one failure of cross-cultural communications before the season began. In common with other foreign managers, Eddie had been asked to come up with a new slogan for the team to go on the programme and on team pictures. At S-Pulse, Steve Perryman had managed to come up with 'Football with Style and a Smile'.

'My son is in advertising,' said Thomson, 'and he suggested "In a League of Our Own". But the marketing people said that wouldn't work in Japanese for some reason. It didn't sound right. So I suggested "Never Give Up" because we are a team that has always battled hard and the boys have a lot of spirit. They said that was fine.'

So no problems there – not until Thomson saw the new season's individual photographs of the Sanfrecce team, including one of himself. Instead of 'Never Give Up', the team's catchphrase for the season had been re-translated into English as 'No Surrender', a slogan associated in Scotland with the predominantly Protestant Glasgow Rangers. As a result, Eddie Thomson, whose uncle is a diehard Celtic supporter, has been unable to send any of this season's photos back to the family in Scotland. It was rather like the Urawa Reds fans and their 'Aryans' signs. But that's globalisation.

Meanwhile, despite Sanfrecce's sixth place, the home crowds remained unimpressive. After all, Hiroshima, unlike Shimizu, has its own baseball team, the Hiroshima Carps, and supporting a football team in the Big Arch Stadium, forty minutes from the centre of town, is not always such fun – as Shimizu S-Pulse and the samba band were about to find out.

I booked into the economically priced Hotel Central, down by the river in an 'entertainment' district called Kanayama-cho, which seemed to attract a disproportionate number of loitering women.

Perryman-san and the S-Pulse team, on the other hand, were staying in the far more salubrious five-star Royal Hotel, which had a lobby the size of a small railway station. They had come down from Shizuoka on the Shinkansen, a journey of around four hours. This time, Perryman had brought his wife, Kim, and their children, four-year-old Ella and two-year-old Jojo. They were installed on the thirty-second floor of the hotel, with a stupendous view over the city and the low surrounding hills. After the game, the plan was to go to Kyoto with some friends for a break.

Kim, Ella and Jojo had room service. Perryman ate with the team in a vast banqueting room set about with an equally vast buffet. As usual, the buffet included an additional serving of vitamin pills for the players. At dinner, not surprisingly, the recent success of the evil Jubilo Iwata came up at the management table.

'I reckon that Jubilo never has foreign referees,' said Perryman over a plate of *yaki-soba* fried noodles. 'They wouldn't stand for what goes on. Look at the Avispa game. Normally they announce referees two weeks in advance. For that game it was only two days in advance. Look at our game against them. That left-back must have kicked our Alex about eight or nine times and no booking. Does that mean that every player on the pitch can kick Alex eight or nine times?' Perryman suggested that Japanese referees don't pick up on the dynamics of a game before it starts – they don't work out in advance what they have to be prepared for.

'The Japanese referees, they look the tree,' added the Japanese assistant manager, Oki-san, in a moment of poetic simplicity. 'They no see the wood. The forest. They always rule-book looking.'

Attention switched to a video of the previous day's epic European Cup final, in which Manchester United had come back from 1–0 down against Bayern Munich to score twice in the dying minutes of the game. Then there wa a complicated discussion of train timetables and baggage movements, and the risks posed to the weekend's trip to Kyoto by the nightmare possibility of sudden-death extra time. 'Now, Matsuba, you speak to Ohta-san. If Ohta-san say no problem, then no problem. If Ohta-san say problem, then problem.'

By comparison, my own domestic arrangements were starkly simple. I wandered back to the dingy Hiroshima Hotel Central stopping along the way to buy a beer from a vending machine. Vending machines, always unvandalised and usually fully stocked, are another of the things that make Japan great, along with the country's 50,000 plus twenty-four-hour convenience stores. The convenience stores are already taking on many of the functions of the state – you can pay your bills at the Seven-Eleven, and buy air-tickets at Lawson's. Eventually, they'll be running the court system. The convenience stores, the Family Marts and the AmPm, are the backbone of the Japanese convenience industry. The vending machines fill in the gaps.

There is a vending machine for every twenty-seven people in Japan. Everyone knows the stories about vending machines selling schoolgirls' used underwear. If they exist, I've yet to find one, although I did once encounter a machine that distributed plastic sex toys, but it only activated itself after eleven o'clock at night, which doesn't seem so convenient. The city of Kobe that year had introduced vending machines with electronic message boards which could flash warnings of earthquakes or tidal waves or other imminent disasters to the consuming public. The drawback seemed to me to be that the machine didn't tell you what to do about the forthcoming disaster. Buy another can of iced coffee? But the most important thing about Japanese vending machines, and perhaps one of the chief benefits of a rigid social order where vandalism is rare, is that they sell beer. They even sell pints of Suntory Whiskey.

Surveying the selection, I decided to extend my knowledge of Japanese beer, the branding of which shifts like the sands. I opted for a can of a new Asahi beer called Silky First Lady. 'Asahi First Lady has satin smoothness' it said on the label. 'Relax and enjoy the time taste'. First Lady is one of a range of new beers brought out in 1999 targeting young women. Another is Beer Water, aimed at persuading consumers that this isn't really beer. The water theme is big; new vending machine products include Leafs Tea Water, described on the can as 'a new refreshment that combines water with a variety of tea leaves'. There's lots of fun to be had at Japanese vending machines.

First Lady is certainly not in the first rank of the world's beers, and buying it made me feel rather effete ('It's not for me; it's for a friend') which is, I suppose, exactly what the marketers want. Luckily, I acquired a can of standard issue, very manly Asahi Extra Dry for back-up. All this ensured a peaceful night in my less than capacious accommodation.

After eating breakfast on my bed the next day (a carton of orange juice, pre-packaged donuts and a banana), I set out for the game at about noon. I took the ASRAM line again, gliding out towards the stadium through the suburbs of Hiroshima. The train was hardly packed with supporters. In fact, it was entirely empty of any supporters whatsoever. So was the station out at the sports park.

The situation wasn't entirely devoid of atmosphere. Purple Sanfrecce flags decorated the empty walkway out of the station, presumably to give you that matchday buzz as you surveyed the yawning openness between you and the stadium. Music was playing too, a jaunty girl-band tune echoing strangely across the concrete, with a chorus in English which went like this: 'I want to see you get that kick. Please let me see you get that kick.' This was the Sanfrecce Hiroshima team song, sung by a locally born J.Pop chanteuse, Aki Murakami, and released back in 1993 at the start of the J.League frenzy. It was a reminder of those hectic days, when Aki Murakami's record was one of many produced to feed the J.League hysteria. At least she came from Hiroshima. The Yoko-hama Marinos ended up with a rather dire anthem called 'Yokohama Fight On!' which I bought at half-price from a sports store earlier in the year. Produced by Sony Music, 'Yokohama Fight On!' was performed by a group of musicians in Paris assembled for the occasion and called B.R.B. – Bleu, Rouge, Blanc, the Marinos colours. The song was entirely in English, and it went like this:

> Here we are
> And the light's burning on
> In our hearts
> There's a feeling
> That will never, never die
> One bright star
> Burning now for so long
> Yokohama fight on
> Keep fighting on.

Overall, Sanfrecce had come out of things rather well.

As I was about to walk on up to the stadium, I suddenly noticed that the music wasn't coming from the station's public address system but from a couple of small loudspeakers that had been taped to part of the roof structure for the occasion. I followed the wire back from the speakers. Eventually, back in the station, on top of the coin lockers, I found a CD player and amplifier plugged into a wall socket and entirely unsupervised. It wouldn't happen at Highbury.

The mood of innocent fun continued up at the esplanade running round the stadium. It was like a school fête. There were children queuing to have their faces painted in Sanfrecce's shock-ing purple. There was a real Italian man selling pizza from the back of a van. There was an even longer queue by a tent where two of the team's youngest players, nineteen-year-old Sachio Yoshida and eighteen-year-old Takanori Ikeda, were patiently signing tee-shirts, hats, balls and whatever else came to hand. They were handing out collector's cards pictures of the two players. 'No surrender' it said at the bottom of each card. At one point, a vast procession of ten and eleven year olds was led off towards the pitch for a group photograph with Sanche-kun, the Sanfrecce big bear mascot. I had some pizza. I drank some cold tea. Everything was lovely.

This was, however, not a game without its tensions. You could even say that the Sanfrecce–S-Pulse game is something of a grudge match, at least as far as the managers are concerned. The previous season, after S-Pulse had beaten Sanfrecce 1–0 at Nihondaira, Ossie Ardiles made remarks to the effect that Eddie Thomson's team played negative football. In the return game, to Eddie Thomson's lasting satisfaction, his boys held S-Pulse to a 2–2 draw at the Big Arch, and then won the penalty shoot-out. Ardiles left in a huff. There was definitely a contrast of styles. S-Pulse played free-flowing, elegant football. Sanfrecce's main aim was to get the ball forward to Kubo, their star striker, and to keep a solid defence. It wasn't always pretty.

I decided that this was a game to be watched from the stands. At the away end, I found the S-Pulse samba band staked out in the centre. They had driven overnight from Shimizu and were looking the worse for it.

'I am very tired,' said Yamada-san, who was manning one of the big surdo drums. He looked tired. It was made worse by the hot glare of the late afternoon sun, which was shining directly into our faces. Small groups of fans were trying to take shelter behind the scoreboard. There was Mr 'Call me Mr Cherry Blossom' Sakura, the number one up-tempo bad boy.

'Ah, Jonasan-san,' he roared, as he bounded enthusiastically towards me. Clearly a few beers had been consumed. I said hello and was led by Mr Sakura over to the shade where we met Mr Koike, the man who had started waving my arms back and forth when I first appeared in the stands at Gifu. I had stood next to Arisa, Mr Koike's ten-year-old tambourine-wielding daughter at that game. Looking at the well-oiled Mr Sakura, I remarked on how varied and different the S-Pulse fans seemed to be.

'Family,' said Mr Koike. 'We're one family.'

At about 2.30, the fans mobilised. It was very, very hot. Far away at the other end of the stadium, we could see the not-so-massed ranks of the Sanfrecce fans and their purple banners. Between us and them stretched a vast acreage of empty seating. To fill up some space, the home side had strung a giant picture of Sanche-kun, the Hiroshima bear, over an entire unoccupied central section of the stand. 'Pour On The Heat' read a small banner next to the bear.

Before the teams marched out, Sanfrecce's all-girl cheerleaders performed a small display somewhere over near the central stand. It may have been good. From where we were standing, it was hard to tell. I remembered what Perryman-san had said before the game – there was a theory that the design of the Big Arch Stadium sucked all the energy out of opposition players, which was why S-Pulse always struggled to win there. Out on the terraces, things didn't feel right.

At this point, I witnessed a particularly bizarre incident involving one of the older S-Pulse supporters. This man's huge orange S-Pulse banner, some ten or twelve feet long, had fallen from where it was resting at the edge of the pitch on to the running track behind the goal. This happens quite a lot at J.League games. The usual etiquette calls for one of the ballboys to pick up the banner and return it to the grateful fan. This time, however, the ballboy wasn't watching, and was in fact kicking a ball around with one of his colleagues. The unhappy S-Pulse fan, who was probably in his fifties, shouted. Nothing happened. He shouted again. Then all the people around him shouted. The ballboy finally got the message, walked over and picked up the flag. But as he tried to hand the pole back to the distressed fan, the man, who had probably been drinking and who had probably spent the previous night driving down from Shimizu, grabbed hold of it and tried to hit the apparently innocent ballboy over the head with the other end, while shouting 'Bakayaro' at him. It means literally 'You're stupid' but has more the weight of 'You're a bastard'. The ballboy, as surprised as I was, disentangled himself from the flag without injury, gave the fan a hurt look, turned round and walked off.

What made this all the more interesting was that none of the entirely respectable citizens standing around said anything at all to the fan in question, who wasn't a particularly dangerous person and whom they all knew. It was as if one of the church wardens on a Sunday school outing had suddenly assaulted a ticket-collector at the station and no one had said anything, not even 'Steady on a bit, Arthur,' or 'That wasn't very nice, dear.' Of course, one could if one wanted build an entire national stereotype upon this incident which would take in everything from Japanese wartime atrocities to the Tokyo subway gas attacks of 1995, all of which could be explained on the grounds that it would have been just too embarrassing to say anything along the lines of 'Hang on a minute, Ishihara-san.'

It was, in any event, an incident which heightened my sense of foreboding as the game got under way. We did our best. We chanted and we sang and we all jumped up and down. Matsuda-san was there on the big bass drum. None of it stopped S-Pulse going one goal down six minutes into the first half, the goal scored by Popovic somewhere at the other end of the pitch. Just over ten minutes later, more disaster struck when one of the S-Pulse forwards, Yasunaga, was carried off with a dislocated toe. Things weren't off to a very good start. But it was only one goal, and S-Pulse, on paper, are a far superior team.

As far as I could make out from the stands while jigging backwards and forwards and chanting 'OOORE OOORE ORE ORE ESS-PULSE!' Hiroshima were playing a hard physical game and S-Pulse couldn't deal with it. The boys in orange couldn't settle down. They couldn't put their moves together. Hiroshima's big defenders, Popovic and Foxe, were all over them, delivering a couple of 110 per cent tackles which had people around me trying to identify the enemy.

'Who's their number 18?' asked an outraged fan near me, as Popovic physically eliminated another attempt by Alex to attack the goal.

'It's Po-po-vee . . . Po-pa-vo . . .' said someone else struggling to work it out from the Japanese script.

'It's Po-po-vitch,' I said.

'Right, Po-po,' said the first fan. 'Po-po,' he shouted, 'is a bastard!'

In the second half, things got worse. Kubo, Sanfrecce's talented striker, intercepted a pass in midfield and beat Sanada to make it 2–0. Perryman and Thomson were both out of their boxes on the running track, going spare and, so it turned out later, abusing each other like it was going out of fashion. It wasn't clear who started it.

'We had a bit of a go at each other,' said Perryman later. 'He's getting at me, yelling, "Stevie, you better get Ossie back because you're not going to win the league if you play like this," and I'm shouting at him, "You know why no one comes to watch you play? Because you're fucking boring." And so on. It's what we do. The Japanese look at us and they can't believe it. We were playing Reysol this year and their big Brazilian goalkeeping coach jumps up and starts shouting at the referee, "Yellow card! Yellow card!" because of a tackle by our Santos. And so I shout at him, "Fucking sit down. You're the fucking goalkeeping coach. Sit down and fucking shut up." Our Japanese players were shocked. Shocked. They couldn't believe it. It just doesn't happen.'

As the game went on, it was clear that we weren't going to have to worry about sudden-death extra time and missing our trains. S-Pulse were about as threatening as my grandmother. Eddie Thomson's low-rent operation might not be pretty, and they might have had thirty-five free-kicks given against them, but they had done for S-Pulse once again. At the end of it, the S-Pulse fans who had travelled so far to see it, just went quiet. A lady standing by me had tears in her eyes (I also suddenly noticed that she was wearing yellow S-Pulse earrings). As the team walked over to bow to their supporters, there was a desolate outbreak of chanting 'ESS-PULSE ESS-PULSE!' But they'd failed. The players knew it, and the S-Pulse fans, despite what some people might say about their antics, knew the team had let them down. I said my goodbyes to the subdued fans and headed for the press conference.

'We saved our worst performance for last,' said an exhausted and disconsolate Perryman-san. 'We were beaten by a stronger, more physical team and our team looked ill-equipped to match their battle. We can play. We can pass. But when it comes to a one-to-one confrontation for the ball, we didn't have it.'

The question had touched the key issue about S-Pulse – they looked good, they could pass the ball, they had great technique, but did they have the will to win? Could they produce what Perryman called 'that little bit more' when the chips were down? 'I sometimes think there's more will to win in my voice than there is in their legs,' he'd said earlier in the season. Before leaving, though, Perryman couldn't resist a bit of a dig at the hosts.

'Maybe I need to teach my team to be more physical so more opposition players finish on the floor.'

There was more bad news for S-Pulse on the big orange bus heading back to the station. Verdy Kawasaki, the team which S-Pulse had beaten in the opening game in March, had defeated the Yokohama F. Marinos. So S-Pulse weren't second now. They were third, two points behind Verdy and four points behind the evil Jubilo. Sanfrecce were still sixth, their highest ranking since 1994, and all without spending any money.

Out on the pitch, the cameras were on Eddie Thomson, and the interview was broadcast around the ground. He was telling the modest crowd of some 6,000 that he hoped they'd continue to support Sanfrecce. His vast picture smiled down from the electronic scoreboard. 'No surrender' it said underneath.

清水

9 ORANGE HAT

After the S-Pulse game in Hiroshima on 29 May, the J.League went
on its summer holidays. Like sudden-death extra time, the league's
two-stage system is in part an attempt to keep the fans happy by
giving them a constant string of possible title dramas – first-stage
champions, second-stage champions and a two-leg championship
final between the two triumphant teams. It also allows the league to
spread its costs between two separate sponsorship deals. But it
doesn't make life easy for managers and players.

'In England, it may take ten or twelve games for a player to
settle in,' Perryman-san said at the end-of-first-stage press conference in Hiroshima, 'but by that time in Japan, someone's the
champion.'

The system also means that the traditional measure of success
in a football league – consistently winning matches through the
whole season – doesn't necessarily apply. It would be entirely
possible for a team to end up with the most combined points from
the two stages, but win nothing at all. Or for the same team to
win both stages of the league, and for there to be no championship final.

It isn't so straightforward for the fans either. A variety of factors ensures that being a Japanese football fan requires a degree in management planning just to keep up with the fixture schedule. In 1999, the J.League planners outdid themselves, engineering new levels of complexity that challenged the imagination. The first stage had been easy enough, with sixteen games in a row, culminating in the triumph of the evil hordes from Jubilo Iwata. But the second stage was a mess, a vast coitus interruptus stretching from August until November.

At the start of the year, everyone knew that the second stage would begin on 7 August and that five games were scheduled for that month. But that was all. The JFA wanted another break to allow Japan to concentrate on the vitally important national task of qualifying for the Sydney 2000 Olympic Games. The only problem was that at the start of the season, no one knew exactly when the break would be. Eventually, by the beginning of August, things had settled down. Japan's Under-22 Olympic team would play Thailand, and more alarmingly, Khazakhstan, in October and November. As a result, S–Pulse were scheduled to start the second stage with a home game against Cerezo Osaka on 7 August. They would then play eleven games through until 23 September, when the J.League would break for the Olympic qualifiers. S–Pulse would play Purple Sanga on 30 October, and break for another two weeks. They would play the four remaining games in the last two weeks of November. Tension? Only if you had a good memory.

At the end of July, I returned to Shimizu ahead of the opening game for a community-based sports event of an entirely different kind. The full heat of summer had descended on Japan. Cicadas were singing in the trees around Hibiya Park in the centre of Tokyo. The city streets sweltered under clear skies. In the evenings, the cab drivers had their radios tuned permanently to baseball; in the Central League, the Tokyo Giants were struggling to keep up with the league leaders, the Chunichi Dragons from Nagoya.

Summer in Japan is a time for traditional night-time festivals.

They proliferate in towns and at shrines across the country as the temperature rises, frequently accompanied by spectacular fireworks displays. That summer of '99, young Japan was going through a 'look East' boom, and traditional festivals were back in vogue. In Tokyo, young women wearing traditional cotton kimono-like robes, or *yukata*, designed in big splashy patterns of primary colours, together with traditional open sandals, fluttered on to the subway carriages clutching fans and tiny handbags just big enough to hold a mobile phone.

Shimizu was not left out. The first weekend of August marks the Shimizu port festival, the traditional event, founded a whole decade previously, mentioned in the town guide. It was another part of the town's effort to boost civic pride in the face of an ageing and declining population, and to draw in more of those big-spending tourists in search of the good times down on the bay. Yamada-san had told me about it at the store opening in Kusanagi back in May. There would be public displays, there would be fireworks, and most of all, there would be street dancing.

When I emerged from Shimizu Station on 31 July, I wasn't at all surprised to find a small crowd in the station plaza just opposite McDonald's, standing in the blazing sun and watching a pair of ten-year-old boys in karate kit attempting to kick each other as hard as possible while a grown man shouted encouragement. A group of giggling schoolgirls in short blue and purple *yukata*, were loitering mischievously by the station entrance.

I didn't know exactly what to expect, but I knew that whatever it was, there was going to be some S-Pulse supporter participation. So I followed a spotty youth in a Number 8 Paul Gascoigne England shirt, who had a small plastic S-Pulse Paru-chan mascot attached to the mobile-phone cord dangling from his rear pocket. Paul Gascoigne led me to the covered shopping street, the Shimizu-no Ginza, where a series of complicated lists was on display, showing exactly who was to go where. This was not going to be your run-of-the-mill, spontaneous-fun-on-a-Saturday-night kind of street dancing. Like making the world's longest sushi roll, street dancing requires organisation. This was a highly organised mass mobilisation of the citizenry of Shimizu, involving an estimated 20,000 or 30,000 people, appropriately divided into over 200 individual groups. According to the list, the S-Pulse Chapéu Laranja supporters club was number 81, located just after the NTT telephone office on Satski-dori, Shimizu's main street.

The event was due to start at around six thirty, and as the sun began to set I walked along the pavements past small groups of policemen and civil defence workers with helmets at the ready, making the final preparations. I found a dozen or so S-Pulse fans gathering their strength for the evening over a few beers and a picnic of meat on skewers. As I expected, my spaced-out friend Yamada-san wasn't there; another group of supporters had allowed their love of football to prevail over civic pride, and had gone down to Osaka for the annual J.League All-stars game, between J.League East (Tokyo and Nagoya) and J.League West (everywhere else). But I'd met Chapéu Laranja's chief of operations, Tominori Endo, before. It was hard not to meet him. Mr Endo, probably in his early fifties, is not so tall, but he is very round, with a serious beer-drinking belly that reflected the size of his personality. Ever cheery, Mr Endo is the one who would lead the group singing in the lifeboat, if it ever came to that. I suspected that he probably plays the accordion at home. In normal life, Mr Endo runs a small business in Shizuoka; his bulk also makes him a stalwart of the back-row bass-drum players in the samba band. Today he had on a summery yellow and orange, short-sleeved, cotton shirt, knee-length shorts, white Puma training shoes and a white towel wrapped around his sweating head.

'Eat! Eat!' said Mr Endo, showing me to the yaki-niku. 'Drink! Drink!' said Mr Endo, handing me a can of Asahi beer.

'Are you sure you like?' said Midori-san, a lady who was also in her early fifties, as I picked up something which I thought was chicken.

'Yes. Very tasty,' I said, until I realised with horror that I'd just picked up a skewer of barbecued tripe.

There were about two dozen supporters, a couple of older women and a few younger ones in S-Pulse football shirts. I recognised Yuki, a shy and thin seventeen-year-old high-school student with long black hair who had rolled sushi next to me back in May, and Mizuho, a young student who was a regular with the band. There was also an older man with short frizzy hair and tinted glasses. He was wearing yellow plastic wellington boots and had dyed his hair yellow and blue for the occasion.

As we chowed down on the pavement, more dancers walked by on their way to their designated dancing locations. A couple of girls walked past in blue tee-shirts with the words 'Dental Team' in English on the back. Most of the teams were pushing decorated carts and small wheeled floats. We had a small, two-wheeled, metal delivery cart, the sort of thing no Asian small trader would be without. A superstructure of yellow boards had been fixed to it, painted in S-Pulse yellow and orange. Yellow S-Pulse flags flew at each corner and an orange sunhat, signed by Alex, had been fixed to the front with three drawing pins, like some primitive trophy.

The weirdest piece of totemistic symbolism was out at the front, like the standard of a Roman legion. A small man who didn't say much was holding a pole to which had been attached four painted figures cut from polystyrene. At the top of the pole, naturally enough, there was a cartoon head of Paru-chan, pointing skywards in his 'Get the Victory' stance. Beneath him, ranged like a trinity of saints, were three other figures. On the left was the bald head of Fabinho, Shimizu's Brazilian striker, fixed on a tiny cartoon body; on the right was the equally bald head of the midfielder Tasaka; and in the middle was the yellow figure of Pikachu, the Pokemon cartoon character that was currently challenging Mickey Mouse's absolute control over the minds of Japan's unruly five to seven year olds. To add to the glorious mix of randomly selected social icons, Fabinho, Pikachu and Tasaka each held in their left hand a skewer of three smiling-faced rice balls. In 1999, it was hard to get away from the three rice-ball brothers craze, the *dango san-kyodai*. It was like something that could only have been conceived, or properly appreciated, under the influence of perception-enhancing drugs.

It was time to start dancing. The S-Pulse fans deployed behind the cart, five abreast. Mr Endo and Mr Yellow Wellingtons waved the big S-Pulse Chapéu Laranja banners in front. The music started and it wasn't at all what I had expected. A male voice boomed out across the loudspeakers rigged up on the lampposts, backed by a weird disco beat mixed with echoes of some kind of wailing Japanese folk song. At the sound of the first notes, the dancers, who were drawn up in ranks which stretched as far as the eye could see, put their left hands on their left hips and raised their right arms together. They stepped forward and back again. Then they did the same thing, raising their left arms. After that, both arms went out to the right, everyone stood on one leg and hopped round in a circle on the spot. It was like English Morris dancing, but on a far more dangerous scale.

I have to say that despite the banners and the orange shirts, the S-Pulse group looked a little ramshackle compared with some of the competition. In front of us danced the massed ranks of the Suzuyo group, wearing matching blue Shimizu FC Lovely Ladies tee-shirts. Across the central reservation, facing back into town, was the 'm.m. jazz dancing club' including a battalion of nine- or ten-year-old girls in pink happi coats, with make-up and perfect hair styles, who were backed up by another battalion of equally well turned out young mothers. It was an amazing sight.

'This is a new song,' said Midori-san, helpfully, as we watched from the pavement. 'It's more difficult to follow.'

The song finished and the whole procession moved forwards about twenty yards. Another song began. It had a kind of chorus, where everyone shouted 'Kappore, Kappore'. I'd never heard this word before. I was told later that it's a general expression, meaning 'Cheer Up'.

'This is the older song,' said Midori-san. 'It's more easy, because it's slower.'

And so we went on, pausing intermittently for beer. At one

point I saw Mr Miyagashima, the mayor, go by in a black and white checked happi coat and shorts. It turned out that there were just three dancing songs, played over and over again as we edged down the street. It was a strange way to spend a Saturday night, but it showed that Shimizu is not to be underestimated.

Of all the groups, my favourite was a group called 'Ringo'. They had all dyed their hair steel grey, which was something of a craze that summer. The men were in full-length robes made of blue with silver edging. The women were bare-shouldered with their hair up. Their upper bodies were wrapped in white cotton banding and they wore long blue and silver skirts. Between their shoulder blades, single Japanese characters were painted in silver. It was a lot sexier than an orange football shirt.

I asked Mrs Midori who they were. She couldn't say, but thought it might be some kind of theatre group. Perhaps. Or the Shimizu Gay and Lesbian Association. Or the trade union from the Hagaromo tuna-packing company. All these groups from Fuji Logitech, the Girl Guides of Japan (Shimizu), City Hall and the local gas company, reminded me that my fan friends with their well-organised sub-groups, were merely repeating a pattern that seemed to extend across the city and presumably across Japan. Everyone, it seemed, was in some group or other. All those people who throng the streets of central Tokyo and crowd on to the commuter trains in the evenings, perhaps they've all got some special costume in the wardrobe, something which says that they're part of something smaller and far more manageable.

As the night wore on, the S-Pulse dancing got sillier and sillier. I fell in with a group of Kenta Club fans at the back, who weren't taking things too seriously. I tried hopping around on one leg. We passed old men sitting on the street benches drinking beer and little girls out with their parents, eating ice cream, wearing their special summer cotton kimonos and looking like tiny butterflies fluttering in the lamplight. No one was too drunk to stand. There were no fights. And just as after the final whistle the S-Pulse fans pack up and go home, so at nine o'clock on the dot, it was all over.

I met Mr Endo again the following Saturday, as I headed towards Nihondaira on the bus for the opening game of the second stage of the season. S-Pulse were playing Cerezo Osaka. We were both almost late.

'I have been drinking beer with some friends,' said Mr Endo, presumably to explain why he hadn't been at the stadium the statutory two hours before the game started. Perhaps he was worried I'd report him. He looked thoughtful. 'Ah, Jonasan-san,' he said, 'tomorrow, we are having a barbecue. On the river. You can come?'

It was a characteristically warm and open offer and not one to be refused. But first there was the football. S-Pulse faced a tough start to the second stage. Cerezo Osaka had beaten them 2–1 during the first stage. Cerezo was managed by René Desaeyere, a tall blond Belgian who had previously coached in South Korea. His team included two South Korean internationals, Hwang Sun Hong, a striker, and Noh Jung-Yoon, the player who'd been sent to Breda in Holland by Eddie Thomson's Sanfrecce. Cerezo were rather like Sanfrecce; they weren't expected to win the championship, but on a good day, they could make life difficult for the best J.League teams. They had ended the first stage in fifth place, two points ahead of Sanfrecce.

'This is an important game,' said a serious-looking Phil Holder when I bumped into him at the stadium. 'Psychologically important. We've got some tough games ahead.'

That was true. The next game was away to Jubilo Iwata, nemesis of all that is good, followed by the Kashima Antlers, the Urawa Reds and Nagoya Grampus, all tough teams. The pressure was beginning to mount on Perryman-san. There were rumblings coming from the Japanese front-office staff. S-Pulse had been expected to win the first stage, and they hadn't. The word was that the club chairman, Mr Yasumoto, had let it be known that he had hoped Perryman-san would continue in the style of Ossie Ardiles, and that this, regrettably, had not been the case. The owners, interested in longer term development, let it be known that they also expected to see more younger players being given a chance in the first team. This, too, was not happening. Perryman had signed a one-year contract when Ardiles went, for less money, and the word was that it would not be extended – unless, of course, S-Pulse could win the second stage.

Talk like this was troubling. Kashima Antlers were in the process of dumping their old Brazilian manager, Ze Mario, who had led them to the championship the previous season. Ze Mario knew he was in trouble when they sacked his translator. In Japan, people don't come up and say, 'Win the next three games or you're out.' Instead, imperceptibly, the victim is edged out of the group into lonely spaces outside. I sensed that this was what was beginning to happen at S-Pulse.

With the daytime temperature pushing up to 34 degrees, the game was due to start at 7.00 p.m. It was a sweaty, humid night, with the western sky still lit by the setting sun and dark storm clouds looming over the hills. The S-Pulse crowd had become a splendid luminescent mass of yellow and orange in the glare of the floodlights. A lot of beer was being drunk. Yamada-san had cut his hair short. 'It's too hot,' he said. Everyone was hot. It was not a night to be playing football.

Before the game, a small ceremony marked the start of the second stage, augmented by a new and rather thrilling feature – an eight-member women's cheerleading team. They gyrated and strutted and high-kicked their way round the centre circle, waving golden pompons, to the backing of the theme from *Star Wars*, while Paru-chan pranced enthusiastically up and down waving an S-Pulse flag. It was not a night to be dressed in a Paru-chan suit, either. 'GET THE VICTORY' flashed up on the electronic scoreboard as orange balloons floated skywards.

My notes on the game are a little bizarre. Cerezo's two forwards, Hwang and Morishima, were apparently looking dangerous.

Sometime during the first half, fireworks started exploding in the sky over towards the summit of Nihondaira. Ichikawa was showing great imagination and running like a madman. Cerezo went one goal up after nine minutes. At one point, the S–Pulse crowd started whistling at their own players for passing the ball around in their own half. Alex equalised midway through the first half. Desaeyere was demonstrating his European origins by dancing around on the touch–line, making 'you need glasses' gestures at the referee. Alex put S–Pulse 2–1 ahead in the seventy-third minute. It looked a certain victory. Six minutes later, Cerezo's Morishima scored from a near-post corner. 'Why does this make me so tense?' I wrote. This was the game when I realised I cared.

The game went into sudden-death extra time. The crowd were samba-ing their hearts out. It looked very much as if the ball crossed the Cerezo goalline from a corner on the right but no goal was given. Then the Korean attacking midfielder, Noh Jung-Yoon, sent a high, long cross in from the left towards S–Pulse's far post. The ball eluded goalkeeper Sanada's attempts to intercept. A Cerezo striker climbed above his marker to head it down towards the left post. The ball hit the foot of the post. We gasped in disbelief. But we could see the inevitable catastrophe coming as if in slow motion. The ball bounced diagonally out again to the right. Cerezo's other Korean, Hwang Sun Hong, was waiting to push it in, right in front of the disbelieving S–Pulse fans. Game over. Cerezo win 3–2.

On my way to the press-briefing room, I passed Shirase Mayumi, the sports journalist who writes the S–Pulse programme notes. She'd been crying.

'Football can be beautiful sometimes,' said René Desaeyere, gracious in victory. 'They had good chances, we had good chances. In soccer sometimes you need a little bit of luck. Sometimes in football, you never know.'

The journalists politely applauded. Desaeyere went off to receive a reprimand from the match commissioner for suggesting the referee needed glasses. Steve Perryman came into the press-briefing room. He looked as completely gutted as I'd ever seen him.

'Of course, very disappointed to lose,' he began, in a hoarse, croaky voice, his eyes watering with disappointment. 'We were positive . . . We created chances . . . Lots of good combination play.' S-Pulse, he thought, had been looking fitter. The game, he reckoned, had been lost when they had given away the second goal. 'It was a fantastic game. Two teams that wanted to play. I'm disappointed to lose. But if you have to lose, lose like this.'

The S-Pulse PR man called for questions. There weren't any. Presumably, to the Japanese reporters, it wouldn't have seemed fair. Perryman-san got up and walked out.

The next day, I found myself discussing Perryman-san's management style with an enthusiastic drunk whose name I don't remember, on the banks of the Tama River in the hills above Shizuoka at the annual S-Pulse Chapéu Laranja summer barbecue.

'Ardiles very strong man,' said my friend. 'He say, "go, go, go," and everyone go, go, go. Perryman-san too much gentleman. He say, "please go, please go." No good. Too much gentleman.'

I felt that Ardiles without Perryman would have had problems getting his ideas across. I tried to make this point but I was having similar problems.

'Ardiles, go, go, go,' said the man. 'Perryman . . . gentleman . . . Ardiles good . . . Perryman too much gentleman.'

I'd met Mr Endo in Shizuoka Station as planned at eight o'clock that morning. It was already hot and sunny. Endo-san was wearing his barbecue gear, a white tee-shirt, capacious shorts and a black-and-white zebra patterned sunhat. He handed me another zebra-hat.

'Take it,' he said. 'Hot day.'

We'd walked out of the station to a parked saloon car. Sitting inside were three fans I recognised – Mr and Mrs Mochizuki, both samba-band regulars, both perhaps in their early forties, and Mizuho, the young student whose front-line dancing skills were exceeded only by her skills on the samba tambourine. I was wedged in the back of the car between Mizuho and Mrs Mochizuki. As we headed out towards the surrounding hills, I noticed I was travelling in a mobile S-Pulse shrine.

There was a miniature furry Paru-chan stuck to the upper left windscreen, above the S-Pulse pull-over parking sun-screen. There were two, even more mini, plastic Paru-chans on springs on the dashboard. The front seats were covered with S-Pulse Chapéu Laranja tee-shirts. The back-window shelf was piled with more yellow, fluffy dolls. If we had a serious accident, we'd end up as one big mangled bloody mass of metal and yellow fluff.

The barbecue site was a broad shoal of stones beside a small river, which cut in beneath a steep craggy slope covered with trees. As we arrived, small teams of relaxing Japanese were staking out positions like settlers in the Wild West, running balls of twine around pegs set in the ground to mark the boundaries of their designated recreational space. I wondered if there was a municipal agency in charge of taking bookings for the river bank, or if this was just spontaneous order. I suspected the latter.

Chapéu Laranja, the largest sub-group of S-Pulse supporters, with a mailing list of around 1,000 families, was not taking this barbecue lightly. There was a small, open-sided marquee in which a woman was sitting behind a trestle table registering arrivals and handing out name tags. Each car party paid 5,000 yen, or about $45, which in Japan would only cover a modest meal of noodles for three. On the other side of the tent, another younger woman was dispensing draft beer and cold tea. Over by the river, two barbecue pits were being prepared. Above the tent, the black and yellow S-Pulse Chapéu Laranja flag fluttered proudly in the breeze. All around, the river bank was filling up with people. Little children were heading for the shallow but fast-flowing river, clutching inflatable rafts and water-wings. A radio was playing. It was a highly sociable affair.

Before we could start, Mr Endo called us all into a circle for the official opening ceremony and introductions. He introduced me as a guest from England, and made everyone say, 'Hello. My name is x, pleased to meet you.' I told them all that I was equally delighted to meet them. And so it began.

The sun was very, very hot. I went for a swim in the river, I drank a few beers, and I discussed Perryman-san's coaching style with the drunk man. The conversation turned into one of those 'things aren't what they used to be' talks. Young Japanese players, he seemed to be saying, could all benefit from a spot of national service. This is a common attitude among Japanese men in their late fifties and sixties, who remember all the hard work that went into the reconstruction of Japan after World War Two, and the unrelenting struggle that eventually turned Japan into the world's second largest economy. For them, J.League football with its hair-dye and its youthful stars posing for screaming girl fans is about as popular as the Rolling Stones and George Best were with readers of the *Daily Telegraph* in the 1960s. For them, the country is going soft. They wanted the Japanese equivalent of Bolton Wanderers and Stanley Matthews and more hard work all round.

Kazuo Imanishi, the general manager at Eddie Thomson's Sanfrecce, had said the same sort of thing to me earlier in the year. 'Japanese people . . . Japanese people not so hungry,' he'd said. 'You understand? In England, people will go to watch football at eight o'clock at night in the freezing cold. But Japanese people are not so strong now. A child wants something, the mother gives it.'

But if Perryman was getting criticised for being too soft on his unruly and wilful charges, he was also getting criticised for trying to do something about it. As the second stage began, S-Pulse had dropped the team's popular right-back, Masahiro Ando. Ando had been replaced on the right by Ichikawa, while the Brazilian Alex had been pressed into service as an attacking left-back. The fans didn't like it. Ando's name provoked lots of teeth-sucking noises, and the sorts of 'Well, I don't know, but it seems to me that he's quite a good player, and perhaps things could be going better' remarks which constitute aggressive criticism in Japan. As I surveyed the chicken pieces sizzling on the barbecue by the banks of the Tama River, it seemed that the fans, like the management, were getting restless.

But now, with the afternoon moving on, Endo-san was calling me over to meet someone new, a tall, authoritative-looking man perhaps in his late fifties, with grey hair, who was wearing brown-tinted sunglasses.

'This,' said Endo-san, 'is Mr Naya.' I wasn't sure, but Mr Naya looked to me like Mr Yellow Wellingtons from the previous week's dancing event.

'Pleased to meet you,' said Mr Naya, handing me his card. 'Seiji Naya,' it said. 'Shimizu S-Pulse Torcida Uniformizada – Chapéu Laranja', it said. 'President' it said. Standing there in my shorts and tee-shirt and my black and white zebra-hat in the blazing sun, I realised with a shock that this was it. I'd finally met Mr Big. It wasn't after all Mr Matsuda, the band organiser, who turned out later to be the leader of the Kenta Club group. It wasn't smiley Mr Tanaka, from Boa Sorte (Brazilian Portuguese for 'good luck'). It certainly wasn't the chortling Endo-san. They were just the generals in the S-Pulse supporters' army. The supreme commander was Seiji Naya. I apologised profusely for having omitted to bring my business cards to the river-side barbecue.

'My business,' he said to me in English, 'is to send Shimizu players to play football outside Japan. To training schools. You know La Coruna, in España?' I said I was indeed familiar with the name of this renowned footballing town in north-western Spain. 'I now have Shimizu players there, twelve of them, at Deportivo La Coruna.'

I was suitably impressed. We made a little small talk, and I got the distinct feeling that the audience was over. Mr Naya began to stare into the middle distance. Then he wandered off. I assumed that making an appearance on a Sunday at the Chapéu Laranja barbecue was probably just one of the many responsibilities of being the S-Pulse all-supporters leader. He probably had things on his mind.

Later that month, I was to find out more about Mr Naya when I sat down for a *tête-à-tête* with Matsuda-san, the band leader. My early concerns about Matsuda being involved in organised crime turned out to be misplaced, but not entirely misguided. He told me he used to be a policeman. Matsuda-san explained that while Mr Naya was indeed the president of the eighteen groups of S-Pulse fans, he himself was a sort of chairman and chief executive officer of the fan corporation, elected democratically every two years by the different groups. Mr Naya was president because of the significant role he'd played at the launch of the J.League. It was, for example, Mr Naya who first thought of creating the S-Pulse samba band.

'President Naya used to go to Brazil before the start of the J.League,' Matsuda-san explained. 'And in Brazil he saw real samba bands playing. When they started S-Pulse, we had a lot of Brazilian players, and so that's how the idea of having a samba band started. We brought over a group of samba musicians from Brazil and they taught us how to play. The people who learned from them taught other people, and so it went on.'

Mr Naya had done more – as the great Shogun Tokugawa had unified Japan's quarrelling local lords in the seventeenth century to create modern Japan, so had Mr Naya created a unified supporters' group out of the chaos of the early years.

'Before, when the J.League began, the different supporters' groups used to fight between themselves all the time. They used to fight for seats and for tickets. And they used to produce their own newsletters and flyers, handing them out at the game and competing to get fans to join the individual group. Mr Naya got the leaders together and said they should form a unified supporters' group, and we should cooperate for the sake of the team.'

Newsletters, it seems, are now banned, except for groups such as Chapéu Laranja, that organise extra-curricular activities, the annual summer barbecue, for instance.

'The object of this is not to suppress the different groups,' said Executive Director Matsuda, 'but to build unity behind the team. The aim now is to respect the individual characteristics of each supporters' group. The different group leaders have meetings an hour before each game and if we have problems to discuss, we have meetings afterwards.'

As the new cooperative relationship developed, the different fan groups settled on their own pieces of territory in the main S-Pulse stand. I realised now that in the home stand at Nihondaira, each sub-group can always be found in the same place – S-Keepers down on the right, K's Club over on the front at the left, the band in the middle.

'It's a kind of unwritten rule,' said Matsuda, 'about who goes where. The samba band is always in the middle and the others are all around. There's no actual organised system, but everyone knows where to go.'

As I stood beside the Tama River, with my brains boiling in the intense sunshine of an August afternoon, I didn't know any of this. Yet I already had the firm impression that S-Pulse fans were a pretty organised group of individuals. Mr Naya's arrival gave them another opportunity to demonstrate that. He'd turned up in a van with what must have been half of the samba band's drums loaded in the back. So, by the banks of the river, on a supposedly quiet Sunday afternoon, with the tiny children cavorting in the shallows, Chapéu Laranja, led by Endo-san, decided to strut its samba stuff. As I stood in the shallows, holding a tamborim in my right hand and a two-pronged samba-tamborim stick in my left, I remember thinking that if you tried starting up an under-strength and slightly off-beat samba ensemble on, say, a British holiday beach, things would probably get rather ugly rather quickly. It's true one extremely drunk young man did stagger over, but he wanted to join in. After all, drumming in public places was included in the current range of youth booms; at times in Tokyo it was hard to get away from long-haired, scruffy guys banging bongo drums while their girlfriends looked dutifully on. So I suppose our little samba excursion was part of something much bigger.

'Tang-tang ting-ting, tangity-tang ting-ting' went the metal cowbell-like agogo percussion. 'Chapity-chapity, chapity-chapity, chapity-chapity' went Mizuho and Mrs Mochizuki on the other tamborim, as I struggled to master the art. 'Boom-boom, boom-boom, boom-boom, boom-boom' went the big surdo drums, one of which had been taken over by the drunk guy. 'Takakattack . . .

takattack . . . takarakatatak' went Mr Endo on the snare drum lead. 'Eh Oh, Eh Oh,' we shouted, 'ESS–PULSE ESS–PULSE.'

It went on for about forty-five minutes, I suppose. I discovered that like the drunk guy on the surdo, I didn't really have the rhythm. I settled instead on the shaking rattling device known as the *chucalho*, which is basically a long thin metal tin full of gravel. I could just about cope with that. In fact, a dribbling moron could probably cope with the *chucalho*.

By now, we'd been at the river bank for approaching eight hours and I was turning crispy red all over. People were clustered desperately around the beer and tea tent. It was time to stop but we needed to be told to stop.

At about 4.30, we were summoned into a circle by Endo-san, who was himself looking a bit bedraggled. He called on Mr Naya to make a speech. Mr Naya made various remarks about upcoming fixtures and tickets and future plans. Then he handed the floor back to Endo-san, who thanked me politely for attending their annual barbecue. He shouted something I didn't catch and raised his hands.

'Jonasan,' he shouted, and clapped.

'Jonasan,' clap-clap-clap, came the response from everyone else. 'Jonasan,' clap-clap-clap. And so on, ending in general applause. I bowed appreciatively. This was a big moment. I said thank you very much. Then I put my arms up, and shouted:

'Chapéu Laranja,' and clapped, clapity, clap clap.

'Chapéu Laranja,' came the response, clapity clap clap. 'Chapéu Laranja.' And so on, ending in general applause.

It turned out that S-Pulse had after all been quite lucky. The 3–2 loss to Cerezo might have been a bad start to the second stage, but worse things had happened to their main rivals. Evil

Jubilo, now without their talented midfielder Hiroshi Nanami who had gone off to play in Italy, had gone down 3–0 to the Yokohama F Marinos. Nagoya Grampus Eight had managed to lose 4–2 to struggling Bellmare Hiratsuka. The Kashima Antlers and the Urawa Reds had both lost. The world appeared upside down.

At Hiratsuka, two Grampus players were sent off, although Dragan Stojkovic somehow managed to escape with just one yellow card for arguing with the fourth official. The next day, Stojkovic launched a verbal assault on the referee, accusing him of killing the match. 'I think the Japanese referees especially do not have a feeling for the game,' he said, 'and it's irritating.'

Despite the victory, Bellmare were facing the threats of bankruptcy and relegation. The team had brought in a new Japanese manager and a collection of foreign players, including two economy-rate Australians – a defender with the wonderful name of Steven Laybutt, who was built like a tank, and a midfielder, Chay Hews.

Elsewhere, JEF United had said goodbye to Gert Engels after just six months. Their battle to avoid relegation was now led by Nicolae Zamfir, a diminutive fifty-four-year-old Romanian who had previously been working as a university coach somewhere in Transylvania. How Mr Zamfir ended up working for JEF in the shadow of the waste incineration plant on Tokyo Bay remained a mystery, but he was to become a feature in the J.League, especially after a game later that season when he performed a standing somersault on the touch-line.

Back at S-Pulse's Hebizuka training ground on the Tuesday after the Cerezo game, the mood was strained after a training session in the hot sunshine. During the practice game, Phil Holder had been concentrating on talking the dreadlocked Alex through his new role as attacking left-back. Afterwards, in the air-conditioned cool of Perryman's corner office, the two were still steamed up, this time over the Japanese defender's approach to passing.

'It's like, OK, have it, there's the ball, that's my job done now you've got it. Finish,' said Perryman to Holder, about a pass out from the defence to the midfielders which had achieved essentially nothing at all.

'Santos says to me he thinks we're doing too many long balls. Fucking bollocks.' Long pause. 'But Santos shouldn't have called for it to begin with and Saito shouldn't have passed it because we've got six back before we've even got to their first two players.'

'Right,' said Holder.

'But if you come with the ball, then the midfielders go forward and go through, and then it's equal numbers, three on three or two on two, and we'll have some of that. We'll fucking have some of that.'

'Fucking right,' said Holder.

'Our back three haven't got it,' said Perryman. 'They think they know it fucking all.'

It wasn't just the backs. One of the forwards who had been substituted in the Cerezo game halfway through the first half, had been put on the second team for the practice session.

'I told him I put him on the other team to take him out of the spotlight. Because I told him he's playing as if he's doing us a favour by being here but he's not doing anyone a favour including himself. He says he's tired. But he lets the tiredness get to him. He hasn't got it up here,' said Perryman, pointing to his head.

'Because by rights he should be a fit young man,' said Holder, 'but we can't leave him on for the full ninety minutes. We got maybe sixty-five minutes last game.'

'If that,' said Perryman.

'And we need eighty-five to ninety and then maybe take him off.'

'Right,' said Perryman.

'We've got a team with no spirit,' said Holder glumly.

There were other troubles, too. One of the youth team's coaches had been making derogatory remarks about one of the junior teams. Perryman wanted to have it out with him, but the offending coach had slipped out early. And Perryman wanted to get his own life sorted out. His current contract was due to expire in just four months, and he wanted to know whether he should be looking around for work elsewhere. The company had promised him a meeting, but only after the game against the dark side of the footballing force, Jubilo Iwata, on the following Saturday. It wasn't looking very positive.

清水

10 THE DEFEATED SAMURAI

Just over 11,000 people turned out that weekend at Nihondaira to watch S-Pulse play Cerezo Osaka. On the same night, a hundred kilometres or so to the north in the vast indoor arena of the Tokyo Dome, 50,000 people watched the Hiroshima Carp baseball team beat the Tokyo Giants 3–0, dealing a further blow to the Giants' hopes of winning the Central League pennant. Amidst the fanaticism of Shimizu, it is easy to forget that soccer remains very much a minor sport in Japan, and that in the real world, especially in the summer, everyone else is watching baseball. According to a government public opinion survey published the previous year, almost 50 per cent of the Japanese population regularly watch baseball, against around 36 per cent for sumo and just 13 per cent for football. Football turns out to be only marginally more popular than watching marathon races. With each of Japan's twelve baseball teams playing 135 games each season, there's plenty of baseball to go around.

That summer in the Central League, the Tokyo Yomiuri Giants were lying second, chasing the Nagoya-based Chunichi Dragons. In the rival Pacific League, the Daiei Hawks, from the southern city of Fukuoka, were on top, led by their coach Sadaharu Oh (as a player, Oh became a living legend in Japan in the late 1970s when he overtook both Babe Ruth's and Hank Aaron's home-run records). The Hawks were being chased by the Seibu Lions, whose line-up included the game's latest star, an eighteen-year-old rookie pitcher called Daisuke Matsuzaka. (Matsuzaka had made headlines earlier in the year, when he signed for the Lions, for boasting that he would be chosen as Rookie of the Year in Japan, even before he'd pitched his first ball, an act of extremely un-Japanese arrogance and another sign that things aren't what they used to be.)

The nightly sports programmes on TV weren't just showing Japanese baseball. That summer, three more Japanese players had made it big in America, following in the footsteps of Hideo Nomo, whose debut as a pitcher for the Los Angeles Dodgers in 1996 created a national sensation. Now Masato Yoshii, formerly of Tokyo's other team, the Yakult Swallows, was pitching with the New York Mets; Mac Suzuki had joined the Seattle Mariners; and Hideki Irabu had signed up with the Yankees.

Despite baseball's well-established dominance, the initial runaway success of the J.League with its glamorous young stars and its exotic face-painting crowds caused rumblings of alarm in the sport. In January 1993, the head of the Central League admitted in the newspapers that baseball was, in comparison with soccer, 'old fashioned'. 'Baseball,' he argued, 'tends to emphasise spiritual aspects, such as hard training and sportsmanship.' Later that year, the Asahi newspaper printed a seventeen-syllable satirical poem from a reader which elegantly claimed 'J.League is action. Pro-baseball is slow motion.'

The teams responded by deciding to loosen up a little. By 1996, several baseball players appeared with dyed hair in place of the regular short back and sides. But the following season, as the J.League boom faltered, baseball's managers seized the opportunity to relapse into their traditional quasi-militaristic ways. Dyed hair disappeared. Baseball ruled Japan again.

Baseball and soccer arrived in Japan at the same time, in the 1870s and 1880s during the great push towards modernisation that followed the social and political revolution of 1868 known as the Meiji Restoration. Before then, Japan had opted to cut itself off almost entirely from contact with the outside world. The proud lords of the Tokugawa Shogunate maintained a feudal system of government which had remained largely unchanged for almost two centuries. While the British public schools were preparing to rule an empire with rugby and cricket, the sons of Japan's samurai practised the traditional arts of swordsmanship and archery.

In 1853, change came suddenly with the arrival of an American fleet led by Commodore Matthew Perry. His instructions were to force the Tokugawa rulers to open their ports to foreign trade. Japan's subsequent humiliation provoked revolt and led to the emergence of a new state, which set out to learn from the West. In came foreign missionary teachers and with them came western ideals of sport and physical training.

In 1873, an American missionary teacher is reported to have begun coaching baseball at Tokyo University. In September that same year, Lieutenant Commander Archibald L. Douglas of her Imperial Majesty's Royal Navy organised what is now recognised as Japan's first game of football at the Naval Academy on Tokyo Bay. Of course, Commander Douglas and his thirty-three men taught the new Japanese Imperial Navy some other things, too. The naval alliance with Britain prepared the way for Japan's successful surprise attack on the Russian fleet anchored at Port Arthur in 1904 at the start of the Russo-Japanese War. The Imperial Navy continued to go from strength to strength, all the way to Pearl Harbor in 1941. Football didn't do nearly so well.

'The Meiji government, under the slogan "rich country, strong army", was seeking to push Japan into the ranks of the advanced nations,' explains a Japanese government publication on the country's sporting history. 'It encouraged the game of baseball because, it thought, the team play heightened the spirit of solidarity.'

In 1919, however, the British got involved again. The previous year, reports had reached London of the first All Japan Schools Soccer Tournament, which had been played in Osaka in 1918 between four teacher-training colleges. Sensing an opportunity for global expansion, the FA dispatched a replica of England's FA Cup as a gift to Japan. According to one of Japan's leading modern soccer writers, Yoshiyuki Osumi, this proved slightly embarrassing in Tokyo.

'The FA sent the cup, but there was no Japanese Football Association there to receive it,' Mr Osumi explained. 'The cup went to the Ministry of Education. But they didn't know what to do. So they ordered various people who were involved in football at that time to form an association. And so the JFA was founded in 1921.'

Mr Osumi, a small dapper man in his forties with small round glasses, was talking to me in the coffee shop of a hotel in Tokyo's Ebisu district. He's something of an expert on the game's roots in Japan. For instance, if I hadn't met Mr Osumi, I would never have known that the reason the Japanese spell soccer 'sacca' when they transliterate the word, and not 'socca', or even 'football', is because the word was brought back from America by an Osaka-based teacher, Tsuboi Gendo, who had travelled to the United States at the end of World War One. 'Sacca', Mr Osumi, explained, mimics the American pronunciation.

The idea that baseball somehow suited Japan was to prove enduring. Over the years, the sport established itself as the main game in the new Japanese system, alongside the modernised martial arts such as kendo, karate, aikido and judo. In the process, baseball itself changed into a kind of new martial art for the new Japan, which would serve the dual purposes of building character and promoting harmony through the rigours of hard work and discipline.

But if baseball is seen by the Japanese as a Japanese game, soccer is still very much a foreign import. Like tasting fine wines, or playing tennis, or dancing to rap music, in football the Japanese seek avidly to learn from the foreign experts, hoping perhaps that one day they can beat the foreigners at their own game. In Shimizu, for instance, they used to call Ardiles *sensei*, or master/teacher (a term, interestingly enough, never applied to Perryman-san, who possibly came across as insufficiently haughty).

'At the beginning of the J.League, they brought over lots of stars,' said former Grampus goalkeeper Dido Havenaar when I asked him about this. 'If the foreign stars fail, no problem, they get cheering, cheering, cheering, and I was very surprised that the supporters were still positive if you play very bad as a foreigner. But in baseball, if a foreigner is playing bad, they say, "Go back to America, go back to the States." In soccer, it is very different.'

That's because in baseball, Japan has nothing to learn. Japanese baseball is as Japanese as judo, something that the American baseball stars who've come to play in Japan find out very quickly. In Japanese baseball, there are no Dungas or Stojkovics, ordering people about and telling the umpires what to do. In baseball, the foreigners are supposed to do what they're told, and to work hard for their money. For while American baseball highlights natural talent, the Japanese system stresses teamwork and rigorous training, differences brought out by an American author, Robert Whiting, in his classic book on Japanese baseball and American stars, *You've Gotta Have Wa*. In the American game, the media focuses for the most part on the personalities of the individual players. In Japan, the managers themselves are the paramount stars. In America, a pitcher with a sore arm is told to rest. In Japan, a pitcher with a sore arm is expected to pitch through the pain – to demonstrate guts – even if this eventually leads to surgery for the damaged arm muscles and early retirement.

Baseball didn't only suit the disciplinarian spirit of pre-war Japan. It fitted in with the new corporate ethos established the next time Japan reinvented itself, as it emerged from the ruins of World War Two. Japanese office and factory workers found their daily struggle, sweat and sacrifice for the sake of the company mirrored in the iron discipline of the company's baseball team, for which players would train hard and long in an effort to improve, always remaining obedient to the stern coach. Baseball, not football, is still the bedrock of popular Japanese sporting culture – the big rock against which the foreign football managers bang their heads over and over again, sometimes without even knowing it's there.

So before the showdown with Jubilo Iwata, I decided to pay my respects at the ultimate shrine of pure Japanese baseball. I'd been to the Tokyo Dome to see the Giants. I'd sat in the outfield of the Jinggu Stadium to watch the Yakult Swallows, drinking beer and eating sushi on a late summer's evening. I'd seen how Japanese baseball fans are even more structured than most Japanese soccer crowds, with thousands of people rhythmically clapping and chanting when their team is at bat. But I'd never been to Koshien Stadium in August to watch the All Japan High-School Baseball Champions Tournament.

Osaka is over three hours from Tokyo on the Tokaido Shinkansen bullet train, which hurtles on from Shizuoka through the industrial cities of Hamamatsu and Nagoya to the Shin-Osaka Station. I realised I was in baseball territory when I saw my first inflatable model of Katsuya Nomura, manager of Osaka's Hanshin Tigers.

Along with 'water'-based drinks, steel-grey hair dye, eye glitter, platform sandals and the three little rice-ball brothers, there was a bit of a Nomura boom going on in Japan at the time. This was partly because of the initial successes of the Tigers, whose fans are supposed to be the fiercest in all of Japanese baseball. It was also partly because Nomura himself, in comparison with the majority of Japan's grim-faced baseball managers, was regarded as something of a colourful and emotional character. But it was mainly on account of his outspoken wife, a member of the Upper House of the Japanese parliament. She was engaged in an open cat-fight with a rival who'd accused her of misleading the public over her academic credentials, thus providing endless material for the gossip-based television chat shows and weekly magazines.

After a promising start, the Tigers had subsequently faded; by mid-August they had sunk to the bottom of the Central League. The Nomura boom was also about to go bust, despite the best efforts of the poor man's wife. However, blow-up figures of the troubled manager were still on sale at the station, still apparently considered legitimate souvenirs of a trip to Osaka. There he sat in effigy, next to yellow and black Hanshin Tigers clappers, and tins of yellow and black Hanshin Tigers biscuits. Later, in town, I stumbled across a food stall selling yellow and black packets of Hanshin Tigers curry sauce.

Koshien Stadium, home of the Hanshin Tigers and the traditional venue for the summer high-school baseball tournament, is about twenty minutes out of Osaka on the Hanshin subway line. The Hanshin line starts, naturally enough, in the basement of the Hanshin department store. Fans of the Kintetsu Buffalos take the train on the city's Kintetsu subway line from the basement of Osaka's Kintetsu department store. Both Hanshin and Kintetsu started off as railway companies. They added the department stores and the baseball teams later, to give people even more reasons to travel up and down on their railways.

'The railway companies made baseball teams to develop their railway systems,' I'd been told in Tokyo by Takeo Goto, one of Japan's leading sportswriters. 'Seibu, for example, built a ball-park outside Tokyo, where the Seibu Lions now play, so their railway could get more passengers.'

Professional baseball in Japan started back in the 1930s, after Matsutaro Shoriki, the owner of the Yomiuri newspaper, invited a team of American professional players on a tour of Japan to play local amateur teams. The touring Americans, including the great Lou Gehrig, drew big crowds, and the enthusiastic public response encouraged Mr Shoriki to establish Japan's first professional team, Dai Nihon, in 1934. After the war, Dai Nihon became the Yomiuri Giants. Five other companies followed suit and Japan's first professional league was created. The Yomiuri group used the new team to promote its newspaper in Tokyo, while the newspaper in turn promoted the team. Both were a tremendous success.

The cosy nature of this relationship makes the row that erupted in Britain when media mogul Rupert Murdoch tried to buy Manchester United in early 1999 seem rather tame. 'But,' said Mr Goto, 'in England the teams existed before the business came along. In Japan, the companies created sports.'

The Koshien high-school baseball tournament, on the other hand, is a strictly amateur affair. Theoretically, at least, it isn't about business at all. It's about youth, or how some people in Japan think Japanese youth ought to be.

I turned up at the stadium in the middle of the afternoon on the fourth day of the two-week tournament. It was clear immediately that this was something bigger than the average school sports' day. The station address system started relaying instructions as the train doors opened, advising the honoured customers what to do and how to do it in the safest possible way. I was marshalled out of the station by a small army of officials in blue uniforms, wielding loudspeakers and flashing batons, directing me to the right exit (there are only two). As I headed for the ticket barriers, I noticed that the station authorities had hung out a board, carrying the results of the day's games so far. Outside in the hot sunshine, more crowd controllers were on hand to flag down cars and wave me and the rest of the new arrivals across the road. The public address system urged me to buy my return ticket in advance to avoid the rush later.

The Koshien Stadium is built of brick with dark-green painted girders, and it is covered with green climbing plants. It looks rather like the old Centre Court at Wimbledon, with a hint of a Cambridge college, if you ignore the adjacent elevated expressway. The stadium opened in 1924. By Japanese standards, I was looking at history.

Lines of people had formed outside the ticket offices. Over to my right, small family groups and gaggles of students were milling around by the assembled flags of the forty-nine participating high-school teams. Above the school banners hung the red and white sunburst flag of the Asahi newspaper group – organiser of the annual event – and the red and white flag of Japan, the *hinomaru*. People were taking photographs of each other in front of the colourful mass, or searching for their school flag. For many schools, just getting to the national championships is worth a photograph in itself. Traditionally, it's not that easy. Expensive, private Japanese schools usually dominate Koshien; they have the money and the space that building a top-class team requires. This year, one state school from Tokyo had managed to get through to the finals, creating a minor media flurry along the way.

Eventually, I found myself inside, sitting on the crowded press benches with Taka Mizuno, the head of the Osaka office of the Asahi newspaper. He had recently returned from an assignment in Washington.

'Today there are more than 40,000 spectators,' he told me. 'Yesterday, we had a similar number. Koshien is very popular.'

As we were settling in our seats, located in a prime position directly behind the catcher, the sound of a loud klaxon wailed out across the ground like an air-raid warning. Two teams in white uniforms and dark caps ran out on to the diamond, which in Koshien is laid out not with sand, but with dark brown earth. The players lined up opposite each other, doffed their caps and bowed. Then the batting team ran back to the dug-out and the fielders ran to their positions. At Koshien, everything is done at a run, army style.

'You are lucky,' said Mr Mizuno. 'The game about to start is between two of the best teams, Toho High School from Hyogo Prefecture, which is from this area, and Takigawa High School from Aichi Prefecture near Nagoya.' I looked as appreciative as was humanly possible.

There's really nothing like it in Britain, or Europe, or possibly anywhere. Koshien is like the playing fields of Eton, *Tom Brown's School Days* and the poems of Rupert Brooke rolled up with Wimbledon and the Oxford and Cambridge Boat Race, perhaps with a touch of the now defunct Royal Tournament and the 1936 Berlin Olympics. It's a celebration of Edwardian ideals of sportsmanship and youthful heroics, packaged and mythologized and played out live to a television audience of millions, with a good dose of traditional, crypto-militarism thrown in for good measure. The opening ceremony, for instance, is broadcast live on national television. All forty-nine teams march into the stadium to the sound of a brass band, each team in step behind its school banner. The banner is always carried by a demure and virginal-looking junior high-school girl. Everyone swears the Koshien oath. Like young kamikaze prepared to give their all for the cause, the players all have identical crew-cuts. Once the tournament gets under way, all the games are broadcast live on radio and television. For those who have to work, the special Koshien programme in the evening brings them up to date and always includes one or two soft-focus portraits of the young would-be heroes of the next day's play. The narrative is usually accompanied by mournful piano music. It doesn't focus on achievement, athleticism or skill. It emphasises the oh-so-sweet melancholia of the forthcoming date with destiny out on the black earth in the bright summer sun.

Out on the field, Toho was first to bat. Over to the right, their supporters started firing on all cylinders, backed up by the school brass band; from where I was I could see at least four massive euphoniums and a handful of trombones. A massed block of students in the centre was chanting 'Toho! Toho!' and waving yellow and green megaphone-clappers, directed by a crowd conductor at the front and by younger students holding up signboards.

But as the teams were changing positions at the end of the first innings, I was taken entirely by surprise. Through the stadium loudspeakers came what sounded like some kind of anthem. It was sung by a male baritone, with heavy vibrato. The words may have been different but I was struck by the fact that this was the sort of musical number to be heard blaring from the sinister black loudspeaker trucks covered with Japanese flags that cruise the streets of Tokyo, operated by Japan's vocal right-wing minority. The people who drive these trucks are not nice people. They think Japan should stop apologising for atrocities committed during World War Two. They think Japan should re-arm. They like judo and kendo and sumo. They don't like soccer.

'The Toho school song,' said Mizuno-san, helpfully. I asked him how he would describe that type of music, getting a little anxious. 'It is . . . mmm,' he paused, 'rather old-style. The school was founded in the early 1920s.'

Out on the field, Toho's pitcher, Fukizawa, was making rather a hash of things. At the end of the second innings, he gave away a home run, the ball whacked over the stadium's fence deep in left field. Mr Mizuno was telling me at the time that the Toho manager was something of a star in the world of Japanese high-school baseball.

'Actually,' he explained, 'the idea of what we call *wa*, of doing something for the sake of team harmony rather than for the sake of the individual, comes more from these high-school games than from professional baseball. The idea that you should be prepared to die for the sake of the team.'

Wa, according to Robert Whiting's book on Japanese baseball, was what the American players in Japan struggled to understand. From what I'd seen, it was what made Japanese soccer players unwilling to get over-demonstrative on the pitch. *Wa* was what was lacking among the troubled supporters of the Yokohama F Marinos.

'But,' added Mizuno-san, conspiratorially, 'I don't like all this stuff. Actually, personally I prefer soccer. Soccer is more individual-istic.' Mr Mizuno was definitely an OK guy.

At the end of the second innings, they played Takigawa's school anthem, which sounded very much like Toho's. Toho's Koshien dreams were looking increasingly shaky and in the third innings, Takigawa managed to get three more runners home. Toho changed their pitcher and promptly gave away another single. With Toho trailing by five runs to nothing and staring defeat in the face, Mr Mizuno introduced me to a fundamental element of Japanese culture, although at the time, it has to be said, I had some difficulty working out exactly what he was talking about. I'd asked him about all the melancholic television coverage I'd been seeing.

'That is what Koshien is all about,' he said. 'It is very Japanese.

We call it "*hoganbiiki*". It means sympathy for the loser. Actually, *hogan* means the defeated samurai, and *biiki* means sympathy.' Defeated samurai? This, as they like to say in baseball, was rather out of left field. 'It's a famous tale,' Mizuno-san tried patiently to explain. 'About Yoshitsune. In the twelfth century.'

I didn't know it at the time, but Yoshitsune, a lord of the Minamoto clan, is as famous in Japan as Robin Hood is in England. But unlike Robin Hood, Yoshitsune's tale is one of great success followed by the most miserable and abject failure. Brought up by a monk in the remote north of the country, Yoshitsune had grown up to be the greatest general of his era, a warrior whose brilliant victories established the Minamoto clan as the most powerful family in all Japan. But in his hour of victory came treachery and defeat. While he was out winning battles, Yoshitsune's liege lord – who also happened to be his brother – had been turned against him by evil and scheming advisers. Yoshitsune was driven from the court and became a fugitive. In 1189, surrounded and outnumbered by his enemies, he killed himself rather than face capture. His tale lived on, enshrined in popular songs and celebrated in traditional Noh and Kabuki dramas. It has a special place in the Japanese imagination.

'The poignancy of Yoshitsune's downfall evokes an immediate response from people of every age,' wrote the American scholar Ivan Morris in his classic study *The Nobility of Failure*, which traces the idea of noble failure in Japan from Yoshitsune all the way through various ill-conceived but highly principled revolts which ended with mass executions and disembowellings, to the suicide pilots of World War Two who crashed flying bombs into American battleships. *Hoganbiiki* is not to be trifled with.

But the youthful flight of Toho had not yet crashed and burned on the black dirt of Koshien. In the fifth innings, the team staged a dramatic recovery. First, a massive hit by some young hero whose name must remain unsung here brought three jubilant runners home. Then came a double to tie the score 5–5. Over in the right-field stands, the Toho fans were in overdrive, the brass band playing something which sounded very much like the theme tune from *Hawaii Five 0*.

Mr Mizuno was called away to deal with some developing newspaper-related drama. I decided to wander out of the stadium and work my way round to the Toho stand to take a closer look. When I got there, I found myself in front of an entire girls' junior high-school band in white blouses and neat blue skirts and sunhats. There were clarinets and oboes, there were trumpets and trombones, and, at the back, there were big brass euphoniums. The band was playing snatches of march tunes, and backing up the chanting of 'Toho! Toho!' An anxious-looking girl, who must have been about fifteen, was conducting. With her back to the action, she took her cues from an older boy who stood in front of the massed ranks of male fans, next to a big bass drum. The phalanx of males was flanked by a line of girl cheerleaders in red and white outfits, waving red and blue pompons. Ranged in front were photographers and television cameramen, for whom the youthful exuberance of the young fans is as important as the unfolding drama on the field. The pictures always show sweating, fanatical-looking young men with short hair, or red-faced, worried-looking high-schoolgirls. On the other hand, I couldn't help but notice the large number of people with dyed hair who seemed to be taking a more ironic approach to the whole affair. This cheered me up considerably.

But when Toho were at bat, it was like a vast, carefully controlled noise machine, prepared to give its all for the full nine innings. I noticed that Toho's operation was not as slick as some of the other fan groups I'd seen on television; Kyoto Toin Academy, for instance, had a group of young junior high girls whose job it was to keep everyone supplied with cold barley tea. Toin had my favourite crowd-chant directors. They operated by using sign-boards. They would wave a 'T' followed by an 'O' followed by an 'I' followed by an 'N' followed by all four together, followed by a single board saying just 'Ah!'

The score remained tied until the bottom of the ninth, and then Takigawa hit what the Japanese call a sayonara single. It was 6–5. The game was over. The air-raid klaxon sounded and the players ran to the centre to form up in two lines facing the scoreboard at the bottom of the field. Once again the Takigawa anthem boomed out as their school banner was hoisted on a flagpole above the scoreboard.

Then the photographers closed in – not, as you might expect, on the winners, who were rushing about throwing people in the air and waving boisterously to their fans, but on the losers. They were on their hands and knees down by their dug-out, shovelling dark soil from the in-field into whatever they had to hand – small bags, batting caps, plastic cups. A mass of cameramen clustered around, seeking the classic Koshien-tears-in-defeat shots.

'The Koshien ground is a kind of sacred place for players,' said Mr Mizuno, by way of explanation. 'So the losers always want to take a piece of the ground back as a souvenir.'

Now the siren was sounding again. Another game was about to begin and the new contenders were sprinting out on to the pitch for their date with destiny. Toho was Koshien history.

Later that night in my hotel room, I watched it all again, this time with the benefit of camera close-ups. It showed so much more – the look of horror on the pitcher's face as the ball soared over for the first home run, the jubilation of the winning team, the sobbing, defeated, dirt shovelling, all the agonies of youth broadcast to an ever-appreciative nation. It seemed a long way from the samba.

Given the predominance of baseball, it's rather surprising that soccer ever managed to get a foot in the door. Most of the game's current bosses have their stories about why they opted for soccer instead of baseball. The man who did more than anyone to set up the J.League, Saburo Kawabuchi, started off playing baseball in the 1950s in Sakai City, near Osaka.

'I was playing baseball up until junior high school,' says Mr Kawabuchi. 'Then the high school I went to had a good soccer team, and the baseball team wasn't up to much. In 1952, things were difficult, and no one got to travel very much. The soccer team was going on a trip to Shikoku [the island off the coast from Osaka] and so I joined the soccer club to take the trip because I wanted to travel. I didn't really know much about the rules, or about how to kick the ball or anything, but they sent me out anyway.'

Mr Hotta, the godfather of soccer in Shimizu, started out as a Little League baseball player, until he had a parting of the ways with his coach.

'I played baseball in elementary school. I had strong arms and I was a good catcher. But we always had to do what the coaches told us to do, and one day I was told to sacrifice bunt [when the hitter hits short, getting himself out in order to advance a runner on the bases]. But I didn't. I hit a home run, and afterwards I was in trouble. So then I joined the soccer team in junior high school.'

Mr Hotta's first football coach had allowed him into the team on the basis of the number of press-ups he could do. 'It had nothing to do with football,' he says. Subsequently, as he fathered the development of football for boys in Shimizu in the 1950s, he set out to encourage other coaches not to make the same mistakes. He even published a book called *Kick Off Life*, a collection of his thoughts on football published in the local coaches' weekly newsletter. By Japanese standards, it's all very revolutionary, preaching the virtues of individual expression, of not putting too much pressure on the young players, and of generally remembering that, after all, it's only a game.

But Japanese baseball and its 'old-style' sports ethics still exert their influence on the new sport of soccer. When foreign coaches and players find themselves perplexed by the Japanese approach to football, the problems can often be traced back to training methods in the school system. In the schools, the game is taught in a way which is not so very different from the traditional approach to baseball. It's a subject which can get European or Latin American footballers extremely worked up very quickly.

'I get some goalkeepers who cannot catch the ball,' says Dutchman Dido Havenaar, now coaching at second division Consadole Sapporo after fourteen years playing football in Japan. 'When they dive for the ball, they always dive with their chests to the ground, as if they were diving for the base in baseball. But come on! You can't catch the ball if you're face down.'

It's not just a matter of technique. In the Japanese school system, guts and commitment still hold sway.

'The problem is in the schools,' says Havenaar. 'They have managers who think in the old-fashioned way. They don't teach them how to build up, how to pass. They only know how to say "*Gambarre, gambarre, gambarre!* You have to fight, fight, fight!" They're always running, running, running. If you see high-school players, they're fit enough. But they can't play football. So the problems start at school, before they come to the foreign coaches in the J.League.'

American baseball players in Japan complain about the traditional 1,000 balls fielding practice, when a fielder has to catch ground balls until he can hardly stand up. Similarly, Japanese high-school soccer training sessions, rather like those Japanese endurance game shows, would reduce most European players to a state of babbling exhaustion. Perryman-san remembers his son coming home one Sunday from a school soccer training session that had lasted about six hours. Dido Havenaar's ten year old had just played fourteen games in eight days, as his team fought its way through the rounds of summer tournaments.

In May at Hiroshima's Big Arch ground, I'd met Ottavio Neves, a young coach who was one of six Brazilians working in the Japanese high-school system on some kind of government-funded scheme. Perhaps there were six Japanese guys teaching baseball in Rio in exchange.

'They train for two to three hours every day,' he said of his school teams, with evident dismay. 'I don't understand why. When a soccer team has maybe fifty members, there are always five to ten guys who are injured. I try to explain to the coaches that they need to allow the players to rest, but it's always "*Gambarre, gambarre,* try your best, try harder." And when they play tournaments, they play two games a day, maybe eight games in four days. The final is something terrible.' Terrible? 'Yes. Terrible. Everyone is so tired they can hardly stand up. The level is good, but the pressure is enormous, everyone saying to themselves, "I'm really so tired, it's a big stress, but we have to win, I have to try harder." '

Japanese baseball makes a virtue of repetition. The great Sadaharu Oh, for example, used to stand in front of a mirror, swinging his bat like a sword over and over again. Baseball, like sumo and kendo, is to some degree a game with a set of moves that can be mastered through repetition. Soccer isn't.

'They repeat, repeat, repeat the same movement,' explained Ottavio Neves, beginning to gesticulate. 'Left foot, right foot, left foot, right foot, again, again, again, again. So if the ball comes to them in exactly the same way every time, they can make a good pass. It's incredible. Incredible.'

I felt that it was probably time for young Ottavio to take a holiday. How much of that sort of thing can a young Brazilian take?

Jan Versleijen, a Dutch coach who spent two seasons at JEF United, told me that when he arrived in 1997, the team was in full-on baseball-mode.

'They had this idea that if they could send one hundred crosses from the wing in a row, eventually they'd be perfect. When I came here, they were trying to train for two and a half or three hours at a time. But you can't do that. It's too long.'

'They're desperate for knowledge,' said Perryman. 'They really want to learn, and part of our job as foreign coaches and players is to teach them. But some things can't just be imitated. I've had players who have missed a volley at goal, and instead of getting back in the game, they've stood there, looking thought-ful, and repeating the kick they missed. Like they were playing tennis or golf.'

All this running and training and repetition and more running and training is at the behest of the high-school coaches. They, like baseball coaches, are the teachers, the *sensei*, who hand down the knowledge of the sacred art. In baseball, no one argues with the coach. In Japanese professional baseball, the coach sits in the dug-out with an impassive face, the face of the wise and powerful master who expects to be obeyed, as opposed to the flustered, hot-under-the-collar, arm-waving frustration of the soccer coach who knows that no one on the field is taking a damned bit of notice because they all think they know what they're doing.

'Discussions? No, no, no, no,' says Havenaar. 'No discussions. In Europe, every player is talking, saying, "What do you mean, coach? No, no, that's wrong. How can you say that?" But not here. It starts in school. The coach is thinking for them, like in baseball.'

'The players always want to know what the answers are,' said Versleijen. 'So I give them a problem, a free-kick position, or a throw-in, and I show them four ways of dealing with it. Then I ask them to think up a fifth way for themselves. They have to develop their own style. But you don't change it all in one day. Look at the elementary schools. Everyone is taught to think as a group.'

At Sanfrecce Hiroshima's training sessions, I'd watched as Eddie Thomson went over videos of the previous Saturday's match, pointing out grievous errors and saying what he wanted done next time. At the end, he always asked for questions. There were never any questions.

'All the young players who join us are very quiet and very regimented. They never question anything, never ask why or where and don't even communicate with other players.

'I think people are comfortable being told they must do a thousand or they must do five hundred of something. All the players want to know what we're doing, how many days we're training this week, what days, what afternoons – they love to be prepared and know that's what we're going to do. So I can understand them enjoying baseball training. A Japanese person would be quite happy thinking, "Oh, there's a thousand balls, so let's go and do it." But soccer's not like that. Soccer requires a lot of individual play, being part of a team whose members communicate with each other. And they find that . . . a little bit difficult.

'The main problem,' he concluded, in a moment of analytical brilliance, 'is getting them to think.'

清水

11 BRAZILIANS

After the day at Koshien, I headed back to my hotel in the centre of Osaka. It was a week night, but the idle non-baseball-playing youth of Osaka were hanging out around the railway station, which was close by. A procession of customised saloon cars cruised slowly past, revving their ridiculously supercharged engines, while heavily hair-dyed young men hung out of the windows. A car slid past with a purple 1970s-style lava lamp in the back seat, alongside a massive inflatable Hello Kitty doll. The girls were pursuing the 1970s look that had emerged that summer alongside cotton kimonos – a sort of souped-up Barbie Doll look which required deep, deep sunbed-induced suntans, long brown or blonde hair, heavy make-up and sparkling dust applied around the eyes, plus huge cork-soled platform sandals.

The platform sandals and boots had been around since the beginning of the year, but they seemed to me to be getting bigger. That night in Osaka, the average height must have been around six inches, or slightly more. Later that summer, the whole Japanese-girls-in-exceptionally-high-platform-soles issue was to erupt into a major controversy in the media, after the shoes were blamed for at least two fatalities – one a straightforward head injury caused by a fall, and the other a fatal car accident involving a boot-wearing driver.

I strolled past two young guys leaning on a hatchback car with the back door open. A vast customised stereo system was pumping out loud rap music with a massive bass beat. This was too much to cope with after a day of old-style baseball. So I bought a dubious take-away from a convenience store and retired to my hotel to watch the baseball highlights and dip briefly into the free two minutes of pay-per-view soft pornography which is an essential part of the business hotel scene, along with all-in-one plastic bathrooms. These occasional two-minute ventures produced a bizarre and not entirely reassuring series of snapshots of contemporary Japanese erotic taste, although the details were periodically obscured by chequered blocking patterns over the key areas. The patterns regularly extended to cover the entire screen. There was a lot of weird manipulating of young women going on, often by old salarymen in white gloves; in one case, which I didn't really have the time or the imagination to work out, it involved clingfilm.

Channel 6, on the other hand, was showing a late-night eel-cooking competition called 'Battle Anago', in which cooks of various nationalities were pitched against each other. The Italians were using mozzarella. Someone else, possibly Spanish, was using melted chocolate.

The next day was hot and overcast, humid and nasty. I swooshed back from Shin-Osaka Station towards Tokyo on the Shinkansen. My destination was Perryman-san's next date with destiny – the local Shizuoka Prefecture derby against the evil Jubilo in the small industrial town of Iwata, located about a hundred kilometres to the west of Shimizu. It was another evening game and so, on the way, I took the opportunity to pause in the industrial city of Hamamatsu, where I had to change from the Shinkansen to take the local line to Iwata.

Hamamatsu is the main city in the manufacturing belt of western Shizuoka, where the major employers include Yamaha, Suzuki and Honda. You can tell this is Yamaha country because on the left as you leave the station, there's an unattended open-plan display of Yamaha musical instruments, with a grand piano just sitting there, ready for any passing commuter to sit down and thump out a few tunes.

Aside from tinkling the ivories, Hamamatsu is also a good place to consider that central question of Japanese soccer culture – why Brazil? Why not Italy? Or Germany? Or even England? Unlike, say, the fads for growing dreadlocks and listening to reggae, or cultivating gangsta-rap dress styles, Japan's obsession with Brazilian soccer is not entirely random. In Hamamatsu I had arranged to meet Mara Nakagawa, a journalist with a local newspaper with the very un-Japanese name of *Folha* (pronounced 'folya') *Mundial*. This is one of two Portuguese-language papers based in Hamamatsu. Two more are based in Tokyo. Between them, they serve a community of almost a quarter of a million Brazilian nationals living in Japan; 70,000 of them, including Mara Nakagawa, live in Shizuoka and Aichi Prefectures, between Shimizu and Nagoya.

As the only northern European male in the vicinity of the main railway station, I was not hard to spot. Mara looked more Brazilian than Japanese, and had a big sense of humour. While I was heading for football, she was going to a concert given by a visiting Brazilian pop singer. We had tea on the eighth floor of the department store adjacent to the station. The slightly rundown restaurant was fitted out to recreate the interior of a European railway carriage. Over tea and a slice of cheesecake, we discussed Brazil and cultural confusion. The setting seemed ideal.

Mara arrived in Japan in 1991. Her father was a Japanese Brazilian, her mother Brazilian. Mara learned Japanese in Japan. Most of the Brazilians in Japan are at least partly Japanese, the descendants of a wave of Japanese emigrants who began to settle in both North and South America at the start of the twentieth century. The communities steadily grew. In Brazil, there are now roughly one million Japanese descendants of the original settlers, while Peru's former president Alberto Fujimori is part Japanese. In the late 1980s, as its economy continued to expand rapidly, Japan was facing a labour shortage. The country needed to import workers but it didn't want to bring in other Asians. Latin America's Japanese seemed to provide the perfect solution – foreigners who were already Japanese.

'So in 1989, they changed the law,' explained Mara. 'They made it easy for second or third generation Japanese to come to work in Japan. They needed workers. They wanted anyone who had two arms and two legs and two eyes to see, to come and work in the factories. They came to this area because there are so many factories.'

Of course, things turned out to be a little bit more complicated when it came to actually dealing with the people the Japanese call the *burajiro-jin*. They had, after all, been living in Brazil for the past ninety years.

'We come from a country where everyone likes to play soccer and drive fast,' said Mara, expansively. 'In Japan, they give their children a baseball bat and a bicycle. In Brazil, we give them a football and a toy car.'

In 1999, with unemployment up at what for Japan was a record high, strains were beginning to appear. On a housing estate near the town of Toyota over by Nagoya, right-wing groups had organised a demonstration against Brazilian immigrants, who were accused of holding loud parties and causing traffic accidents. The Japanese found the Brazilian Japanese disturbing. They hung around in groups, talking Portuguese. They played noisy card games. They stayed up late.

'For the Japanese, we look like them, but we don't act like them,' said Mara, 'and they don't know who we are. It is confusing for them because we don't behave the way they expect us to.'

The historical links of this strange trans-Pacific odd-couple relationship had fed Japan's grassroots enthusiasm for soccer. In Shimizu, Mr Hotta and his schoolteacher friends started sending Japanese boys to summer soccer training camps in Brazil. Shimizu's goalscorer Alessandro dos Santos, aka Alex, speaks Japanese because he first came to Japan on a scholarship aimed at bringing over talented Brazilian players to improve the quality of Japanese high-school teams.

In the J.League, the Brazilian contribution is huge. Since the start of the J.League, more than 130 Brazilian players have appeared in Japan, roughly half of the entire foreign presence. The Kashima Antlers, guided by the awesome Zico, have only ever fielded Brazilians as their foreign players. Kashiwa Reysol, Verdy, S-Pulse and even Kyoto Purple Sanga have historically opted for Brazilians. Brazil has provided the J.League with stars – world-famous players such as Dunga and Zico, who moved to Japan at the end of their careers, and the big-in-Japan players who might never have made a name for themselves in Brazil but who are national celebrities in Japan. In 1999, Dunga left to return to Brazil, but Zico was still 'technical adviser' to the Kashima Antlers, the club he'd worked to build up at the start of the J.League. Despite being sent off for spitting on the ball during the 1993 championship play-offs – for which he had, of course, apologised – Zico went on that same year to become the first foreigner in the history of Japanese sport to be awarded the Prime Minister's medal for sporting achievements. He'd subsequently become a sort of honorary Japanese.

Two other Brazilians went even further than that. Japan has a cautious approach to giving away citizenship to anyone whose family can't trace their roots in Japan back at least to the thirteenth century. This has been particularly galling for the country's long-established Korean community, many of whom, like the Japanese in Latin America, have been living in Japan since the nineteenth century, but who are still regarded as foreign residents; they're not allowed to vote, they're excluded from all significant public office, and are generally treated as second-class citizens. A Japanese might have become president of Peru but the chances of a Korean becoming prime minister of Japan are just about zero.

But in 1993, Japan's national team was fighting to qualify, for the first time ever, for the World Cup finals, to be held in 1994 in the United States. Japan was also trying to persuade FIFA that it should be allowed to host the 2002 World Cup. At the time, a thirty-six-year-old Brazilian midfielder, Ruy Ramos, was playing for Verdy Kawasaki. Ramos had arrived from Brazil in 1978, just out of high school, to join the old Yomiuri FC. Initially, he struggled to adapt to Japan but then settled down. He learned Japanese; he married a Japanese woman; he started riding a bicycle around town; and he showed he could eat the most challenging food Japan could lay before him. People began to think of Ramos as Japanese, even if he did have long blond hair and a name dominated by the letter 'r'. So in 1993, just in time for the crucial World Cup qualifiers, the government made Ruy Ramos a Japanese citizen. When Japan took to the field for the final round of Asian qualifiers in October in Doha, Qatar, Ruy Ramos was in the line-up. (Similar moves were under way to convert Dutch goalkeeper Dido Havenaar, then at Nagoya Grampus Eight, into a two-metre tall, blond-haired Japanese goalkeeper. Unfortunately for Japan, Havenaar's papers came through too late for Doha.) Ruy Ramos wasn't enough. A tragic 2–2 draw with Iraq meant Japan were eliminated in favour of South Korea, probably to the delight of all those non-Japanese foreign residents.

By the time Ruy Ramos retired at the end of the 1998 season, he was probably one of the best-loved players in the whole of the J.League. He'd even formed a band and had dabbled with making records. Around 40,000 people turned out to watch his testimonial game played at the National Stadium. The man was big in Japan, but he was still not so big with the Brazilians.

'I went to a party once,' said Mara Nakagawa, 'and Ruy Ramos was there, singing with his band and everything. But only the Japanese who were there made a thing of it. The Brazilians didn't care.'

Having successfully persuaded their own fans and FIFA that Ramos was Japanese, in 1997 the JFA tried the same tactics again. This time the candidate was twenty-eight-year-old Wagner Lopes, a striker at Bellmare Hiratsuka. The first part of Lopes's story is classically Brazilian; born in the city of Franca, he spent his early teens working in a shoe factory before being recruited by a big-name team and going on to play in Brazil's national Under-17 team. At the age of eighteen, Lopes moved to Japan, claiming afterwards, perhaps improbably, that he made the decision after reading a book by the founder of Sony, Akita Morita. After five years playing in the Japanese second division, Lopes eventually made it to Bellmare in 1997, establishing himself as a goalscoring striker just as Japan was in the midst of another campaign to qualify for the World Cup. So Wagner Lopes became a Japanese citizen. 'It's hard to explain,' Lopes told the press, 'but I feel I was Japanese in my previous existence.'

Just over two weeks later, Lopes was playing against South Korea in front of 57,000 fans in a blue national team shirt. This time, after various ups and downs involving Kazakhstan, Uzbekistan and Iran, Japan qualified for their first World Cup finals. In France, Lopes played for his newly acquired country for the final twenty-two minutes of Japan's distinguished 1–0 defeat by Argentina. His appearance resulted in both teams having a player on the pitch called Lopes, which must have confused the commentators, even after they'd explained what a Brazilian with a German name was doing playing for Japan. Young Wagner's moment of World Cup glory was to come in Japan's final game, against the Reggae Boyz of Jamaica. Japan lost 2–1, but Lopes's header set up Japan's only goal of the entire competition.

Shimizu S-Pulse, of course, have their own trio of Brazilians, led by midfielder Carlos Santos. Santos was someone for whom Perryman-san had nothing but praise, seeing him as a sort of anti-Dunga. 'This player gave the young players at S-Pulse something to look up to. He's a foreign player who has a clean image, a perfect professional. He looks after his body, and that's why he's still playing at thirty-eight years of age.'

Santos turned professional in Brazil at the age of seventeen and played for the São Paulo club Botafogo before coming to Japan at the age of thirty to play alongside Zico and Alcindo at Kashima Antlers. He transferred to S-Pulse in 1995 after three years.

'I am very good in Japan,' he told me one day after training at Hebizuka. 'My life good. I like Japan. I have many, many friends in Kashima, in Shizuoka.'

Santos suffered from the usual shock at the early J.League. 'At the start of J.League . . . many, many, many problems because soccer just starting in Japan. At Kashima, we were good, we have Zico organisation. But some games, I look, the ball goes left, maybe twenty-two players go left. Ball goes right, twenty-two players go right. Very interesting because Japanese players don't understand position. Just run, run, run. Now they have better position. Now for me, for Stojkovic, for Alex, more easy. Before many difficulties. Before many foreign players go bye-bye Japan.' Santos knows that the comparative lack of pressure from fans and from the media in Japan has meant that foreign players have had to force themselves to play their best. 'If I'm no good for one maybe two games, the supporters say, "Never mind, Santos, next game, next game." In Brazil, no. In Brazil they say, "Now". Very important for foreign players in Japan not sleeping because no pressure from supporters. In Brazil, players don't sleep. There's pressure from the fans, the commentators. In Japan, no pressure. In Japan, commentators not understand. Only understand base-ball. Maybe sumo. Japanese soccer is very interesting.'

Now, with two young children, Santos is thinking about the future. 'If team give me another contract, I stay in Japan. No problem. But if next year, my body says no more, problems start, and I don't enjoy, I stop. But now I'm having luck, luck, luck. Every day, I say, "Ohhh, thank you, thank you, thank you God." But if my body has problems, maybe then that is my God telling me to stop. And then I go back to Brazil to finish my education, maybe six months of one year, I finish university in physical training.'

Before I left Mara at Hamamatsu Station to continue to Iwata, I asked her what the Brazilian Japanese thought about the J.League and the Brazilians who played in it.

'They don't take any interest at all in the J.League,' she said dismissively. 'They watch Brazilian football on satellite television.'

We chatted for a little longer and then we had to leave. She said that if I was interested, the Brazilian community in Hamamatsu was holding regular open-air barbecue parties every

Saturday during the summer, generally starting around midnight, with loud music and lots of dancing. I was sure the neighbours were really happy about that.

Mr Matsuda, the kendo-practising, Mount Fuji-climbing head of the S-Pulse samba band was another who recognised that, culturally speaking, Japan and Brazil are really not so close. As he'd explained, a group of Brazilian musicians had come over to Shimizu to teach the S-Pulse fans how to play samba in the first place, but Shimizu samba had then evolved all on its own into something rather different.

'Now we have our own style,' Matsuda told me one day. 'When the band began, it was real samba. Now you could call it samba Shizuoka-style.' What did that mean exactly, in musical terms? 'Well, Japanese culture is different from Brazilian culture. Brazilian people express themselves very well, but we Japanese don't. So Shizuoka-style samba is maybe a little less exuberant. In Brazilian samba, you should smile and laugh. Our style now is like Japanese culture – it's harder for the players to express themselves, so it's a more orderly style.'

When I arrived at the stadium in Iwata, taking the obligatory shuttle bus from the station through the charming industrial garden suburbs of Iwata, the samba band was in position, crowded behind the goal. The hot, humid, nasty day had turned into a hot, humid, nasty evening, and the oppressive, claustrophobic atmosphere was amplified by the Iwata Stadium, which is cramped. The ground has the sort of atmospheric quirkiness that is entirely suited to the English second and third division. It is built into the side of a slight hill, so the side opposite the main stand is exceptionally steep, while the away supporters' end, open to the elements, is unusually narrow, but so close to the pitch that you feel as if you could reach out and touch the back of the net. There were now over 17,000 people packed in.

The stadium is located in the grounds of the Yamaha motor company. It's surrounded by the company's fenced factories and adjacent to Yamaha's main office buildings. There's a big red Yamaha sign above the old-style manual scoreboard, and blue Yamaha signs all around the ground. In the main stand, top company executives in suits were being guided by office ladies in smart uniforms towards a specially reserved lift that would whisk them to the spacious air-conditioned executive suite. Everyone and everything else had a wedged-in feel.

In the main stand, the S-Pulse front-office managers went by, looking like the poor country cousins who expected to lose. After all, Perryman's team had lost at home during the first stage, in the infamous 5–2 game, and S-Pulse had never ever won away against Jubilo. Feeling daunted, I went out to visit the orange and yellow masses. On the way, near the beer and snacks stand, I noticed a group of men in S-Pulse shirts standing in a small circle. Matsuda-san was talking to them. Naya-san, the president and supreme commander of all supporters, was standing just behind him, nodding his approval. This was the pre-game heads of supporters' groups meeting, which given the history of occasional crowd trouble between the two rivals, was presumably particularly important tonight.

I had spoken to Matsuda about the mild trouble at Nihondaira after the 5–2 defeat in the first stage, when fans had started throwing plastic bottles. He attributed this behaviour to extremists, rowdy individuals who were outside the control of the organised supporters' groups structure.

'The difficult thing,' he said, with all the weight of a former law-enforcement officer, 'is that ordinary supporters who aren't attached to any group are hard to control. The people who threw the plastic bottles didn't belong to any specific group. Some supporters sometimes get too excited, but if they do, after the match they have to apologise or they won't be allowed into the group at the following game.' But this didn't mean that Mr Matsuda was going to allow opposition supporters to take all kinds of liberties.

'Sometimes, you need to fight,' he said, with evident commitment. 'Like when we had a fight with the Jubilo supporters two years ago. There was a big fight at Nihondaira. Some Jubilo supporters surrounded a young woman S-Pulse supporter on a motorbike and wouldn't let her go. And they tried to scratch the cars of anyone who was an S-Pulse supporter. Another time, some away supporters got into the lower level of the home stand with team banners, where no flags are allowed, and some of our supporters went down and started a fight.

'But the Jubilo supporters apologised and since then we haven't been fighting with them. Sometimes in Japanese culture, after you fight someone, as in judo or kendo, you can be closer to them.'

In fact, the various fan organisations in the area were working on mutual confidence-building measures. There were ambitious plans for a joint S-Pulse–Jubilo–Grampus union of supporters' clubs. All three mascots – Paru-chan, Grampus-kun the whale and Jubilo's rather dodgy-looking bluebird – had been seen together over the summer at Nihondaira, advertising the forthcoming union in a festival of regional cuteness.

'The difference between Japanese and foreign supporters lies in the unique style of the Japanese fans,' said Matsuda, reaching for the broader sociological analysis. 'In Japan, it's not just old people or young people. Everyone can take part. We get excited. Some people even try to be like hooligans in England, but that's not the Japanese style.

'We understand the social background to hooliganism in England – maybe people don't have jobs, and they're under stress – but here in Japan we don't have those kind of problems. We have no violence. And we hope our style will continue.' And if there was any violence, whoever did it would certainly have to apologise.

As I surveyed the assembled ranks behind the goal, I had to agree he had a point. In Britain, the narrow confines of this stand would probably have caused problems with crushing. Here, a man was holding up a toddler directly behind the goal. The child did almost get whacked by the end of an S-Pulse supporters' banner, but it would have been an accident.

Yamada-san was up at the back with the big surdo bass drum. He smiled a classically diffident greeting. I could never tell if I was embarrassing him or not. Suddenly he produced a small booklet of folded white printed papers.

'The S-Pulse supporters' unofficial matchday programme,' he said. 'I'm sorry we don't have an English version.'

Even without an English version – Perryman, Holder, possibly their wives and I would have been the only readers – it was pretty impressively produced. I assumed Yamada-san had got the official permission of the eighteen-member supporters' council before rushing into print. The unofficial matchday programme included background on Jubilo's record. More interestingly, there was a fan's view of the forthcoming game. The fan predicted a 2–0 win for S-Pulse and suggested that both goals could come from Ando, the attacking right-back whom Perryman had controversially dropped from the first team. Ando, known as An-chan to his fans, was on the subs' bench again.

I decided to spend the first half down with the Shimizu fans. This time, I'd come prepared. At the last game at Nihondaira, I'd bought myself an orange S-Pulse tee-shirt with blue and yellow on the shoulders. On the back it said 'NOBORI' in blue letters, with his number, 10. I boldly stripped off my more serious shirt and shifted into orange mode.

I was just to the left of the goal, standing next to a woman I recognised from the Sanfrecce and Gifu games, and to the left of the band. I was possibly in K's Club territory, but at an away game it was hard to tell. On my way in to the ground, I'd already seen my friend Mr Oba, who was again taking a front-line leader position. I was beginning to know pretty much what to do, without someone having to grab my arms – except for one particularly tricky clapping routine that I was still struggling to master.

My talk with Matsuda had also helped to clarify a few matters regarding the art of Shizuoka-style samba. Initially, he'd explained, there used to be some fairly complicated chants and songs, often in Brazilian Portuguese, but the crowd had found this hard going. Some people still got the words wrong – like me. I discovered I had been foolishly singing, 'OOOOOOOH FORZA ESS-PULSE . . . OOH OOH OOH FORZA ESS-PULSE!' when I should have been going 'OOOOOOOH HOSSA ESS-PULSE!' I now know that there are currently twelve different samba music chanting routines, and that each one has a specific name, and that each one is deployed at particular times. Even Mr Matsuda is hard pressed to list them one after the other, but when you hear them, you know them. So, when the boys in orange walk out to warm up, we start with the basic 'ESS-PULSE! Cha-cha-cha ESS-PULSE! Cha-cha-cha ESS-PULSE!' The same chant is used again at the start of the second half, and when the players come over to the crowd at the end of the game. It's our way of saying hello to the players. It's pretty easy stuff.

After the greeting, and before the kick-off, we go directly into one of our happiest and most sophisticated tunes, nicknamed for some reason which no one could explain, 'Guriko'. This is the standard European-style 'OHH-LEEE! O-LÉ-OLÉ-OLÉ! ESS-PULSE ESS-PULSE' but with a rapid syncopated beat from the band, and preceded by a few spontaneous Shizuoka-samba cries of 'EHH!' as the band strike up, and it's accompanied by waving our arms above our head and clapping.

When I was trying to get Matsuda to tell me all the names and to put the names to the tunes in a desperate attempt to satisfy a deep internal longing for order and categorisation that could one day see me standing in railway stations in an anorak, I asked about one of my favourite tunes, a sort of swinging march that they sing when things are going pretty well and S-Pulse are moving the ball around in midfield and there's a clear view of Mount Fuji.

'We call it "March",' he said, using the English word. 'It's from a film, about a bridge.'

'*Bridge over the River Kwai*?' I said.

'Yes,' he said.

Of course.

Defensor has a slow-clapping beat, with a rocking, long, powerful 'OOOOOH OOOH OH OH OOOOOH' that I suspect is in a minor key. They sing Defensor when the team is losing, presumably to steady their jangled nerves and develop resolve. At the Jubilo match, they decided to deploy Defensor if they were winning, presumably to steady nerves and develop resolve.

It was going to be a tough game. There was, though, one element of hope. At the end of the first stage, Jubilo had sent their best Japanese player, Hiroshi Nanami, on a short-term transfer to Venezia in the Italian *Serie A*. Nanami had been one of the bright spots in Japan's World Cup performance, along with the great Hidetoshi Nakata, who was now beginning his second season with another second-string *Serie A* club, Perugia. During the first stage, Nanami had to a certain extent adopted the mantle of Dunga as the club's main playmaker. Could the team adjust to his absence?

Perhaps Jubilo had lost that old magic; but during the first half, viewed from behind the S–Pulse goal on that hot, humid, nasty evening, it certainly didn't look like it. I later read accounts of the game which said the balance of the first half was in S–Pulse's favour, but from behind the goal, there seemed to be a stream of Jubilo blue shirts running towards us in dangerous positions. It was nervous stuff. Even the samba leaders seemed a little tense.

Our crowd leader for the evening was a certain Mr Tsuyuki, the leader of Kenta Club, who could be identified by a single feather stuck in his orange headband. Maybe it was because the action was fast and fragmented, maybe it was because we weren't high enough up to see the action properly, but the S–Pulse crowd seemed slightly out-of-whack. Mr Tsuyuki was struggling to move us from one chant to the next fast enough to keep up with the action. We'd be chanting 'ALEXU! ALEXU!' to show our appreciation of an artful run at the Jubilo goal which led to a corner, but the corner would have been taken by the time we'd shifted gear to the chant that sounds like 'Ji-ber-abu-ji-bera-bu GO! GO!' reserved for threatening dead-ball situations.

The first half ended scoreless. Just twenty minutes into the game, S-Pulse's Kuboyama, who was playing up front with Yasunaga, had suddenly walked off the pitch feeling unwell. Perryman-san had brought on Shimizu's third Brazilian, Fabinho. At half-time, Yamada-san wasn't happy.

'I don't know why Perryman brought on Fabinho. I like him personally,' he explained, 'but I don't think he's so good as a player.'

I had hoped that being down with the fans would allow me to be more relaxed about whether Shimizu S-Pulse beat Jubilo Iwata, but it wasn't working. I was still tense. I still cared. For the second half, I moved up to the main stand press seats, hoping to get a better view, and to monitor the action on the S-Pulse bench.

At half-time, the Jubilo fans unfurled a massive banner over the heads of the crowd. 'WE ARE THE CHAMPIONS OF ASIA' it read in English. It was bloody irritating.

As the second half started, Jubilo fell upon S-Pulse with gusto. About ten minutes in, their eighteen-year-old forward, Takahara, who is a product of the Shimizu high-school system, slipped through to go one-on-one with the veteran S-Pulse keeper Sanada. A few minutes later, Jubilo almost had a penalty when their attacking midfielder, Nishi, went down just inside the box. Disaster was brewing.

It struck roughly fifteen minutes into the second half. As Jubilo continued their pressure, S-Pulse's veteran midfielder, Santos, was beaten by Jubilo's twenty-one-year-old, Fukunishi. As Fukunishi went past, Santos sort of fell over on him. It looked like a deliberate foul and deserved a yellow card. Unfortunately, Santos had done pretty much the same thing in the first half. He was off. I was sitting behind my friend Shirase Mayumi, sports reporter and S-Pulse programme notes writer. She was looking tearful again. I felt extremely glum.

It was a terrible blow. For Santos, it was the first time he'd ever been sent off and this game marked his two hundredth appearance for S-Pulse. With just ten men, S-Pulse didn't have a chance. The S-Pulse crowd was booing, and Santos was refusing to leave the field until Perryman-san had time to reorganise. Off came an attacker, Fabinho, who hadn't done much, and on went Oenoki, a Japanese version of Santos – thirty-three years old, a club veteran and not a man to panic. S-Pulse fell back and braced themselves for the storm. There was half an hour left, followed by half an hour of sudden-death extra time. They were doomed. Perryman-san's chances of having his contract renewed were looking increasingly bleak. The S-Pulse crowd settled into the Defensor chant.

Perryman-san was up and down like a yoyo. Jubilo were pulling their old niggling tactics. They still knew how to cheat and dive and mess with the referee. At one point, S-Pulse's defender, Morioka, dispossessed Jubilo's number 6, Hattori, with a committed sliding tackle. As they lay on the ground, the Jubilo player kicked Morioka in the face, pretty much in front of the referee. Perryman-san was probably about fifty feet away but I could hear him – 'REF! YOU SAW IT! REF! YOU FUCKING SAW IT!' The fourth official was moving towards him. There was a mounting sense of injustice around.

'Jubilo are crap,' I said in English to the reporter next to me, a Jubilo man, who looked a little worried.

Then, with just ten minutes left, a Jubilo defender was on the side-lines receiving treatment for an injury. Teruyoshi Ito, a player known for his short, bright yellow hair, suddenly managed to lose his marker and break through. As the Jubilo goalkeeper came out to challenge, Ito slipped the ball through towards the left post. Alex was there to push it in.

'YES!' I shouted, and banged the table. 'UN-FUCKING-BELIEVABLE,' I shouted to the man next to me, who was looking even more worried.

The S-Pulse crowd was in full jubilation mode, olé-ing and dancing. Below me, Perryman-san and the rest of the bench were jumping up and down. And that's how it ended – S-Pulse 1, Jubilo 0. An historic victory.

It seemed to me that it was mostly Jubilo's fault. When they were one man up, they hadn't changed their tactics to take advantage of the additional player. Their defenders had stayed back. They hadn't used the wings. They'd just carried on playing the same style of game. It was the old Japanese problem of not being able to change the pace and the tempo of the game. With Dunga and Nanami gone, there was no one to show them what to do. At the start of the season, Jubilo's Japanese manager, Takashi Kuwahara, had inherited a team built by Dunga, but the roof was beginning to leak.

The general manager of Sanfrecce Hiroshima, Mr Imanishi, when discussing the merits of foreign managers, had predicted that Jubilo would start to deteriorate without Dunga.

'Japanese managers are fine when a club is winning,' he'd said. 'But not when they start to lose.'

Mr Imanishi, who is a wise old bird, was proved right. Jubilo, it turned out, were at the top of a long and slippery slope. By the middle of the season, they would be down at the bottom of the table, alongside Bellmare and JEF, in a sudden and catastrophic collapse, despite still having some of the best individual players in the J.League.

Similar things had been happening over at the Urawa Reds, another well-financed team with great individual players, who had ended the first stage fourth from the bottom of the table after a massive 8–1 thrashing at the hands of Grampus in the last game of the stage. Urawa had now removed their former manager, Hiromi Hara, and brought in a big Dutchman Aad de Mos, whose previous career included stints at PSV Eindhoven, Ajax Amsterdam and Liège in a bid to stop the rot.

But at the Iwata Stadium, it was Perryman-san triumphant. Regrettably, I arrived late for the post-game seminar. The reporters were asking why he'd brought on Kenta Hasegawa in the final minute in place of Yasunaga, rather than Ando instead of Ichikawa. It was detailed stuff, none of which really mattered because S-Pulse had beaten Jubilo, and just before Perryman was due to start discussing his contract with the front-office management. It was a big win.

12 ULTRA MAN

After vanquishing the dark powers of Jubilo, S-Pulse advanced
with renewed confidence.

'It was an important win,' said Perryman-san much later.
'When we were down to ten men at Iwata, halfway through the
second half, we were staring down the barrel of defeat. We'd have
lost the first two games in a row. But, as it happened, we won it.
As I see it, there are fifteen games to play, and if we can win four
out of every five, we can be champions.'

The victory over Jubilo was followed by wins against the
Kashima Antlers and the Urawa Reds. Then came Nagoya Grampus
Eight. Grampus had made a bad start to the season, losing the first
three games and as a result, losing their manager, the charming and
philosophical Gerard Depardieu lookalike, Daniel Sanchez.

The Grampus game turned into a gut-wrenching re-run of the
dramatic last-minute S-Pulse victory back in May in Gifu, when
I'd made my first appearance on the terraces. The game ended 4–3
to S-Pulse, the winner set up by a brilliant, perfectly weighted
through ball from Alex, and blasted in by Fabinho from just inside
the penalty area. After five games, S-Pulse stood second in the

league, three points behind the still unbeaten Yokohama F Marinos. The S-Pulse front office decided to open negotiations with Perryman-san on the renewal of his existing one-year contract. There were ten more games to go.

After the post-match press conference which followed the Grampus game, I took the shuttle bus from the stadium to Shizuoka Station. The bus got stuck in a traffic jam of happy fans, and as a result I managed to miss the last train back to Tokyo. This was more than usually annoying because in an earlier fit of enthusiasm I had bought a $350 return ticket to fly from Tokyo's Haneda Airport to the northern island of Hokkaido at 11.00 a.m. the next day, so I could watch Consadole Sapporo play Tokyo FC in the Japanese second division. Now at Shizuoka Station, the last local trains were leaving and the station plaza was emptying of people fast. On the pavement by the main entrance, two young men were playing the guitar and singing Bob Dylanesque dirges in Japanese, while their girlfriends sat opposite, looking on appreciatively. If the right record promoter walks out of Shizuoka Station at 11.00 p.m. on a Saturday night, these guys could be famous.

Things were looking bleak but all was not lost. As far as I could make out from the station timetable, a special night train passes through Shizuoka at 2.00 a.m. and arrives in Tokyo at about 5.00 a.m. every Sunday. This would allow me to get to the airport in time, and even to get home and take a shower on the way. I could spend $100 on half a night in a hotel, or I could hang around in moody bars and noodle joints, which certainly seemed much cooler. I decided to wait up and take the train. Besides, the Japanese like to give names to their trains and who could resist one called the Moonlight Nagara Express?

So I whiled away three hours in the mean streets around Shizuoka Station, eventually ending up drinking beer at a noodle stand under the railway arches in the hot, humid night, next to a table of nightshift railway workers in blue overalls and wellingtons. I felt like a character in a Japanese detective film. The only serious downside was the Moonlight Nagara Express, which didn't live up to its promise of romance. Instead of moonlight, there was the glare of the carriage lights exposing a gaunt-looking collection of hungover late-night revellers and day-trippers, slumped and snoring. Instead of express, we stopped at every available station, chugging through the darkness towards Tokyo. I tried to sleep, but it didn't work. It was the train of the damned.

This whole Hokkaido business was the fault of Consadole's Dutch goalkeeping coach, Dido Havenaar. When I'd first met him the previous season, Dido had inspired me with tales of packed stadiums and mass enthusiasm beneath cool, spacious northern skies, in a place where life was good, where people had space and cows had room to wander, at least when they weren't buried under feet of snow. 'It's a bit like Holland,' I seem to remember him saying, 'only with mountains.'

Consadole's moment in the sunshine of the J.League had been brief. After just one season, at the end of 1998 they had been relegated into the new second division. But in the moment of defeat, the team had managed to score a surprise late winner by recruiting Takeshi Okada as their new manager, the man who had managed the Japanese national team at the 1998 World Cup in France, and who, for one brief summer, had been one of the most famous people in Japan. So Mr Okada was another reason to travel to Hokkaido.

Eventually, in something of a daze, I arrived at Tokyo's Haneda Airport. It was packed. It always is, even at nine o'clock on a Sunday morning. Whenever you travel by air in Japan, you'll generally find at least 50,000 people with the same idea. After checking in, I made my way to the departure gate, bought some nasty Japanese instant coffee and settled down to wait for the flight, trying not to nod off and feeling vaguely nauseous.

Luckily entertainment was on hand. As I struggled to retain consciousness, a small group of fans wandered into view, clearly heading for the same plane. There were about a dozen of them, all wearing blue, red and white soccer shirts. It was the Tokyo FC away crew, dedicated travelling supporters of the club that used to be known, rather unfortunately, as Tokyo Gas, now a strong contender for promotion to the J.League's first division. I'd seen Tokyo FC fans in action before, up in the stands at the Edogawa Stadium on the east side of Tokyo, standing behind a big banner proclaiming SEXY FOOTBALL, chanting and whistling and singing 'You'll Never Walk Alone' before the start of the second half. But this was no rowdy crowd of testosterone-crazed soccer fans, out to have as much fun as possible as fast as possible with minimal regard for public order. No one in this group was talking to anyone else. 'Surely they know each other?' I thought to myself. 'At least by sight?' Instead, they looked like a sad group of lonely and shy individuals, or possibly a long line of sulky schoolchildren. I suspected that they hadn't been properly introduced. I was pleased to see that they were following a man holding a small blue and red Tokyo FC pennant and a clipboard, whom I assumed to be the tour guide. At least they had a leader.

If I'd had more than one and a half hours of sleep, I might have chatted to them, and maybe made some introductions. We could have had some fun, running up and down the aisles of the Japan Airlines 747 singing 'You'll Never Walk Alone' and drinking so much beer we got sick, and all before noon on a Sunday morning. Instead, I sat and stared out the window at another JAL plane. It had been entirely painted over with pictures of the four long-haired, slightly effete-looking members of a wildly popular boy-band called Glay, who had, just a few weeks previously, performed in front of about 50,000 screaming teenaged girls in Tokyo. 'Celebrating the tenth anniversary of the Tokyo–Hakodate Route' it said on the side of the plane. More evidence of the purchasing power of Japan's fickle youth, I thought. Back in the old days, if Japanese children had wanted to paint an airliner, they'd have had to design, build and pilot it themselves. The old codgers were right. Japanese kids had it too easy these days.

I boarded my own, conventional 747 and fell asleep, dreaming of effete long-haired Japanese pop singers in Tokyo FC shirts.

清水

During the summer of 1998, Takeshi Okada's bespectacled face had been on television pretty much every night. As Japan prepared to play Argentina, Croatia and Jamaica in their first-ever appearance in the World Cup finals, the Japanese media set out to tell the public more about Okada than they ever realised they wanted to know; about his career, and his family, and the time he'd spent in Canning Town getting his coaching licence at West Ham. Mr Okada is possibly one of the few people in Japan, or perhaps anywhere, with fond memories of Canning Town. But after all the drama of the World Cup, Okada had turned his back on the bright lights. Rather than taking a job with a big-name club, Okada opted for humble, second-division Consadole. Who better to explain the odd relationship between Japan and its national soccer team?

'The performance of the national team is one of the main forces behind the development of soccer in Japan,' I had been told by Mr Osumi, the football journalist and historian. Baseball might be the country's most popular spectator sport, but when the national soccer team plays, Japan goes entirely crazy. During the national team's three games in those World Cup finals in France, the television audience ratings were around 60 per cent, the highest for any single sporting event since the entire ratings system began.

It's not just the World Cup which pulls these big football crowds. Earlier in 1999, in the first round of Japan's qualifying campaign for the soccer competition for the 2000 Sydney Olympics, 40,000 people turned out in Tokyo to watch an Under-22 team beat the Philippines 13–1. Similar numbers turned out for games against Hong Kong and Nepal. English fans would have to be paid to watch Nepal. As for the Olympic soccer competition, well, frankly, we have better things to do.

Japan has had something of a special relationship with the Olympics – perhaps it's because those lofty Olympian sporting ideals of peace and love and the glory of taking part mirror the hopes of international pacifism and global friendship embraced by Japan's own post-war constitution; perhaps it's because, after World War Two, the Olympics provided ordinary Japanese with their first chance to cheer for their country without feeling bad about it; and perhaps it's because the staging of the 1964 Olympics in Tokyo was a hugely significant event in the development of modern Japan, the arrival of the Olympic flame symbolically marking the country's recovery from the devastation of the war and its return to the community of nations. Such was the national importance of the Tokyo Games that the Japan Football Federation decided they could not afford to risk any humiliating Philippine-esque 13–1 defeats. A German coach, Detmar Clammer, was hired to take charge of the country's young amateur players and to knock them into shape.

Herr Clammer's collection of gentlemen players and university graduates did very well indeed back in 1964, crowning their triumphant performance with an heroic 3–2 win over footballing giant Argentina, a victory that provoked nationwide celebrations. The scorer of the second goal was a youthful Saburo Kawabuchi, the man who went on to become the J.League's chairman. Mr Kawabuchi says he still considers that goal is his biggest achieve-ment. According to Mr Osumi, the national soccer team's performance galvanised the nation as never before.

After the 1964 Olympics, Japan had its first soccer boom. Soccer schools were set up all over Japan and young boys started to play football. Detmar Clammer told the JFA that they needed a national league, which led to the start of the Japan Soccer League, the JSL, in 1965, with its company-owned teams.

More Olympic glory was to follow. In the 1968 Olympics, Japan successfully made it to the final four, and managed to beat the hosts Mexico to bring home the bronze medal in the country's greatest international soccer success to date. Japan's next Olympic appearance wasn't until Atlanta in 1996 when once again the team pulled off its Latin American giant-killing act by beating Brazil 1–0.

This is the point when Mr Okada takes centre stage. At the Atlanta Olympics, and during the first stages of Japan's attempts to qualify for the 1998 World Cup finals, Mr Okada was the national team's assistant coach, working under the then manager, Shu Kamo. The pressures on Japan to qualify for the finals for the first time had been dramatically increased by FIFA's decision to award the 2002 World Cup jointly to Japan and Korea. But things didn't go well. When a disastrous away draw against Kazakhstan in the distant steppes of Central Asia left Japan on the brink of elimination, Shu Kamo suddenly resigned. Takeshi Okada had no choice but to take over the team. Eventually, with a little luck along the way, Okada steered Japan to a nail-biting 3–2 victory over Iran in a play-off game in November, in the unlikely setting of the southern Malaysian city of Johore Bahru. Japan qualified for the finals. Mr Okada became a national hero.

Dido Havenaar was right. There were indeed 17,000 people crowded into Consadole's Atsubetsu Stadium on the outskirts of Sapporo, beneath a sky that was high with fluffy white clouds. In contrast to the hot, muggy weather of Tokyo and Shimizu, everything here seemed clear and bright, especially to someone suffering from the hallucinatory effects of sleep deprivation. A cool breeze from the mountains that ringed the northern horizon blew across the stadium. Everyone I saw seemed to have healthy, ruddy, open faces, the look of people who are used to lots of healthy living. Sapporo seemed to be my kind of place. Blearily, I thought about moving there and settling down in the cool mountains to rear cows.

It turned out that this Sunday also happened to be the day of the Sapporo marathon, so the wide downtown streets were full of people looking even more exhausted than me, wearing plastic bags and wrapped in aluminium foil. But football was holding its own. At the subway station nearest to the stadium, I was confronted with a long but fast-moving queue of perhaps a hundred people, lined up in front of a folding table where a man in a subway company uniform was taking their money as fast as was humanly possible. A man with a loudspeaker was on hand to move along dawdlers and to chivvy anyone who fumbled with their change. Small groups of fans were clustered around, eagerly examining whatever it was they'd just bought, and saying things like 'Great!' and 'Wow!' in Japanese. Intrigued, I edged closer to the man with the loudspeaker and asked what all the fuss was about.

'Subway travel cards,' he said. 'For 5,000 yen. But with pictures of players.'

This was not a second-division level of enthusiasm. In fact, Consadole's average home crowds were higher than most J.League teams, including S-Pulse. There was something worrying about this. Perhaps there really is nothing else to do in Sapporo. I was beginning to review my resettlement plans.

The stadium has the obligatory athletics track running around it, which doesn't help the atmosphere, but the home fans, ranged over to my left in a mass or red and black and white, were more than compensating, with their banners trailing across the athletics track. There was the usual selection of English slogans – ULTRA SAPPORO, ATSUBETSU GOAL RUSH – and two salutes to the star local striker, twenty-two-year-old Kota Yoshihara – LOVELY SMILE KOTA and KOTA MAKES REVOLUTION. Consadole's mascot, a sort of white eagle called Doriku, was prancing up and down, flapping his wings in front of the home crowd. Doriku was actually more of an off-white colour, and looked as if he could do with a trip to the dry-cleaners but the fans didn't mind. They especially didn't mind when Doriku was joined by Consadole's high-kicking, cheerleading team, wearing glamorous red and black knee boots, who strutted around to the sounds of 'Born to be Wild'. Then the two teams ran out to start warming up. Dido Havenaar ran out with the goalkeeper, and waved to the crowd to whip up the enthusiasm. 'CONSADOLE,' thundered the appreciative fans. 'CONSADOLE!'

Then the pre-match entertainment sequence began in earnest. Eighteen ballboys ran on to the pitch in yellow and blue tracksuits. The cheerleading team lined up in front of the main stand. The loudspeakers started up again, breaking into Consadole Sapporo's unofficial anthem: 'Young man,' it went, 'doo-doo do-do-do doooh. I say, young man . . . doo-doo do-do-do dooh.' In the centre stand, on each side of me, husbands and wives and little children were all clapping in rhythm. Out on the pitch the ballboys and the cheerleaders were doing the gestures. 'Down at the WHY . . . EMM . . . SEE . . . AY!' went the loudspeaker. 'Doo-do-do-do dooh.' In my critically spaced out state, I began to smile and chuckle like a mad man in my seat, but suddenly I noticed that no one else in the press box was laughing. I tried to look more serious.

Now the teams were marching out behind the fair play banner. Mr Okada himself walked out to the touch-line, a small figure in a neat, light grey suit, followed by three television cameras. 'CONSADOLE,' screamed the fans while at the home end they held up huge letters spelling out L-I-V-E F-O-R-E-V-E-R. How much more fun could you have on a Sunday afternoon in Sapporo? It certainly seemed to beat watching marathon races. At the other end, two or three hundred away fans, hopefully including my tour group from the plane unless they'd got lost on the way, were looking a little overwhelmed, ranged defiantly behind their SEXY FOOTBALL banner.

The match was a marked improvement on the last time I'd seen Consadole play a few weeks earlier, against Montedio Yamagata. (One of the joys of the Japanese second division is that the teams have an entirely new selection of totally wacky names to compete with the admittedly high standards set by the first-division competition. Amused by first-division Kyoto Purple Sanga? Try second-division Albirex Niigata. Tickled by Avispa Fukuoka?

Switch to Oita Trinita. You think Nagoya Grampus Eight is a strange name for a football club? Then try Ventforet Kofu, Sagan Tosu and Vegalta Sendai.)

Most of the second-division clubs are based outside Tokyo in smaller industrial towns and cities that are a long way from the nearest baseball team. Yamagata, lying in the mountains about 200 miles north of Tokyo, is surrounded by ski resorts, while the plain around the town is covered with apple orchards and vineyards. Yamagata is linked to Tokyo by a special mini Shinkansen train, called the Tsubasa, which winds its way at rather less than bullet speed up the side of mountains and through tunnels to the city. Montedio — named in honour of a nearby sacred Buddhist mountain shrine — plays at the Yamagata track and field stadium, which is modern and new and unhelpfully located in fields several miles north of the town centre, surrounded by yet more apple orchards and a vast, empty car park.

Presumably sometimes the Yamagata track and field stadium is filled to its 20,000 capacity, perhaps when teenage-heartthrob, effete boy-bands come to play open air concerts in the summer. That night, I could hear the fans chanting from the car park, but when I emerged at the side of the pitch, they had all disappeared. I was looking at a floodlit pitch surrounded by empty stands, as if the crowd I'd heard a few minutes earlier had all been abducted by aliens. The entire opposite side of the stadium was empty. So were the two ends behind the goals. Then I realised. They were behind me. In an effort to create something of a sociable atmosphere, the 4,000 crowd had been packed into the main stand. The pitch was perhaps fifty yards away.

It was a dreadful game. Consadole eventually managed to beat the home side, but I forgot to write down the score. It didn't seem to matter. This was football dangerously close to the point where everyone could suddenly decide that the whole thing was a waste of time and head for home, like an English fourth-division match in November when it's raining, although a crowd of 4,000 like this one would be good going for the fourth division. Undeterred by the dismal lack of action on the distant pitch, the home crowd's hardline supporters, about 200 of them, kept up a relentless and mind-numbing drum beat throughout the ninety minutes to the tune of Gary Glitter's 'Rock 'n' Roll Part One' except that the words went 'MON-TE-DI-I-I-O, MON-TE-DI-I-I-O' repeated over and over and over again. Because there was nothing better to do, I calculated the rate of drum beats per minute, and found that it was averaging around 200. If you multiply that by ninety, you get 18,000. It was that sort of a match. The only bright spot was the referee who was so bad that he threw the home fans into something of a frenzy and they hurled guttural rustic abuse at him as he left the field.

Consadole's stadium is football heaven in comparison, and the game was a cracker. Tokyo FC, who were pushing for promotion into the first division, opened up by hitting Consadole's post twice, provoking anxious, high-pitched, rising 'Ahhh!' noises from the home fans, half hysterical scream, half orgasmic shout. Tokyo went one goal ahead with five minutes of the first half remaining, only for Consadole to equalise four minutes later.

Every time Consadole had a corner or a free-kick at the other end, the whole stadium started chanting, 'GOA-RU! GOA-RU!' as one, with all the supporters in the main stands cheering and banging their plastic clappers together. This was crowd participation on a level which even exceeded what I'd seen in Shimizu, where the shouting and singing are usually restricted to the end behind the goal. People in the centre stands tend to restrict themselves to quiet harrumphing and teeth-sucking and the occasional shout. If you were to take away the running track, Consadole's Atsubetsu Stadium could be Japan's San Siro, a boiling cauldron of sound which would strike fear into any opposition.

Eventually, with the crowd screaming him on, Consadole's Portuguese striker, Roberto de Assis, put them ahead. Then with five minutes to go, the home team's nineteen-year-old forward, Kawamura, made it three, with a spectacular strike from outside the area which smashed in off the underside of the bar. Assis made it four, blasting a thirty-metre free-kick into the back of the Tokyo FC net, beating the wall and the goalkeeper. It was a good day for the home fans and a good day for life in the second division.

After the game, I caught up with Mr Okada, who ushered me past his adoring fans, first into the team bus and then into his car, which he drove at breakneck speed to a downtown hotel. For a quiet guy in a grey suit, Okada certainly liked to motor. He complained that that was one of the problems of being the national manager. Everyone started to tell him he should use a driver and sit in the back, like the chairman of a big corporation. 'But I like to drive myself,' he said, as we narrowly swept through a changing traffic light. I asked him why he'd chosen Consadole.

'Consadole is a young team, so I can do everything myself. And I like Hokkaido. I like nature, and the people here are very kind. Plus economically, Hokkaido is having a very hard time now and Consadole gives them hope. If Consadole do well and get promoted to the first division, it will make people here very happy. The club is a symbol.'

Clearly the team was big in Sapporo. So was Okada. At his post-game press conference there'd been six television cameras and perhaps two dozen reporters, all hanging on his every word, while a squad of photographers tried to work out new ways of taking a picture of a man in a grey suit and glasses sitting behind a table.

'In Sapporo, I am more famous than the prime minister of Japan,' he said, at least partially in jest. 'Normally at second division J.League news conferences, there is maybe one camera. In Hokkaido, we get more.'

But did he miss the drama of being national coach?

'I was national coach for only one year. That was a special experience for me. But my work here, this is normal. Being the national coach now seems a long, long time ago. I would *never* go back to the JFA,' he added, with evident feeling. 'I don't like it. The national coach has no real involvement in player development. And too much pressure on my family, that was another reason I didn't like it. Japanese newspaper and magazine reporters don't ask about football. They ask about my salary. They ask about my relationship with individual players. They ask about my family. I can't face it.' He shook his head in dismay at the awfulness of it all. 'They think I am a football coach and that is the same as a movie star. But it is different.'

There is indeed not much to distinguish the media hysteria surrounding football and its handsome young stars from the blanket coverage of Japan's pop idols, the *idoru*, the stars of bands like Glay who are created by the country's entertainment industry and whose popularity often has more to do with marketing than it does with talent.

'Many young good players, they have ability and potential, but they are brought down by the media,' Mr Okada continued. 'For example, in our team, Consadole, we have Kota Yoshihara. He is only twenty-two years old but in Sapporo he's on the front page of the newspaper every day, and everyone is saying "Kota! Kota! Kota!" He drives a Porsche. And he gets money from advertising. So it is very hard for young players.'

'Look at me. I was forty-two years old when we beat Iran and qualified for the World Cup. When I heard everyone saying, "Okada! Okada! Okada!" I used to go back home and look at myself in the mirror, and ask myself, "So. What happened? Have I become better than I was?" And of course the answer is no. It's very difficult for a young player to keep his head. It's a Japanese problem. All the foreign coaches have found it to be a big problem here.'

Shimizu S-Pulse had been subjected to their share of media hysteria the previous season, when Mr Okada named Shimizu's attacking full-back, Daisuke Ichikawa, in the national squad for France. Ichikawa is a gangly, mop-headed kid who also happens to tackle like a ton of bricks and run like a train. That year he was just about to turn eighteen. His boyish, innocent looks make him ideal media material, and for a few weeks, the whole of Japan wanted to be his mother. Perryman-san, then assistant manager to Ardiles, travelled with Ichikawa to Tokyo on the train after he'd been named for the national squad.

'It was amazing,' he said. 'There were photographers and cameras when we left the training ground to go to Shizuoka Station. There were photographers at the station and on the platform and when we got to Tokyo, they were waiting to meet us. They followed us to the hotel. I'd never seen anything like it.' In the weeks before the World Cup, Ichikawa was surrounded after each match by a moving block of television crews and cameramen, asking him question after question about pretty much everything.

'Well, a lot of people who'd never been particularly interested in me started coming and talking to me,' said Ichikawa, looking back on it all a year later after training one day. 'It was wonderful to be in the national team, but at the same time it was a bit confusing. My parents were worried about me.' Ichikawa is a player who wants to improve. 'I always watch European football on television, and I buy the soccer magazines. I admire that style of football, with its technique. I want to get better, and then go to Europe.'

The problem, according to Mr Okada and others, is that all this media attention in the majority of cases breeds complacency. Japanese stars find themselves appearing in the glossy weekly soccer magazines, next to profiles of Michael Owen or Ronaldo or Dennis Bergkamp. After a while, they start to think they're as good as Owen or Ronaldo or Bergkamp.

'All young players should go to Europe now,' says René Desaeyere, the Cerezo Osaka coach, 'but they just don't care because here they are spoilt. They have many good young players – twenty-one years old, or twenty-two, many young players. But they need to make another step if they want to get better. And they are not going to do it. Here they think they're big stars. But they should all go outside Japan so they know what's really going on.'

Back in May, I'd travelled north from Tokyo to the Japan Football Association's J.Village training facility in Fukushima Prefecture, to have a look at Japan's best young soccer stars preparing to play for the Under-22 national Olympic team.

The J.Village was worth a visit in itself. Purpose-built at a cost of $100 million, it was opened in 1997. It has ten full-sized grass pitches, two of them floodlit, and a small stadium with 5,000 seats. It has one full-sized pitch with an artificial surface and a 400 metre running track, plus five half-sized artificial pitches, an indoor gym and swimming pool, and an indoor arena. It's built pretty much in the middle of nowhere, so the planners threw in a hotel and lodge which can accommodate around 250 people, a 160 seat auditorium, a cafeteria and the Moonrise coffee bar. When there's no football going on, the J.Village doubles up as a convention centre and a venue for weddings, presumably with a romantic reception afterwards at the Moonrise coffee bar.

Next to the cafeteria on the ground floor, there's a small football museum. You might wonder what the Japanese Football Association could put in a small football museum, and the answer is not much. There's a FIFA fair play award from the 1968 Mexico Olympics, and another one from UNESCO for the World 1994 Youth Soccer Championships; there's a plate signed by the 1964 Olympic team; there are a couple of football shirts from the 1998 World Cup; plus a number of highly technical video games which don't really have much to do with actually playing football. I didn't think it was worth the 300 yen I'd paid to get in. I decided against buying any J.Village memorabilia, such as a tin of J.Village biscuits or a J.Village phonecard. After all, I already had my Paru-chan biscuits and my Paru-chan phonecard.

The money to build all this came not from the Japan Football Association, but from the Tokyo Electric Power Company, TEPCO, which happens to own the adjacent Hirano oil-fired power station. The massive concrete chimneys tower over the J.Village site. TEPCO also operates the nuclear power plants at Tomioka, five miles up the road. TEPCO says the J.Village was just a way of saying thank you to a prefecture which uses about a quarter of Tokyo's electricity, in line with the company's stated policy of 'co-existence with the local community'. Sceptics suggested the offer to build the J.Village was linked to TEPCO's simultaneous push for permission to build two new reactors at the adjacent nuclear plant.

Either way, the J.Village was built, and if anything ever melts down in Fukushima, Japan's national team will be the first to know about it. Every time the national teams train there, the Tokyo press corps has to make the long journey into the deep north, although it's actually rather pleasant. From Tokyo's Ueno Station, the delightfully named Fresh Hitachi Express runs along the coast towards Sendai, through a landscape of green hills and woods and paddy fields and nuclear power stations.

When I arrived at the J.Village on a rainy midweek afternoon, I found I wasn't alone. The presence of the national Under-22 team had attracted a handful of dedicated young women who were hanging around the public areas in the lobby, hoping to catch sight of their favourite stars. By the time the team took to a rain-sodden training pitch adjacent to the main building, the crowd in the public viewing area was perhaps 200 strong, most of them armed with cameras.

The media turnout was even more impressive. As the Under-22s practised corner kicks, there were more than sixty reporters and photographers in attendance, and seven television cameras were trained on the pitch. Mr Okada's French successor, Philippe Troussier, who is around six feet tall, was running about in a black and white Adidas tracksuit, with his French to Japanese translator in hot pursuit. S-Pulse's Toda was there, with his short brown summer haircut, and so was Ichikawa. Troussier was with the forwards, physically pushing and shoving them, as the corner kicks came in. 'Leeetle bit more, leeetle bit more,' he was shouting in English. 'Mo chotto, mo chotto,' shouted his translator, as the cameras rolled.

At the end of the training session, the players trooped off to be interviewed by the media and to sign autographs for the fans, who shouted the players' names as they walked past. This was just the tip of the iceberg of Japanese national team support. Most of these supporters, as far as I could make out, were fans of the individual players whose autographs they craved. But when Japan play both at home and away, they draw a dedicated army of supporters, led by the Ultra Nippon hardcore supporters' group. Ultra Nippon was at the forefront of the tens of thousands of Japanese fans who travelled to France for the World Cup in 1998, leading the long, steady chants of 'NIIII-PON, NIIII-PON' and waving the light blue polythene rubbish bags that have become the hallmark of the national team supporters. Japan may not have won a match at the World Cup, but the Japanese fans certainly impressed the world with their garbage-handling skills.

Like any self-respecting Japanese supporters' group, the Ultra Nippon have a leader. The current boss is Asahi Ueda, aged twenty-seven, who works at a sports shop in the Sendagaya area of Shibuya in Tokyo, on the other side of the railway tracks from the National Stadium.

'There's no organisation in the Ultra Nippon,' he claimed when I met him at the shop one afternoon. 'It is, uhhh . . . a movement.'

'So you travel to see Japan play?' I said, provocatively.

'Uzbekistan, Kazakhstan,' he said, obviously beginning with the easy ones, 'UAE two times, Saudi Arabia, Italia for training camp, Spain for training camp, Korea two times, Malaysia and Johore Bahru for World Cup qualifier and for Under-20 World Youth Games. Also Thailand three times. And Paraguay. And France.' He was losing track, and called for help from some other Ultra Nippon adherents.

'South Korea,' said one.

'UAE three times,' said another. 'And Oman.'

'The United States,' said another.

'Mmmh?' said Asahi, the boss, looking a little uncertain.

'Atlanta,' he said, 'Olympics.'

'Ahh,' he said, 'United States. Atlanta Olympics. I forgot.'

'Qatar?' I said, recalling the scene of the great disaster, 1993.

'Ah yes,' he said, 'Qatar.'

Dedicated European fans might make a few trips to Rome or London or Stockholm, but Japanese national team fans are in a frequent-flying category all of their own. For the forthcoming Olympic qualifiers, one company was offering supporters a trip to see the away game against Kazakhstan in Almaty on what was advertised as a three days no nights basis. The lucky fans were to leave Japan on a Friday, travel overnight to the game on Saturday, and leave immediately so they could get back to Japan on Sunday in time for work on Monday. This tour was reportedly quite popular.

In 1998, before the World Cup, I'd met a Japanese couple who were due to get married on a Saturday in June. It turned out to be the same day Japan was to play Argentina. Undeterred, the husband brought his friends over to the luxury hotel wedding suite to watch the game, which started around midnight in Japan. The happy couple then went off on their honeymoon to France, so that they could watch the games against Croatia and Jamaica. When I met them a year later, they were perhaps remarkably still married, and the wife said it had been all quite lovely, apart from a nasty outbreak of rioting in Marseille.

I asked Mr Okada why he thought Japan, a baseball-playing nation, could get so comprehensively fired up over their national soccer team. After all, I argued, it doesn't happen in America where soccer has the same sort of limited popularity it has in Japan. This was something he'd thought about before.

'We have a bit of a complex about nationalism,' he said straightaway, 'and football is a way of beating this complex. For young people, when they come to the football stadium with the national team, they find their identity in the stadium in a way which is not possible in normal life.'

In the past, the Japanese may have succeeded in wrapping up the problematic relationship between nationalism and sport in the security blanket of Olympic idealism. But football, that most nationalistic of all sports, brings to the surface issues of patriotism and nationalism which still make the officially peace-loving Japanese uneasy. That summer of '99, the ruling conservative Liberal Democratic Party finally passed legislation which officially recognised the *hinomaru* flag, the red disk on a white background, as Japan's official flag, in the face of opposition from left-wingers who saw this as a step towards Japan abandoning its post-World War Two pacifist constitution. Japanese sports teams might have been using the *hinomaru* flag at international sports events since the 1950s, the flag might hang outside the United Nations, and the rest of the world might not have realised there was a problem, but constitutionally the *hinomaru* flag was technically a strictly unofficial national symbol and a subject of controversy. Fierce battles have raged between right-wing groups and left-wing teachers over whether to raise the flag at school graduation ceremonies. Earlier in the year, a headmaster in Hiroshima who was entangled in one of these disputes had taken his own life.

Similarly, when Japan played in the World Cup finals, before each game the band played the mournful tones of the *kimigayo*, Japan's then unofficial national anthem. The anthem praises the emperor. 'You have "God Save the Queen",' the Marinos dissident Kazu Miyazaki told me when we met in March in the Shinagawa Denny's. 'Why shouldn't we sing the *kimigayo*?' The same legislation that approved the *hinomaru* flag also finally recognised the *kimigayo* as the official national anthem, despite the protests of left-wingers who said it was associated with pre-war militarism and emperor worship. When the *kimigayo* is played in the stadium, it echoes in a ghostly kind of way, and it's very hard to hear anyone actually singing it. Kazu Miyazaki, on the other hand, says he began a campaign to get Japanese fans to sing along back in 1993. He used to sing it all on his own, banging a drum at the same time, which probably led a lot of people to move quietly away from him.

For the *kimigayo*, like the *hinomaru*, is a sensitive subject. When a Japanese punk rocker, Kiyoshiro Imawano, released a loud and obnoxious version of the *kimigayo* with his band Little Screaming Revue in August 1999, his original record company refused to release it and Japanese radio stations refused to play it, fearing attacks by right-wing extremists who still think the emperor is god despite being repeatedly told that this is not, in fact, the case.

'I don't like *kimigayo* because the arrangement is gloomy and the words incomprehensible,' Imawano told the press. 'But I don't mean any disrespect. I only wanted to make the anthem rock. But they are too scared to play it.'

'When you're picked for the national team, as a player you wouldn't think twice about singing *kimigayo*,' says the J.League's Mr Kawabuchi of the anthem issue, 'or about the *hinomaru* flag. I think it's a general characteristic of soccer that it is involved in national feeling. And now in Japan no other sport attracts such crowds. So I guess you could say that soccer is connected to our national identity. But that's something very different from the militarism and patriotism that we had during the war years. I think it's a good kind of national awareness. These days, watching soccer may be the only time when people think about their nationality.'

Sports journalist Takeo Goto remembers being surprised when he went to Malaysia for the key 1997 game against Iran, and saw so many Japanese flags among the crowd, alongside the blue binliners.

'It was probably the first time that so many Japanese flags had been taken to that region since the Japanese military invasion in 1942,' he told a local newspaper. 'The young probably don't associate the flag and the anthem with the dark implication of the past. For them, it's just another way of cheerleading.'

Japan's star midfielder and renowned free-thinker, twenty-two-year-old Hidetoshi Nakata, caused something of a row when he was seen not singing the *kimigayo* during the World Cup qualifying rounds. 'I think it's unfashionable, depressing and not the kind of song to sing before going on to the field,' he told the press afterwards. But when it came to the finals in France, with the blue binbags of the Ultra Nippon flying in the breeze, orange-haired Hidetoshi was singing along with the rest.

清水

13 IDORU

S-Pulse continued to play well, winning the magic four out of the next five games. Then the J.League broke off to allow the Olympic team to concentrate on the supreme national task of beating Kazakhstan and Thailand to qualify for the Sydney Games. On the last Saturday before the break, S-Pulse beat Verdy Kawasaki and went to the top of the league, one point ahead of the Yokohama F Marinos. Things were looking good at S-Pulse. But the F Marinos still had that F, despite the best efforts of Kazu Miyazaki. Things had, however, moved forwards. After the public meetings earlier in the summer on the steps of the Yokohama International Stadium, Kazu and his dissidents had set up a group entirely dedicated to continuing the struggle.

'It's called the Supporters' Society to save Marinos and Japanese Football Culture,' Izumi-san told me when I met her at Shinagawa Station. We were on our way to a full meeting of the new society in Kazu's flat. (This in itself was yet another sign of Kazu's very untraditional and somewhat revolutionary approach to life – Japanese people very rarely invite anyone into their houses, let alone organise meetings in their front room.)

'That's where Kazu used to live,' said Izumi as we walked along, pointing to a building site surrounded by a high fence. 'He lived in a very old apartment building,' she explained. 'But they knocked it down, and so now he lives over there,' she pointed across to a huge apartment block over by the river. 'On the twenty-ninth floor.'

After stopping at a convenience store to stock up on soft drinks and snacks, we entered the lobby of the low-income housing block and took the lift. On the way up to the twenty-ninth floor, I noticed that the residents had very kindly placed four or five traditional fans on the handrail of the non air-conditioned lift, for the cooling convenience of lift-users.

Five or six people had already arrived and were sitting around Kazu's somewhat chaotic front room, including Kikuchi-san, who had the Nissan van with the television, and a young couple who were cuddling on the couch. Kazu himself was sitting on the floor by a low table, eating a take-out pizza. A collection of football shirts adorned the walls, like washing hung out to dry. One was from the Marinos' captain, Ihara, given to Kazu after they won the 1995 J.League championship. An Argentinian national team shirt was signed by Gustavo Miguel Zapata, who had played for Marinos for three seasons, and there was a Club Atletico del Rio Plata shirt from the occasion when they played in Tokyo.

'Ah,' said Kazu, as he saw me inspecting his miniature figurine of Peter Schmeichel. 'There are a lot of memories here in these things.'

The most spectacular thing was the view from the window. Kazu Miyazaki has perhaps one of the best views in the whole of Tokyo. From the balcony of his modest flat, you can look out on the lights of Tokyo's high-level Rainbow suspension bridge, sweeping traffic up over the Sumida River, where the tugs and small freighters churn along in the darkness, over to the bright lights of the futuristic office blocks of O-Daiba on the other side. A small subway train was edging its way up on to the bridge; ahead, the navigation lights of a plane making its final approach into Haneda Airport winked red and white in the night sky. It was a vast, awe-inspiring panorama of metropolitan density, of housing and office blocks packed with people in one of the world's great mega-cities.

It made me even more of a fan of Kazu Miyazaki. How could he, every morning, look out at a view that showed him the immensity of modern Tokyo, the huge vastness of the status quo, and carry on with this crazy campaign? It reminded me of another tale in the Ivan Morris book about Japan's love affair with noble failure. Yoshitsune Minamoto's dismal performance in the twelfth century had been matched in the nineteenth in the years before the Meiji Restoration by an unfortunate Confucian scholar called Oshio Heihachiro. He had attempted to organise a revolt in Osaka at the height of a massive famine. The revolt, wrote Morris, turned into an unmitigated fiasco. 'But,' he went on, 'there is another type of hero in the complex Japanese tradition. He is the man whose single-minded sincerity will not allow him to make the manoeuvres and compromises that are so often needed for the sake of mundane success.'

In the pursuit of single-minded sincerity, Kazu's new football culture club had decided to take their campaign against the F Marinos right to the top. Kazu was writing a letter to Carlos Ghosn, the chief executive of Nissan. Within a few months of his appointment earlier in the year, Ghosn announced the most dramatic corporate restructuring scheme seen in Japan since the country was bombed flat by the Americans – 20,000 jobs would go and five Nissan factories were to be closed down. But Monsieur Ghosn still hadn't clarified his views on the F issue. Ambitiously, the letter was in French. Unfortunately, it was also completely incomprehensible, despite having been translated by a friend of a friend of Kazu, who claimed to be a French teacher. I set about making things at least a little clearer, aware that my involvement would not look good if the whole thing eventually ended in violent hostage taking, or a rocket attack. But in the end, more or less, after about half an hour at the computer, Monsieur Miyazaki sent Monsieur Ghosn his most sincere and humble salutations, and asked him to clarify his intentions with regard to the club, while seeking to highlight the current problems with the existing management who had continued to disregard the fans.

So Kazu Miyazaki, the exiled leader of all the Marinos fans, the Che Guevara of the anti-merger struggle, was sticking to his guns. Or was he? Kazu, it seemed, had modified his ideological position in the tradition of all great revolutionaries, to adapt to political realities. The initial campaign had, he explained, mainly been focused on consciousness raising. But now the Save the Marinos society had established four new critical campaign objectives.

'First,' he said, 'is to support the Marinos as the Marinos and not the F Marinos. And to let the players know that we support them as Marinos, but not as the F Marinos. Second, is to write letters to some of the players, so they understand. Third, is to keep the campaign going against the club management because otherwise they will think they have won. And fourth, is to explain all this to the ordinary supporters.'

Phase two had already started. Kazu said that a letter had been smuggled to a Marinos player through another friend of a friend, explaining this new position. The letter asked the players to say whether they accepted the fact that some supporters were supporting them as Marinos and not F Marinos. Who knows what the players would have made of it had they seen it. The letter ended up in the hands of the management; the unofficial conduit had been neutralised. So Kazu decided on direct action. Latest intelligence indicated that the Marinos' nationally renowned goalkeeper, Yoshikatsu Kawaguchi, who kept goal for Japan during the World Cup, would be taking the train to Osaka for the All Stars game at the end of July. Kazu decided on an intercept. The target was supposed to be taking the train at 8.23 a.m. from Shin-Yokohama Station. Kazu, wearing a smart suit, was in position at 7.40. The target arrived on schedule. Kazu made his move.

'I walked up to him,' Kazu recounted to the eager circle of fans gathered in his front room, 'and I said, very politely, "Excuse me, are you Mr Kawaguchi?" He said he was, and when he looked at me I said, "I am a supporter. My name is Kazu Miyazaki." And he was astounded.'

It was a potentially tense moment, given Kazu's formidable reputation as an activist of the terraces. Luckily, Kawaguchi was not so astounded as to call the police.

'I explained that I was going to buy some chicken in Nagoya,' said Kazu. He thought this would put the young goalkeeper at ease. 'And then we started talking about football and the Marinos. The train arrived and we got on together.'

If Kawaguchi was hoping to snooze quietly in his first-class carriage all the way to Osaka, it was not to be. According to Kazu, they chatted about this and that, standing in the corridor of the Shinkansen train, all the way to Nagoya, which is about an hour and a half from Yokohama. Kazu tried to explain his problems.

'When I told him about the letter, he said he was very happy to know that there were supporters who cared so much about the Marinos,' said Kazu, getting a little emotional. 'I was touched. In fact, I almost cried. And at the end, he said he'd do his best to get the Marinos back.'

The fans in the front room nodded, clearly quietly impressed. Kazu had scaled the mountain and returned to tell the tale.

It was a strange and weird story, and one which once again proved that Kazu Miyazaki is capable of anything. But at the same time, I realised that the new campaign objectives represented a move away from absolutist rejection of the merged team. Consciously or not, Kazu and the Pirates were preparing the ground for a bid to return to the centre of the Marinos supporters' group, and to oust the illegitimate upstart, Mr Okayama and his Yokohama Big Shout boys.

I thought the whole Kawaguchi story was encouraging. For Kawaguchi was one of the super-heroes of Japanese soccer, whose performance in the net at the 1998 World Cup had earned him the gratitude of the nation. Yet here he was, taking time out to talk to a fanatical supporter whose ideas might be regarded as a little offbeat. It was nice to know he was still travelling without personal bodyguards.

After the World Cup, Kawaguchi had traded the youthful mop haircut that had won hearts across Japan for something spikier, and he'd taken to sporting trendy stubble. He was endorsing an energy drink, and was assumed to be making money. It is, however, not so easy for a Japanese star to turn his fame into hard cash. Japanese footballers sign contracts which require them to pay around 70 per cent of any profits from advertising work to the club, against around 20–30 per cent in Europe. This holds even if the player is shown sitting at home in front of the television, or playing golf, and it's something that annoys Robert Maes of IMG.

'If you're a player in Japan, you're controlled very strongly by your club,' he complained to me in his office one day. 'On endorsements, the percentage that goes to the club reaches criminal levels.' In the transfer market, he explained, conditions were equally Dickensian. 'A player might want to leave the club, but he will have to work within the system. He needs to get the club's approval first. If a player goes against the system . . . well, you might not want to say that they can break his career, but they can certainly cause problems.'

In the J.League, as in the professional baseball leagues, the players are treated pretty much as the property of the club for which they first sign. In October, for example, at S-Pulse, Perryman's decision to play Ichikawa as attacking right midfielder in place of Masahiro Ando, which had caused so much anxiety among the fans, eventually led to Jubilo Iwata approaching S-Pulse and expressing an interest in buying Ando. The club initially turned down the offer, without consulting either Ando or Perryman-san, leading to something of a scene when the disconsolate Ando found out what had happened. Eventually, Ando was transferred. Like salarymen in a traditional Japanese company, joining a club can almost be a commitment for life, or at least for a playing career. Most players are on yearly contracts with the average player making about 25 million yen ($270,000) annually. But if a player isn't happy and wants a transfer, it's not easy. Only a handful have their own agents. All transfers are arranged by mutual agreement among the mafia of general managers who control the J.League clubs and who have links with agents who work the high-school system picking up new talent. Transparency is not always a feature of these transactions.

'You can't just buy a player,' said Sanfrecce's Eddie Thomson. 'I might want to buy a player, but if the general manager says no, we don't want to release him, that's the end of it. I'm not allowed to contact the player directly. The players have got no choice but to stay where they are. If they want to move, or cause trouble, other clubs don't want them. But players have got to be able to move. It would make it much fairer.'

It's a closed system which flourishes because the players have nowhere else to go outside the J.League.

'Where does a Japanese player go? To Korea?' asks Robert Maes. 'There's nowhere else to go in Asia where they can play at this level and make the same money. But a French player can go to Germany, or to England, or anywhere in Europe.'

There are signs that this system is beginning to break down. Over in the world of professional baseball, a handful of agents have set up shop, trying to pick Japanese players who could make it big with clubs in the United States. It's a microcosm of what's happening to the whole Japanese economy, as foreign competition begins to break down the old cosy system, theoretically to the advantage of the consumers or, in this case, the players.

In baseball, the pitcher Hideo Nomo became the ultimate career model for Japanese professional players after his outstanding success with the LA Dodgers in 1996. Soccer has its own Nomo – Hidetoshi Nakata, then in his second season with Perugia in the Italian *Serie A* league. Nakata may have been absent, but he was always on my mind – and on everyone else's. Back in May, I picked up a copy of the *Sankei Sports* newspaper from outside my local convenience store. My attention had been caught by a big, colour, front-page picture of Japan's favorite national midfielder, wearing a smart grey jacket and dark glasses. 'NAKATA' screamed the headline in big blue-coloured Japanese characters. 'TWO BILLION YEN' it howled in yellow and red. 'Perugia will sell' it said in between, in smaller yellow and blue, 'to Bologna'.

Well, in fact, Perugia didn't sell Nakata to Bologna; nor did they sell him to Barcelona or Manchester United (although later in the season the did sell him to Roma). But that didn't stop the colourful Japanese sports tabloids from writing about him at every available opportunity. For Nakata is more than just a football player. He is the pride of the new Japan, the hope for the future, the thinking Japanese footballer, a player whose brilliance and creativity smash all the stereotypes about Japanese players being lazy, complacent automatons who are entirely unable to think for themselves.

'Nakata,' said Mr Okada in Hokkaido, 'is a player who can take responsibility. He can make up his own mind.'

'You know,' Nakata told the press before the World Cup, 'in Japan people tend to suppress originality and uniqueness in an individual. And it's not part of our traditional virtues to stand up for yourself. So that's maybe why I appear different.'

Nakata first burst into the national consciousness in 1997 as he led Japan's push to qualify for the World Cup, excelling in the famous game against Iran. He was subsequently voted Asian Footballer of the Year for 1997. The following year, his 144-page book, *Nakata Speaks*, became a national bestseller, while his masterful and self-confident World Cup performance in midfield held Japan together and guaranteed his position as a fully fledged national institution.

After the World Cup, Nakata became the first Japanese player since Okudera in the 1980s to succeed in Europe, joining Perugia for $3 million and scoring two goals against Juventus in his first game. In 1998, he was voted Asian Footballer of the Year for the second time.

With his dyed hair and his stubble and his trendy imitation spectacles, the Japanese media and the Japanese people were prepared to love Nakata to death. But Nakata wasn't about to let them. He has maintained a frosty relationship with the Japanese media. In his occasional press conferences, he's dismissive of questions that don't have much to do with football. He has an agency in Tokyo to represent him, called Sunny Side Up. It's run by Ezuko Tsugihara and her assistant, Mina Fujita. Along the way, Nakata has become the role model for a new generation of young Japanese.

'I think he's become basically Japan's hero,' said Mina Fujita when I met her at the Sunny Side Up office in Tokyo. She showed me a file stuffed with Nakata press clippings. 'We always say that he's got the weight of the nation on his shoulders. And he's very, very independent, and he's very mature, and he's very sure of his opinions, and that's unusual for a Japanese.' It did seem rather startling.

'He doesn't play football because he wants to be famous,' she continued. 'He plays football because he wants to be good at football, and he's so good that it sparked his fame. But he doesn't think that being a football player makes him a star, in the way that the Japanese expect.' Even more astounding. No wonder he left the country.

But the Japanese fame machine carries on regardless. You can go to Italy, Hide, but you can't hide. There were thirty Japanese reporters and camera crew in Perugia for his first game; half that number are stationed there on permanent Nakata watch throughout the season. Around 1,500 Japanese tourists used to attend every home game in Perugia, doing wonders for tourism in an otherwise sleepy region of Umbria.

'Perugia used to be hardly known at all here,' said Mina. 'Now it's a household name.'

Each time Nakata comes back from Italy, there are on average fifty photographers waiting to meet him at the airport. 'It would be impossible for Nakata to have lived an ordinary life in Japan after the World Cup,' said Mina.

Nakata can sometimes seem too good to be true, although I have to confess that I am a true believer. While giving the Japanese media a hard time, he's set up his own home page, which he kept updated during the World Cup, so that he can communicate directly with his fans. During the World Cup, according to Mina Fujita, Nakata's home page was getting 2.5 million hits a day. What the fans get is perhaps not that amazing. After all, Nakata is just a footballer. But he does think. In October, for example, readers of Hide's home page were treated to his views on the Japanese media hysteria surrounding Perugia's game against Venezia, when for the first time in the history of the world two Japanese players appeared on opposing teams in a European football game (with Venezia fielding Nanami, freshly acquired from Jubilo). It was as if two British blokes were squaring off in the great spring sumo tournament. The Japanese media went crazy. But Hide wasn't impressed.

'To me,' he wrote, 'the match is important for one reason, and one reason alone. Perugia suffered a defeat in our last match, and it's crucial that we win against Venezia. End of story. If the camera crews were a regular fixture at all of our practices, I'd accept. Yet here we are . . . and suddenly the Japanese media behaves as if it's Mardi Gras. Makes me wonder if they ever think about the rationality of their actions.'

Perugia won the clash with Venezia 2–1, played in heavy rain. Nakata was named most valued player in the game. Then, to young Hide's evident exasperation, the Italian press got in on the act, asking him how he felt about the first-ever European game involving two Japanese players. This, he told his cyber fans, just shows that Japanese players are not yet fully accepted in Italy. What did nationality matter? It was the football that mattered.

All this, of course, makes him an even more attractive commercial property. Nakata's endorsements are sparing and selective; in 1999, he was backing Subaru cars, the Asahi Eau+ energy drink (cashing in on the water boom) and Fila sports shoes, with a bit of work on the side for DirecTV, the satellite network that was broadcasting every one of Perugia's *Serie A* games live in Japan. The presence of Nakata in Italy also more than tripled the value of television rights to *Serie A* in Japan, from around £3.5 million to around £12 million.

Hidetoshi Nakata is probably a very rich young man by now; but, like the tamagotchi virtual pet, there are risks in having a boom, especially when it's your own boom. In 1996, when Nakata played in the Olympic team in Atlanta, he shared his hotel room with the team captain, Masakiyo Maezono, who at the time was Japan's most famous footballer. Maezono was the first soccer player to be represented by the Sunny Side Up agency, and it was through Maezono that Nakata made contact with the agency when he was playing for Bellmare Hiratsuka.

But after the successes of 1996, Maezono's footballing career took a turn for the worse; some commentators argue that he started to believe all the hype, and became complacent. He was dropped from the national team after a disagreement with the manager, Shu Kamo, and he was dropped by the media like a hot brick.

'Japanese fans are very quick to get bored,' says Mina Fujita. 'Like when the J.League started. And that's what is scary about stardom in Japan. A player can be as good as he always was from the beginning, and then suddenly find no one is interested any more. It requires a lot of character to be able to cope. To be put on a pedestal, then dropped. It can destroy a player.'

In 1998, Maezono had gone to play in Brazil for Santos. After that season he'd been reported heading for somewhere in Portugal. He was last heard of heading for PAOK Salonika in northern Greece. Japan hardly noticed.

There is one other footballer in Japan whose fame might rival that of Hidetoshi Nakata. Nakata would have been just three when Ozoro Tsubasa first took to the field in 1981 as a twelve-year-old player for a local boys team called Nankatsu, based somewhere in Shizuoka Prefecture. Over the next six years, Captain Tsubasa, as he became known, rose through the ranks of Japan's youth system to become one of the most famous figures in Japanese footballing history.

'In elementary schools in Japan now, they have more soccer instead of baseball,' says the J.League's chairman, Saburo Kawabuchi, 'and one of the reasons is Captain Tsubasa.'

'The performance of the national team is one of two factors behind the development of soccer in Japan,' says football journalist Mr Osumi. 'The other is Captain Tsubasa.'

Captain Tsubasa's footballing adventures are featured in thirty-six volumes of *manga* cartoons created by an artist called Takahashi Yoichi. Between 1979 and 1986, the weekly adventures of Captain Tsubasa appeared in the big thick weekly *manga* anthologies which are standard reading for Japanese of all ages. *Manga* are an essential part of Japanese popular culture; they cover everything from historical romance to sci-fi, fantasy and sado-masochism to tips on how to improve your golf swing.

'According to chaos theory, the fluttering of a butterfly's wing can cause a hurricane,' says Kazuko Horikoshi, a young graduate student who is an expert on *manga* in general and Captain Tsubasa in particular. 'I think that the appearance of Captain Tsubasa was the fluttering of the butterfly's wing which led eventually to Japan qualifying for the last World Cup.'

It's a good theory. The Captain Tsubasa boom swept Japanese classrooms in the early 1980s, when current national team players were playing for Under-12 boys teams in competitions such as Shimizu's All Japan Boys Soccer Championship which attracts scores of teams from across the country every August.

'Sure,' said S-Pulse's Daisuke Ichikawa after training one day, 'when I was a young kid, I used to play football with my friends and we would shout the different names Captain Tsubasa uses for his shots – drop shot or power shot – before we hit the ball. We used to do that a lot.'

The early matches between Captain Tsubasa's Nankatsu school team and rival Shutetsu, with its brilliant but arrogant goalkeeper Wakabayashi Genzo, take place during the local prefectural soccer competition. The two teams vie to represent Shizuoka in the national schools championships. Captain Tsubasa even calls in foreign coaching assistance in the form of a Brazilian former player called Roberto Hongo. The whole thing culminates in a clash between the representatives of Shizuoka – home of S-Pulse and the evil Jubilo – and Saitama, home of the Urawa Reds.

The first series of Captain Tsubasa comics ended in 1987; but in 1993, amid the excitement of the J.League, Captain Tsubasa reappeared in a new series. Now aged eighteen, he plays alongside many of his old rivals in Japan's national youth team, which vanquishes all comers. (This somewhat fanciful scenario has turned into reality. In the 1999 World Youth Under-20 Championships in Nigeria, Japan reached the finals, only to lose to Spain 4–0). In keeping with the new spirit of what one soccer executive called 'internationality', the later series includes an appearance by Ruud Gullit, who appears after one of Tsubasa's friends, Aoi Shingo, ends up playing for Inter Milan. Goalkeeper Wakabayashi Genzo signs for Hamburg. Tsubasa opts for the Nou Camp and is now playing for Barcelona.

As I leafed through one of the Tsubasa books, in which the long-legged eighteen year old weaves his way through the Saudi defence in the Asian qualifying rounds of the World Youth Tournament, it struck me that Tsubasa is another part of the atmosphere of almost boyish fantasy which surrounds Japanese football. 'They want it all now,' Perryman-san had said as we watched Manchester United snatch victory from Bayern Munich in the final of the European Champions' Cup back in Hiroshima in late May. 'They want to run before they can walk,' says ex-footballer Robert Maes.

Takeshi Okada, the former national coach, has more modest goals. 'In the future, Japanese football may become middle level. The first division is Brazil, Germany, Holland and Italy. But I think we will be in the second division, no?'

But if Japan fails to emerge as a first-rank footballing power, they still have Captain Tsubasa. English football fans might not have heard of him, but Tsubasa is big in France, where he's known as Oliver Atom. In the Arabic version, published in

Kuwait, he's known as Captain Maajid. He has fans in Latin America, and he's appeared in Thai, Chinese, Bahasa Malaysian and Korean. Ms Horikoshi, the *manga* expert, argues that Captain Tsubasa is Japan's biggest contribution to world football culture. Even Hidetoshi Nakata can't compete with that.

The Olympic team eventually beat Thailand and Kazakhstan and qualified for the Sydney Olympics. S-Pulse resumed their campaign after the long break with a victory over Kyoto Purple Sanga. Two weeks later, they beat Bellmare and Avispa Fukuoka; and on Tuesday, 23 November at Yokohama International Stadium in front of 40,000 people, S-Pulse beat the Yokohama F Marinos 2–1 to win the J.League's second-stage title. Twenty thousand S-Pulse fans turned up for the game.

The F Marinos had one of their full-backs sent off halfway through the first half, for two bookable fouls on Shimizu's Alex, much to the dismay of the F Marinos fans, still led by Mr Okayama's Big Shout boys. Kazu, and the dissident Marinos Pirates faction, still hadn't returned to the fold, although of course they went to the game. 'We were supporting S-Pulse,' said Mr Kikuchi, afterwards.

The F Marinos game was played in the afternoon, since it was a public holiday. When S-Pulse arrived back at Shizuoka station that evening, they were welcomed by several thousand people, and by Shimizu's mayor, Mr Miyagashima, the man with the strawberry-scented visiting cards. He noted that it was appropriate that the local team had won its first championship, or at least half of it, in the very year that Shimizu Port was celebrating its 100th anniversary. Then the team retired to the Nihondaira Hotel, Shimizu's finest, and known for its hot baths, for the traditional 'beer shower' in the hotel garden, a victory ritual adapted from professional baseball.

'I didn't know what was going on,' said Perryman-san. 'We went to the hotel and changed into our training clothes and went into the garden, and there were all these tables covered with hundreds and hundreds of bottles of beer, and all the press and television cameramen, wearing yellow mackintoshes and water-proofs and what have you. Then we all started pouring beer over each other. It was a bit cold, though.

'Then we went in, and had hot baths. Lovely. And then we got dressed up for a sort of reception, with the sponsors and so forth. A sort of political affair. But it didn't go on very long. Then we went home.'

The following Saturday, another 8,000 rallied at the newly opened S-Pulse Dream Plaza down on the Shimizu waterfront on the following Saturday night. 'Our dreams have come true,' Yamada-san told me. 'We are champions.'

But not quite. Over the two halves of the season, S-Pulse had won more games than any other club in the J.League. But to win the overall 1999 J.League Championship, Shimizu still had to play a two-leg final, at home and away, against the team which had won the first stage – the evil Jubilo Iwata.

清水

14 CHAMPIONS

We were glorious burning orange and gold in the floodlights. We were the dancing samba tunes singing and swaying in the still cold December air. We were the just and the righteous, the guardians of the pure, the children of light. We were Shimizu S-Pulse, with our team below marching out there on to the green grass arena of the Nihondaira Stadium.

They were the slick and the clever, the cold and the calculating, the divers and the niggle-merchants. They were the evil Jubilo Iwata.

And tonight, in Shimizu's Nihondaira Stadium, the final battle was beginning.

'J.League Championship, 1999,' boomed the loudspeakers as the teams marched out, 'Final game. Second leg.'

The ground was sold out, with a capacity crowd of just over 20,000. The evening match was being shown live on NHK national television. There were more than 500 journalists crowded into the stands. A mass of photographers had formed up along the touch-line now, as the two teams lined up for the opening presentation, setting up a wall of white flashes.

When I'd arrived that afternoon to meet Yamada-san six hours before the kick-off, the steps running up to the Nihondaira ground were already lined with a long crocodile of camped-out fans. There were perhaps 5,000 or more already there, all with tickets, but still braving a strong and chilly wind to be sure of the best places in the unreserved seating behind the goals.

S-Pulse and Jubilo fans were sitting happily together, as if before some cheery footballing Last Night of the Proms, all fully equipped with thermos flasks, packs of cards, sleeping bags and blankets. One group was playing a game of *shogi*, a kind of Japanese chess, on a small folding table. Some benighted young women from Jubilo had embarked upon a little open-air arts-and-crafts session, cutting out the Japanese characters for their favourite players' names in light blue and black cardboard. Perhaps the origami and bonzai tree maintenance classes would be starting later.

A local sushi store had set up on the street leading to the stadium, offering a tempting selection of raw fish and rice for only 500 yen, plus a can of barley tea for free. 'S-Pulse special?' I asked, as they handed me my order in a neat plastic bag, with a couple of wooden chopsticks. 'I love you,' shouted one of the young sushi sellers back to me, in English. It was that kind of happy day. After all, two years after almost going bankrupt, S-Pulse was on the brink of glory.

And in the background loomed that perfect view of the snow-covered peak of Mount Fuji, clear as crystal in the cold December air, with the stiff wind to whip the clouds away. The weather had been clear all week, making you realise just how big a thing that mountain really is. Even here, fifty miles or so away, it seemed a vast presence, visible on such a clear day even from the platform of Shimizu station, soaring above the oil waste storage tanks. In the morning, I'd gone for a walk on the black volcanic sand of Shimizu's Miho beach, by the pine trees around the shrine where the *hagoromo* angel danced naked for the local fisherman in the old story. There was the blue sea, and the black sand, and the green pine trees, and there was Mount Fuji all covered with snow across the bay. It was like Japan is supposed to be, but rarely is completely, on account of all the convenience stores and the pachinko parlours and McDonald's and the accumulated urban clutter. At the *hagoromo* shrine, I lobbed a lucky five yen coin into the stone offering bowl.

At the ground, I eventually found Yamada-san up at the head of the queue, chatting with a group of S-Pulse fans, some of whom had arrived the night before. 'And they've been here for three days,' he said, clearly a little shocked, indicating a small gaggle of Jubilo women at the very head of the queue.

'This match is very important,' said Yamada-san, when I asked him for his thoughts on the game, in a sort of litmus test of fan feeling. For it had suddenly struck me that while Perryman-san, Phil Holder and I had all decided that Jubilo represented the dark side, and that the evening's game would represent another clash in the eternal struggle between the forces of good and evil, this was a very western way of looking at things. Maybe Japanese fans like Yamada-san saw the Jubilo question differently. Perhaps, for them, Jubilo was, in fact, just another football team.

'Of course, Jubilo are . . .' Yamada continued at his usual deliberate pace, '. . . special.' He paused. 'They are from the same region. They are a very competitive side.'

He paused again. This was hardly a crushing moral indictment.

'I don't like . . .' I could see he was reaching for the exact expression, '. . . the way they play.'

Yamada-san paused again. After a while, I felt it was time to ask him what he meant.

'Jubilo want to win,' he said. 'Every side wants to win. But Jubilo . . . umm . . . doesn't care much about how they win. They don't play good football. And there are dirty tackles. And . . . umm . . .' He made a little flipping gesture with his hand.

'Diving?' I said.

'Yes, diving.'

This was more like it.

'That is why this game is very important,' he continued, warming to the theme. 'If Jubilo win . . . um . . . then maybe many, many people will go over to the Jubilo style of football. Which is not to play football.'

Proof of a universal morality! Jubilo are bad because they're bad. And if they won the match the world in general, and the J.League in particular, would be a sadder, badder place.

'I think the whole of Japan wants us to win this game,' Perryman-san had said, getting down to basics earlier that week down at the Hebizuka training ground. 'We're what the J.League wants. We play nice football. We've got a good disciplinary record. We've got community involvement.'

By normal standards, S-Pulse had already proven they were the best team in Japan that year. Jubilo may have won the first stage of the league, but they'd finished dismally in the second stage, ending up fourth from the bottom. And if you put the two stages together, which we committed S-Pulse fans tended to do, then S-Pulse were still top, eight points ahead of Kashiwa Reysol. Over the whole season, Jubilo were sixteen points behind, in sixth place, a fact highlighted with yellow marker on the league table posted on the noticeboard at the S-Pulse training ground.

But that's not how the system works in Japan. And then, having elected to have a championship-deciding game between the winners of the two stages, rather than having just one final game to decide it all, there are two. As my friend Takano-san of JEF United had once thoughtfully observed over a bowl of spaghetti vongole, in the J.League, more is better.

The first leg of the championship play-off had been played the previous Saturday afternoon, over in Iwata on the other side of Shizuoka Prefecture, in the shadow of the Yamaha factory. It was another lovely clear day, with bright low sunshine streaming across the cramped, atmospheric Jubilo ground. Once again, the samba band was squashed in behind the goal at the away end. Once again, before the match, the Jubilo supporters held up their irritatingly smug 'WE ARE THE CHAMPIONS OF ASIA' banner, and then put on an impressive display of precision polythene binbag waving, picking out the word 'JUBILO' in blue and black along the upper stand.

I was watching from the crowded press seats, opting for supposed objective distance. But it was no good. I was a tense wreck. I'd clearly crossed over. I desperately wanted S-Pulse to win. I hated Jubilo.

And now, at this key moment, S-Pulse were also labouring with injury problems at the back, with their two strongest defenders, Morioka and Toda, both out. Morioka had broken his toe in a practice game at Hebizuka in November. Toda had come down with a heavy flu, and was reported to be barely able to stand on the morning of the game.

Toda was also suffering from a severe case of bad hair, having changed styles for the fourth time that year, opting now for a vast white *bouffant* do which made him look like a 1970s glam rock star. Worse, even Ichikawa, the thinking man's Captain Tsubasa, hadn't been able to stay away from the hairdressers; his boyish and innocent black mop had now turned into a brown-frizzed perm, which made him look as if he'd been dragged through a car wash.

That afternoon at Iwata, Toda's place had been taken by Oenoki, a thirty-four-year-old S-Pulse veteran, while twenty-five-year-old Junji Nishizawa was playing for Morioka, having stepped in for the last couple of league games and acquitted himself well. 'He's got a big heart, that boy,' said Perryman-san, of the young Nishizawa. He was going to need it.

After a display by the local marching band, the game began, with the Shimizu fans settling into the slow, rocking swing of their Defensor tune, seeking to settle our boys down in the hostile Iwata environment. 'OOOOOOOH OH OH OH OOOOH! OOOOOOOH OH OH OH OOOOH!' The Jubilo fans were relying very heavily on the triumphal march from Verdi's Aïda, with a chorus of 'FORZA JUBILO, OH OH! OH OH!, FORZA JUBILO!'

The match was played with all the intensity of a cup final and a local derby rolled into one. Both sides looked jumpy, frightened of making mistakes. S-Pulse were still giving the Jubilo defence all sorts of problems, while Jubilo were also looking pretty handy. Ando, the former S-Pulse player, was now playing as an attacking right-back, testing S–Pulse's shaky defence with diagonal head-high crosses into the centre. Overseeing it all was the JFA's Scottish referee, Leslie Mottram the Lawgiver, standing no non-sense, and pouncing on any evidence of incipient attitude coming from the Jubilo boys.

Since the start of the second stage, Perryman-san had settled for a combination of two central strikers. Yasunaga and the smaller, nippy Kuboyama. Alex was attacking from the back up the left wing, and Ichikawa doing the same on the right, chasing balls dropped into the corner over the backs.

Thirty minutes into the game, Jubilo's Ando sent in a perfectly weighted cross towards his thuggish looking captain, Nakayama, who stole in between two S–Pulse defenders to head it home. Sanada, the S–Pulse goalkeeper, had no chance. A hysterical scream, reminiscent of the sort of orgasmic noise made by young women in Japanese porn movies when they're wrapped up in cling film, broke from the blue ranks of the Jubilo fans.

S–Pulse equalised just four minutes later, the captain Sawanobori blasting in a twenty-five-yard shot with his left foot, curling the ball past the Jubilo keeper. The orange army, rewarded for its faith, swung into the happy goal song. 'OLEEEH OLÉ OLÉ OLEEEEH! ESSS-PUUULSE . . . ESSS-PUUULSE!' Sawanobori, trailing S–Pulse players, ran towards the bench, and jumped joyously into Perryman-san's arms.

And that was how the score remained at the end of ninety minutes, as the sun set and the floodlights came on and the temperature dropped: 1–1. For S–Pulse, an away draw would have been a good result. But since in the J.League more is always better, that wasn't the end of it, even for a two-leg final. We still had sudden-death-goal extra time to look forward to. The two teams huddled out on the pitch, wrapped in long bench coats, and surrounded by anxious coaches and training staff. The two crowds threw themselves into a frenzy of chanting. The Jubilo rubbish bags were out again. I was tense.

Six minutes into extra time, big Les Mottram booked Jubilo's captain, Nakayama, for diving on the edge of the S–Pulse penalty area. It was a satisfying moment. Two minutes later, Jubilo's striker Fukunishi broke into the S-Pulse penalty area, running at S-Pulse's new defender, Nishizawa, and crossed into the centre. The ball struck Nishizawa's trailing hand.

Mottram instantly awarded the penalty, and booked the hapless Nishizawa. 'He's been known to miss them,' said a journalist next to me in the press box, glumly, as Nakayama stepped up to the penalty spot. As Nakayama scored, another vast orgasmic scream of relief exploded from the Jubilo fans. Nakayama did an aeroplane run in front of the home fans. The Jubilo bench was cavorting with joy. Jubilo had won, in characteristically devious fashion. But it wasn't so bad. It was, after all, only the first leg. The overtime win meant that if S-Pulse beat Jubilo in ninety minutes in the second leg at Nihondaira, S-Pulse would win the championship.

'Despite the defeat, I'm not so disappointed today,' Perryman-san told the assembled reporters afterwards. 'We kept good shape. Defensively, no big, big problems, bearing in mind these are good players we're playing against. So the dressing room is positive.'

Scores of pens scribbled earnestly away. The cameras rolled.

'We believe we can win this next game in ninety minutes. But, as I said to the players, if before the first ball was kicked of this season, someone had said we'd be one win in ninety minutes away from the big championship, I think we'd be delighted in that. We're going to be even more positive in our tactics . . . If we win this tournament, we're going to do it playing football.'

The following Tuesday at the S-Pulse training ground, Perryman and Phil Holder still had the air of cats that had eaten the cream, as they reflected on the events of the previous two weeks over coffee in the corner office.

'The supporters can jump up and down and get silly about it, but we can't. That's not our style,' said Perryman-san wisely, from behind the desk.

'Nah,' said Holder, who'd just come in, flushed from the training field.

'Because in football, you have enough bad times. So you've got to enjoy the good times.'

'And the bastard days are always just around the corner, Steve.'

'So you've got to enjoy it. But on the inside. And enjoy that feeling. But a little leery of it at the same time. Because it doesn't last forever.'

'Right. Because in football, the sack is always just around the corner.'

Winning the second-stage championship didn't mean all was sweetness and light at S-Pulse. The end of the season brought the start of contract renegotiations with players, and the breaking of bad news to those whose contracts wouldn't be renewed. Those on the way out included Kenta Hasegawa, the thirty-four-year-old striker, and a thirty-three-year-old defender Takumi Horiiki. Both were favoured local sons, products of the Shimizu school who'd come back home to play in the new professional team at the start of the J.League. Rather than following the traditional Japanese approach of leaving it to the front office to break the bad news to the players, Perryman-san had done it himself.

Surprisingly, since he'd spent most of the second stage on the bench, Kenta seemed taken aback by the news of his retirement. He'd subsequently complained to the press about how he'd been treated, not by Perryman-san, but by the club's management. This had embarrassed the Suzuyo company so much, that they'd announced the creation of the 'Suzuyo Lifetime Soccer Achievement Award', for players who'd played more than 200 games for the club, which naturally included Kenta and Horiiki.

Then, possibly because they thought their championship-winning manager might feel left out or embarrassed, the front office told Perryman-san that he too had qualified for a Suzuyo Lifetime Soccer Achievement Award.

Perryman-san's footprints had already been recorded on a brass plate on the pavement of Shimizu's S-Pulse street, along with all former players' and managers', put in place at a small ceremony on a rainy day in August. Now his name was to be enshrined in a new Shimizu soccer hall of fame in the soccer exhibit down at the new S-Pulse Dream Plaza shopping and entertainment complex, a few floors above the Shimizu sushi museum. Plus there was a bonus award of one million yen.

Things had worked out rather well for the players, too. All eleven first team members had been named as possible candidates for the J.League's All Star Eleven selection, to be announced at the annual league awards ceremony later that month. Dreadlocked Alex, who'd come from Brazil to Japan as a high school player, was in the running for the most valuable player of the year award. There was talk, too, of the JFA trying to get Alex a Japanese passport to make him eligible for the 2002 World Cup, following in the distinguished footsteps of Wagner Lopes and Ruy Ramos.

As Saturday approached, Shimizu held its breath. The city hall contacted their counterparts in the sister city of Stockton, California, and told them that they should have a congratulatory telegram ready for the mayor in the event of an S-Pulse victory on Saturday. 'Of course we had to explain what it was all about,' said one of the city officials. 'But when they understood, they were very enthusiastic. Maybe they were more enthusiastic even than we are.' S-Pulse Dream Plaza, which had opened in October, was festooned with S-Pulse flags and pictures of Paru-chan, and was receiving busloads of day trippers, who had added a trip to the sushi museum and the Kiddies Land toy shop to a visit to the top of the Nihondaira plateau, and a walk on the black sand beach. Shimizu was having a very good year.

Toda recovered his health. Jubilo went into secret training sessions somewhere in Yamaha land. Perryman-san kept talking the talk to the Japanese media at the Hebizuka ground.

'We come out of that first game very confident that we are on the right road,' he told a group of television cameras after a light training session on the Wednesday. 'And with the belief that we have had all year that we will get what we deserve. If someone deserves it more, then they will take the championship. If it's Jubilo, they will have to be good.'

'What about the home support?' asked the man from NHK. 'Will that be an advantage?'

'We always have good support, at home and away. When I say we will get what we deserve, I actually mean, the club, the company and the supporters. They drive us on, they give us power. And if I can ask them something, I want them, number one, to enjoy this game. Don't be too tense. Don't be too nervous. The same message to the players. Enjoy this experience. Because in this game, we are going to make history.'

The reporters smiled, perhaps nervously, at the notion of enjoyment, rather than suffering, being the key to sporting success in Japan. But the man from White Hart Lane was enjoying his moment.

'This club has in the past had money problems. It nearly went out of existence. This club has returned to this game because of the company, the quality of the players and because of the power of the supporters. One more step. Drive us there. Enjoy it.'

Saturday night. Nihondaira Stadium. I was standing at the front of the S-Pulse crowd, next to Mr 'call-me-Mr-Cherry-Blossom' Sakura. I couldn't tell if he was enjoying it. As the teams walked out, and the cameras flashed, Mr Sakura's eyes looked a little glazed. Perhaps it was uppers. Perhaps it was downers. Perhaps he was just paralysed by the sheer total bloody tension, the awful terror of it all.

This was my first ever appearance as a home supporter on the sacred stands of Nihondaira. Before deciding to invite myself along, I had thought seriously about whether my presence might disturb the gods of footballing good fortune. But I knew I was beyond watching from the press box. I had on my orange and blue number 10 Shimizu S-Pulse tee-shirt, with Nobori's name on the back. Oba-san, commander of K's Club, whose ranks I'd joined at Gifu and Hiroshima in May, had invited me to join his group. I showed him my orange shirt, and he threw me another K's Club orange shirt so I'd fit in even more than I did already. Mr Sakura, on my right, was part of the similar but different Kenta Club; he had a drum strapped around him, which he'd started to beat fiercely as we chanted the names of each player. Each had his own tune, like characters in a Wagner opera.

'CAAR-LOS CAAR-LOS SANTOS!' (BOOM BOOM) 'SANTOS!' we went, to the tune of 'We will, we will rock you. Rock you.'

'KEN-TA KEN-TA HA-SE-GA-WA! HA-SE-GA-WA! HA-SE-GA-WA!' we went, to the tune of the chorus from 'Yellow Submarine'.

'OHHHHH! FA-BI-NHO FA-BI-NHO FA-BI-NHO! OH-OH-OH!' we went, to the theme from *The Sting*.

I had spent the hour or so before the game up on the stands, watching the fans get ready. In front of the central area, where the band would play, there were piles of cardboard boxes, some loaded with yellow and orange streamers and with piles and piles of cut-up newspaper confetti. People were scurrying around, busily preparing. There was Endo-san, from Chapéu Laranja, who'd invited me to the summer barbecue, looking cheerful as ever; Chapéu Laranja had a new, multi-coloured S-Pulse banner, which everyone was admiring. Eventually, Mr Tanaka, who was to be crowd leader for the night, organised a squad of young fans to start distributing the streamers and the confetti, with the orange streamers selling for 100 yen a time. I bought two, and was given a fistful of newspaper. The streamers, I was told, were to be released only in the hour of victory. For some reason, I couldn't find Yamada-san. Perhaps he'd decided it was all too much to take. Or perhaps he was in one of the side-stands, co-ordinating support.

Then Matsuda-san, the band leader and supporters' chief executive, arrived, calling together the sub-group leaders for the pre-match meeting, stressing above all the need for good behaviour, as Shimizu was tonight before the eyes of all Japan. Everyone listened earnestly. Matsuda had shaved his head after S-Pulse won the second-stage championship, presumably fulfilling some vow to the gods. After all, it was currently too cold to climb Mount Fuji again.

On my right were two young women whom I didn't remember meeting before, who said they were called Tomoe and Aki. In front, on the railing, was Oba-san. Wandering around in a bit of a daze was Mr Koike, whom I did remember, father of the twelve-year-old Arisa, another veteran of the Gifu game who was now down at the railing. At the other end, I could make out a Jubilo banner which said, rather unsportingly, in English: 'STEPHEN! NOW IS THE TIME TO LOSE.'

'SA-NA-DA! (BOOM BOOM BOOM),' we went, 'SA-NA-DA!'

The whistle blew. S-Pulse kicked off. We threw our newspaper confetti into the air in a vast orgy of premeditated littering. A storm of paper flew over Sanada in the S-Pulse goal just in front of us. As the paper fluttered about in the stiff night breeze, it struck me that this was not such a good idea. We might be putting him off.

We opened up with a couple of straight rounds of 'ESS-PULSE! (BOOM BOOM BOOM) ESS-PULSE', trying to work through the tension, and then went rapidly into the upbeat 'Deo Deo', where we divided into sections. Over at K's Club, we were crouching down when everyone else went 'DEH-OHH, DEH-OHH', (which I had first heard as 'EH-OHH EH-OHH' but now knew better) and jumping up to scream 'ESS-PULSE ESS-PULSE!'

There were too many people to hear the samba band as much more than a deep beat – down at the front we were definitely missing out on the full acoustic experience, but Oba-san was maintaining visual contact with crowd conductor Tanaka-san, who was standing on bottle crates with Matsuda beside him in the central aisle. I no longer needed advice on the movements. I knew what I was doing.

S-Pulse launched an immediate assault on the Jubilo goal. They were holding possession well enough, and passing it around. I convinced myself they looked more settled than during the first leg. Then Jubilo's Ando got the ball, trying to get past our right back Nishizawa. 'Ando . . . *kuso-tari*,' screamed a man behind me, with feeling. Technically, this indicated that he believed Ando, once our beloved An-chan, to be a smelly lump of rotted fish sauce. In Japanese, this is about as obscene as you can get. I joined in the general booing.

Jubilo weren't making much of an impression on the S-Pulse defence, although about half an hour in, Nishizawa almost let us down. Under pressure in the left corner down below us, he under-hit a back pass to Sanada, almost allowing a Jubilo player to intercept. Sanada threw himself at the ball as the Jubilo player moved in, and our hearts rotated. The ball ricocheted into a high loop, towards the goal, but fell eventually just wide of the post. We almost died.

'SA-NA-DA!' we thundered, wretchedly grateful, 'SA-NA-DA.'

But then, a minute later, perhaps in one of those strange time-slippage things, or perhaps because this time he thought he could get the back-pass to the keeper just right, Nishizawa managed to do almost exactly the same thing again. The action went into slow motion. Jubilo's Nakayama pounced on the error, and crossed the ball back to Fukunishi on the edge of the area, who laid it off to Hattori, who struck a solid first time shot with his left foot. The ball screamed past Sanada, and into the back of the net. Jubilo had scored.

Sanada fell to his knees and doubled up with pain and despair.

Sudden deathly silence fell over the stands. The S-Pulse players looked completely horrified. It was a nightmare.

But this is where our training came in. We could stand about and be dismal. Or we could get back up there. After all, it was only one goal down. There was plenty of time left. We could still win. We were a better team. And so, after the initial gut-wrenching shock, we settled into a nerve-steadying rendition of Defensor as the game restarted. The low, solid chant was thick with desire, a plea to the players to keep going, to keep believing as we did that this match could still be ours. From the centre spot the ball went forward to Alex, our elegant and exotic hope of glory, who moved forward towards the edge of the Jubilo box. He tried to dance towards the goal, and Jubilo's big defender, Miura, brought him down. We bayed for justice, and Japan's World Cup referee, Mr Masayoshi Okada, blew for an S-Pulse free-kick.

The two players, Alex and Miura, fell with their legs in a

tangle. From where I stood in the stands, perhaps a hundred yards away, I saw it all. Alex's boot raised, as he lay on the ground. Alex's boot kicking out into the chest of Miura. Players running in from all directions. Pushing and shoving. Alex was on his feet. The Jubilo crowd booing. The red card. Probably, he'd been provoked. Probably, he was retaliating. Probably, he was just a total and absolute moron.

'Alex is always on the edge of doing something,' said Perryman-san afterwards. 'Often, of course, it's something very special. Sometimes, very, very stupid.'

In the stands, we stood amazed, hoping it was not true. Alex had been sent off. Initially, he refused to walk. He was surrounded by Jubilo players, supposedly trying to calm him down. For a while it looked like a general mêlée might ensue, broadcast live on national television, compounding the humiliation. Eventually, Alex headed for the touch-line, pinching tears from his eyes.

We were one-nil down; we had ten men; there were at least fifty-two minutes left. We were doomed.

Sawanobori took the free-kick, awarded for the foul on Alex. He struck a hard shot which curled over the wall, past the Jubilo keeper, and into the top right-hand corner of the Jubilo net. Exactly one minute had elapsed since Jubilo's goal. Nobori had scored.

The whole of Nihondaira's orange masses swept joyously into a chorus of wild Olés. I may have kissed Mr Sakura. There were still ten minutes left in the first half. And we were still one man down.

There's only so much you can take, and I don't remember much of what happened after that. We knew that S-Pulse had beaten Jubilo with ten men at Iwata in August. So every time they approached the Jubilo goal, there was always that absurd hope, best not to think about, that they might actually score again, and still win in ninety minutes, and we would be the champions of Japan. And every time Jubilo had possession in our half, there was that sick gnawing certainty that the odds were now inevitably and unjustly stacked in their favour, that all it would take would be one more goal to turn the evening into a humiliating rout, like that famous 5–2 defeat back in April.

We lived in a strange place of high anxiety and fear. Mr Sakura, beside me, had clearly gone into an even more far and distant place. He was hardly chanting at all. Just staring at the pitch, transfixed now with the horror. We were certainly making history, as Perryman-san had said we would. But were we enjoying it?

Our repertoire in the stands had become very urgent. I remember at one point we tried 'Hossa S-Pulse', which starts all slow, and then speeds up. It wasn't right. It was too slow. It was too relaxed and too Brazilian. It felt all wrong. Mr Tanaka didn't try that one again. We needed insistent, driving beats, punk head-banging samba. Best of all was the one that began with what sounded like 'Jiber-abu-Jiber-abu GO! GO!' which was our attacking dead-ball speciality tune. The respectable middle-aged woman behind me had developed her own variation on this. In between each massive shout of 'GO! GO!' she'd scream 'Nobori! Nobori!' in my ear in the most amazing high-pitched shriek. Maybe she was his mum.

About halfway through the second half it was still one-all. Perryman took off Yasunaga, and sent on Fabinho. Nine minutes later, Fabinho beat his man, and crossed to Kuboyama, who sent a high lob dropping towards the upper right-hand corner of the Jubilo net. Our hearts soared. It hit the post.

Then, at the other end, Jubilo put the ball in the net. Offside.

Off went the unfortunate Nishizawa and Kuboyama. On came Kenta Hasegawa, for what was to be his final appearance with S-Pulse. And on came Oenoki at the back. And then it was full time. S-Pulse had held the score one-all.

The two sides withdrew into the centre of each half. Perryman was rallying the troops, making gestures which showed he wanted them to drop balls over the Jubilo backs for Fabinho to run on to. Holder was sorting out the defenders. The massage team were working overtime. It had been heroic, but this was a tired team. In the stands, we willed them on, with another burst of power chanting.

Extra time began. More clouded madness. All that really matters was that in the ninth minute, Oenoki picked up the ball in the centre from Ichikawa, and slotted it through to Fabinho. Fabinho blasted the ball again towards the upper left-hand corner of the Jubilo net, right in front of us. There was an instant of disbelief. The ball had gone in. The impossible had in fact happened. S-Pulse had beaten Jubilo. With just ten men.

Hysteria broke out in the stands and on the pitch. I lobbed my orange and yellow streamers. I shook hands with Mr Sakura, who was now smiling catatonically. We all jumped up and down. When it had settled down, I walked over to Oba-san, and hugged him. I realised I had tears in my eyes.

'I'm extremely proud of the players who continued on the pitch after the sending off,' said Perryman-san in the press conference later. 'They had power. They had belief. They did their job.'

So had we.

But of course it wasn't over yet. Because, as Mr Takano had said, in the J.League more is better. S-Pulse had won, like Jubilo, in extra time, which meant that the two-stage championship was now tied. Forget nine months of league football, and being sixteen points ahead. It was time for the penalty shoot-out.

The next day, I paid one more trip to Yokohama. In December, after all the excitement of the J.League championship, the world of Japanese football turns its attention to the Emperor's Cup, the Japanese equivalent of the FA Cup. The Sunday after the J.League championship was devoted to the third round, when the J.League's first division teams find themselves up against the comparative minnows from the second division and from the third division, the Japan Football League.

The Yokohama F Marinos were playing Mito Hollyhock from the north of Japan, who had just won promotion from the JFL to the second division, along with Honda Gikin, in the process considerably enriching the J.League's store of wacky club names. (Mito is a town in northern Japan. The hollyhock is the symbol of the great Shogun Ieyasu Tokagawa, who unified Japan in the seventeenth century. Honda, on the other hand, is the name of a rather ordinary small Japanese car.)

And what of Yokohama FC, the little JFL club? Well, the Fulies and Pierre Littbarski actually ended up six points clear of both Mito and Honda at the top of the league. But since the JFA had only admitted them into the league on short notice as an associate member, who didn't really exist, Yokohama FC had to stay down in the football basement for one more year.

But that's by the way. The main reason I'd come to Yokohama was to catch up with Kazu and the Pirates, to see whether they'd returned to the ranks of actively supporting the Marinos, and ousted Mr Okayama, since we'd last met in August.

The game, wonderfully, was being played not in the vast emptiness of the Yokohama International Stadium, but at the old Mitsuzawa ground, where I'd first seen the Marinos play Consadole at the start of the previous season. Mitsuzawa was far smaller than I remembered, which, with a crowd of just over 5,000, was not a bad thing.

The game had nevertheless attracted a flurry of sports media interest. There was a negotiating team from a Madrid club, who had decided to take the F Marinos' irritating striker Shoji Jo on loan. The local Spanish press had suggested the move was linked to efforts to attract Japanese fans and to sell television rights, rather than by purely footballing considerations. The game was also to be one of the last appearances of Marinos' ageing full back, and former national team captain, Ihara, the man who Kazu Miyazaki had carried shoulder high after the championship win of 1995.

I searched for my friends behind the F Marinos goal, among the *bandeiras*. They weren't there. Okayama and the Big Shout boys still reigned supreme. Okayama himself, clad in a loose red, white and blue hockey shirt, was down behind the goal, shouting instructions with his famous megaphone to the fickle masses.

Eventually, I found them up to the right of the goal, near the corner. There was Kikuchi-san, who'd dyed his long hair brown. There was Kozue and Yuki, who had wanted to know about pride. There was the blind supporter, with his folding white stick, who knew a lot about English football.

'Mr Kazu,' said Yuki, 'is sick. He had to go to hospital. He has a problem.'

It seemed that Kazu, with all his wonderful energy, was fighting a complaint, which had laid him low, and which periodically needed hospital treatment. It seemed quite serious. Kazu had been ill for a week or two now, and without him, things certainly seemed a little sadder. It also turned out that Mr Shimada, the blond-haired old biker who liked to drink more coffee than was possibly legal, had been hit by a car on his bike, and was in hospital with multiple fractures.

The new phase of the anti F Marinos campaign was bogged down, too. The letter I'd helped write in French to Monsieur Carlos Ghosn of Nissan Motors hadn't been delivered yet, owing to some problems with his schedule and access through the underground contact in the front office. I felt I was attending on the death of a dynasty. But Kazu's faithful retainers were still loyal to the core.

'We're not here to support the F Marinos,' said Yuki, when I asked. 'We're here to support the old captain of the Marinos, Ihara, because it may be his last game.'

It had been announced at the end of the league season that the F Marinos were to continue the Argentinian theme in the coming campaign. They'd signed Ossie Ardiles as manager, formerly of Shimizu S-Pulse, now fresh from Croatia Zagreb. I asked Izumi-san if that made her happy.

'I would be happy,' she said, 'if Ardiles was to come to manage the Marinos as they used to be. But not the Yokohama F Marinos.'

The F Marinos won the game. Afterwards, we went to the Skylark restaurant near the station. And there, amid the faceless urban sprawl, we sat down and ate, and drank a lot of coffee, and the members of the Supporters' Society to Save the Marinos and Japanese Football Culture listened carefully as I tried to explain the differences between England and Scotland. 'Being Scottish,' I said, 'is rather like being from Hokkaido. Only a bit different.'

After the Jubilo game, the journalists clapped as Perryman-san entered the room, in his smart grey suit. The veteran of eighteen years at Tottenham Hotspur and two FA Cup finals was looking a little dazed, his voice hoarse and emotional. 'I don't think,' he said, 'I've ever experienced so many emotions before as during that ninety-nine minutes, and the penalty shoot-out.'

The penalties had been taken in the goal in front of us. It was best of five.

'SA-NA-DA!' we chanted, 'SA-NA-DA!' But they scored.

'NO-BO-RI!' we chanted, 'NO-BO-RI!' He scored.

'SA-NA-DA!' we chanted, 'SA-NA-DA!' They scored.

'SAN-TOS!' we chanted, 'SAN-TOS!' The keeper saved it.

'SA-NA-DA!' we chanted, 'SA-NA-DA.' They scored.

'TE-RU!' we chanted, 'TE-RU!' He scored.

'SA-NA-DA!' we chanted, desperately. 'SA-NA-DA!' Sanada almost got his fingers to it. But it went into the top left corner. Sanada hit the ground with frustration.

'FA-BI-NHO!' we chanted, 'FA-BI-NHO!' Fabinho blasted it wide.

We were silent yellow and gold. They were jubilant blue. The far end dissolved into a mass of blue streamers. Jubilo's bench were running towards their players, just in front of us. All around me, the S-Pulse fans had been turned to stone, standing there transfixed as the trophy was awarded. Aki and Tomoe were holding their hands in front of their mouths. Oba-san was holding his head, and looking down. No one was looking at anyone else. But we stood and took it. There wasn't even any booing, not even when the Jubilo supporters unfurled a newly adapted massive banner, saying 'WE ARE THE CHAMPIONS OF THE J.LEAGUE 1999 AND ASIA.' Not when they named Jubilo's captain, Nakayama, as the man of the match, adding insult to injury.

'Well of course from our point of view it's a tragedy,' said Perryman-san at the press conference. Then he paused. 'And I feel a bit of a cheat with the players. Because I always tell them you will always get what you deserve in this game. But tonight, and over the last nine months, we have not got what we deserved.'

When he eventually walked out, the assembled reporters gave him another round of applause.

清水

EPILOGUE

S-Pulse had lost. But in a way, they'd still managed to win. Perryman-san was named Manager of the Year at the J.League awards on Monday, and paid tribute to the influence of Ardiles on the team. Twenty-three-year-old Alex was named Player of the Year, despite having cost his club the championship. People said he had a great future ahead of him. Six S-Pulse players were named to the J.League all-star selection. Eddie Thomson's Sanfrecce beat S-Pulse 2–0 in the Emperor's Cup just before Christmas and went on to the final, eventually losing to Nagoya Grampus Eight on New Year's day 2000. Steve Perryman's contract at S-Pulse was renegotiated, and extended for one more year.